Mastering the PMI Risk Management Professional (PMI-RMP) Exam

Risk Management Professionals seek to identify, analyze, and document the risks associated with a company's business operations, as well as monitor the effectiveness of risk management processes and implement needed changes. The PMI Risk Management Professional (PMI-RMP)® certification not only highlights the ability to identify and assess project risks, mitigate threats, and capitalize on opportunities, but it also enhances and protects the needs of the organization. Gaining distinction as a PMI-RMP sets the Risk Management Professional apart from other professionals and brings credit to an organization.

The exams from the Project Management Institute are not easy, so whether you are running a course as an instructor or studying by yourself, you need a good study guide to maximize time spent studying and one which enhances the chances of passing the exam. Test takers sitting for the exam need a study guide that suggests which study materials are best to read in preparation for the exam, presents exercises to enhance learning and understanding, and provides sample exam questions.

Most study guides just explain the contents of the exam without providing the tools to maximize learning. Klaus Nielsen, an Authorized Training Partner with PMI, translates the PMI examination content outline for April 2022 into what people need to do and know in preparation and provides them with exercises and prep questions as a quick and easy check to ensure they are on the right path in preparation for taking the exam. This book helps maximize the chance of passing the exam.

Mastering the PMI Risk Management Professional (PMI-RMP) Exam

Complete Coverage of the PMI-RMP
Exam Content Outline and
Specifications Updated March 2022

For Exams Taken after April 1, 2022

by
Klaus Nielsen, PMP, PMI-RMP, PMI-ACP and PMI-PBA

A PRODUCTIVITY PRESS BOOK

First published 2023
by Routledge
605 Third Avenue, New York, NY 10158

and by Routledge
4 Park Square, Milton Park, Abingdon, Oxon, OX14 4RN

Routledge is an imprint of the Taylor & Francis Group, an informa business

ISBN: 978-1-032-30227-0 (hbk)
ISBN: 978-1-032-30226-3 (pbk)
ISBN: 978-1-003-30401-2 (ebk)

DOI: 10.4324/9781003304012

Typeset in Garamond
by Deanta Global Publishing Services, Chennai, India

Contents

Preface

Thank you for buying this handbook. It is my sincere goal with this book that you will be successful at the PMI Risk Management Professional (PMI-RMP) exam and that the way leading to the exam has been manageable and fun. I completed my first PMI certification more than 10 years ago, the Project Management Professional (PMP) exam. I failed it the first time as I considered myself to be an experienced practitioner, so how difficult could the exam be? But the actual exam included processes, inputs, and outputs I only read about briefly. I went home reading the *PMBOK Guide* – Third Edition again, and this time all the pages. Shortly after passing the PMP exam, I completed the PMI-RMP exam with little extra effort.

Since then, I have worked as a practitioner, at universities, and training participants to pass the various PMI certifications exams. During these years, I have been buying and using a wide range of exam prep books, some better than others but all in all greatly needed resources for supplementary materials for courses or when preparing for an exam without taking a course.

As you may know, the PMI-RMP is changing to reflect the needs of the market, which are great, and the new PMI-RMP certification will become even more relevant for many practitioners. When I run my training courses, I tell participants to sign up for a PMI membership to get access to the PMI materials and at the same time receive a discount on the PMI-RMP exam. This advice is very important. As mentioned, I have used various prep books for various certifications; however most, if not all, of them include the same content already found in the literature, in this case the *PMBOK Guide* – Sixth Edition; *The Standard for Risk Management in Portfolios, Programs, and Projects* (2019); and the *Practice Standard for Project Risk Management* (2009).

This handbook is to some extent unique. I have not repeated much content already stated in the *PMBOK Guide* – Sixth Edition; *The Standard for Risk Management in Portfolios, Programs, and Projects* (2019); or the *Practice Standard for Project Risk Management* (2009), but I will explain what you need to read and where you can find it in these PMI publications.

The PMI-RMP exam now includes agile and hybrid content, which are not documented in great detail in *The Standard for Risk Management in Portfolios, Programs, and Projects*, nor the *Practice Standard for Project Risk*

Management, so I have written the missing content in this book. It now covers all you need to pass the PMI-RMP exam.

Besides reading, the high value of a prep book is good exercises and plenty of sample exam questions which all have been written, so no extra resources are needed besides this handbook and the PMI publications.

Best of luck preparing and passing the PMI-RMP exam.

I hope you will enjoy being part of this journey and would love to hear from you at LinkedIn.

Klaus Nielsen

Acknowledgments

Acknowledgment is the recognition or favorable notice of an act or achievement, which were numerous in creating this work. My only plea is forgiveness for all not mentioned but not by any means forgotten. First, I would like to extend my thanks and gratitude to the people who have helped make this work a reality. By doing so, I want to acknowledge the work done by the Project Management Institute and the amazing team at Routledge. Thank you Kriss for believing in me and for making this dream possible and a wonderful experience. This work would not have been possible without the support of all the people who have taken part one way or the other in ensuring the content and quality of this work. Thank you. I owe you my greatest gratitude.

Many people have contributed over the years to the evolution of this book, as many of the ideas in this book have been formed, sharpened, and aired at meetings, training, debates, and lectures around the world.

My deepest appreciation goes to Nina, the most patient and supportive wife any author or man could ever dream of. Molly and Julie, my loved ones.

Finally, my family has put up with my absence for more birthdays and evenings than I like to think while writing this book. Thank you Dad and Mom for being who you are!

Any errors, of course, are mine.

> With grandiose resolve a man endeavors to soar above all obstacles, but thus encounters a hostile fate. He retreats and evades the issue. The time is difficult. Without rest, he must hurry along, with no permanent abiding place. If he does not want to make compromises within himself, but insists on remaining true to his principles, he suffers deprivation. Never the less he has a fixed goal to strive for even though the people with whom he lives do not understand him and speak ill of him.
>
> **(Book of Changes, "Darkening of the Light")**

About the Author

Klaus Nielsen holds a master's degree in e-commerce from the IT University of Copenhagen, Denmark, which was supplemented with a year in Cambridge (UK) and later dual MBAs (human resource management and technology) in the US. He has worked in project, programs and portfolio management, plan-based, and agile for more than 20 years and still embraces many of the international best practices for years.

Author of the books *I am Agile* (2013), *Mastering the Business Case* (2015), *Achieve PMI-PBA Exam Success* (2015), *Agile Certified Practitioner Exam* (2016), and *Agile Portfolio Management* (2019) and writer of several industry articles published worldwide, Nielsen has been a subject matter expert (SME) on various publications from PMI and Axelos and recently a PMI core team member on the *PMBOK Guide* – Seventh Edition.

Nielsen is the cofounder of Global Business Development (gbd.dk), a PMI Authorized Training Partner (ATP) and Scrum/DevOps training company, where he trains PMI Authorized Training Partner Instructors and consults businesses ranging from small start-ups to top 500 companies worldwide.

Since 2012, Nielsen has taught part time at the IT University of Copenhagen as a faculty lecturer and is a frequent speaker at events, conferences, and tradeshows. Nielsen holds a wide range of certifications from various Scrum organizations, PMI, Axelos, DevOps Institute, LeSS, Disciplined Agile, Kanban, SAFe, and others, in which he has trained many of them for years.

For a complete listing of Nielsen's programs, products, high-profile clients, and speaking schedule, visit the Global Business Development website at www.gbd.dk.

To book Klaus Nielsen for your next conference, event, or in-house training, please contact Global Business Development on LinkedIn or the company website.

Introduction

How This Book Is Organized

This book is organized around three core values: value, support, and retrieval. Value is the goal alignment and learner's perspective of the PMI-RMP exam. Preparing and going for the PMI-RMP exam is an emotionally charged endeavor and is fully supported by this content of fundamental knowledge value found in Chapters 2, 3, and 4.

The support value focuses on the mastery of the core content for the exam, which is supported with additional background content. This is done with meaningful tasks and relevant information found in Chapters 5, 6, 7, 8, and 9, and Appendix D, supported by content found in Appendices A, B, and C.

The retrieval value has an emphasis on reflection and practice tests, which I call passing the exam, and is supported by sample practice exams found in Chapters 10 and 11. Appendices E and F are additional supporting content for broader understanding and easier recall.

The full list of content is shown in Table I.1.

Table I.1　How This Book Is Organized

	Chapter	Fundamental Knowledge	Mastery of the Content	Passing the Exam	Background Content
	1–10	Value	Support	Retrieval	Support
How This Book Is Organized	Introduction				
Pretest Knowledge Assessment	1	X			
PMI-RMP Certification Overview	2	X			
Study Tips	3	X			
Domain I: Risk Strategy and Planning	4		X		
Domain II: Risk Identification	5		X		
Domain III: Risk Analysis	6		X		
Domain IV: Risk Response	7		X		
Domain V: Monitor and Close Risks	8		X		
PMI-RMP Full Practice Exam 1	9			X	
PMI-RMP Full Practice Exam 2	10			X	
Appendix A: Agile Mindset and Principles					X
Appendix B: Scrum and Risk Management					X
Appendix C: Hybrid Risk Management					X
Appendix D: Code of Ethics and Professional Conduct			X		
Appendix E: Cross-Reference Guide				X	
Appendix F: Tasks Placemat				X	
Glossary of Terms and Acronyms				X	
References					X

Tip: I know from experience that this book, in addition to the PMI readings, covers all you need to read, know, and practice to pass the PMI-RMP exam. However, it is always sound practice to use multiple resources.

Chapter 1

Pretest Knowledge Assessment

The pretest includes 15 PMI-RMP sample exam questions. Use no more than 20 minutes to complete this pretest knowledge assessment. The questions are found in Section 1.1, while Section 1.2 has the answers and explanations. Table 1.1 includes the alignment of the sample exam questions to the five domains found in the *PMI Exam Content Outline and Specifications* (updated March 2022).

The pretest is a good way to test your knowledge before getting really started and to see which strengths and weakness you want to exploit. You may also save the pretest knowledge assessment for later use. The pretest has three sample exam questions from each of the five domains and is a mix of the three approaches (predictive, hybrid, and agile), like you will experience at the real PMI-RMP exam. Table 1.1 contains the full pretest knowledge assessment breakdown.

Table 1.1 PMI-RMP Pretest Knowledge Assessment Breakdown

Domain	Split	Questions	Agile	Hybrid	Predictive	Test Questions
Risk Strategy and Planning	22%	3	1	2	3	1–3
Risk Identification	23%	3	4	5	6	4–6
Risk Analysis	23%	3	7	8	9	7–9
Risk Response	13%	3	10	11	12	10–12
Monitor and Close Risks	19%	3	13	14	15	13–15
Summary	100%	15	5	5	5	1–15

DOI: 10.4324/9781003304012-1

Tip: The PMI-RMP exam will not use least likely, not, or negative questions, however, these types of questions are still good for practice as these types of questions highlight three important correct aspects of the content.

1.1 Pretest Knowledge Assessment Questions

1. Pete, the product lead for an agile team, is having his first workshop with the key stakeholders. He has started working on the risk strategy and planning. Which of the following is the least important topic to discuss with the key stakeholders before the first iteration planning session with the team?
   A. How the preliminary document analysis should be conducted
   B. Input for the assessment of the project environment for threats and opportunities
   C. The key stakeholders' risk thresholds based on risk appetites
   D. The approval of the risk management strategy

2. Anne is the project manager for a hybrid construction project. During the work documenting the risk management plan, the team lead for the agile team asked which risk management activities should be conducted next. What is the best approach for Anne to take?
   A. Anne will plan the predictive risk management activities, while others will facilitate the agile activities, and when both are done, they will align all activities.
   B. First, we need to reconsider which project methodology is needed (e.g., agile, waterfall, hybrid).
   C. We need to list the key risk management activities (e.g., who, what, when, where, how).
   D. We need to develop a common risk breakdown structure (RBS) that can support everyone on the project.

3. Thomas is the project manager of a large healthcare project. Currently he is analyzing the different environmental factors to be considered in the planning phase. Which of the following tools and techniques would be most valued for this task?
   A. Force field analysis
   B. PESTLE
   C. Decision trees
   D. Benchmarking

4 Pete, the product lead, is working with his Scrum master on a concept for his team where the team members need to brainstorm risks, then draw them and explain them to the other team members. The next steps have yet to be finalized. All are very excited about this kind of workshop. What is really the purpose of the workshop?

A. Conduct risk identification exercises

B. Examine assumptions and constraints

C. Recognize the relationship between assumptions and/or constraints, and project objectives

D. Assess and document risk triggers

5 Anne is the project manager for a hybrid construction project and is planning the first risk identification workshop with the key stakeholders. When planning, she and her team need to identify some initial risks. Which of the following would be the least applied tool or technique for that task?

A. Conduct meetings

B. Interviews

C. Focus groups

D. Conduct the qualitative assessment

6 Thomas is the project manager of a large healthcare project. Currently he is examining assumptions and constraints. He has identified these four tasks. What is the best sequence of these tasks?

1. Leverage the results of the assumption and constraint analysis

2. Categorize assumptions and constraints

3. Assess the risk associated with each assumption and/or constraint

4. Recognize the relationship between assumptions and/or constraints, and project objectives

The best sequence is

A. 1, 2, 3, and 4

B. 4, 3, 2, and 1

C. 2, 1, 3, and 4

D. 2, 1, 4, and 3

7 Pete, the product lead, is performing a qualitative analysis with some key stakeholders. When measuring impact, what is the most relevant project constraint for his agile team?

A. Time

B. Cost

C. Scope

D. Quality

8 Anne is the project manager for a hybrid construction project. She has performed the qualitative assessment and is now on her way to perform the quantitative assessment. However, her stakeholders need the risk budget, which covers monetary values for the main risks. Which tool or technique could support this work?

A. Monte Carlo

B. Decision trees

C. Critical path

D. Expected monetary value

9 Thomas is the project manager of a large healthcare project. He and his team have just finished identifying threats and opportunities. Next, they need to assess project risk complexity, but what tool should they use?

A. Monte Carlo simulation

B. Ishikawa diagram

C. Sensitivity analysis

D. Benchmarking

10 Pete, the product lead, and his team have managed to remove a negative risk from the risk board due to technical expertise. The risk response was a major success. What strategy was applied?

A. Exploit

B. Avoid

C. Mitigate

D. Contingency planning

11 Anne is the project manager for a hybrid construction project and has just encountered a risk. The risk response was triggered, but it failed greatly. She has no other responses left. The risk is still severe. What should she do next?

A. Activate the risk response plan

B. Execute the contingency plan

C. Execute the fallback plan

D. Escalate to the steering committee

12 Thomas is the project manager of a large healthcare project. He mitigated a risk, but by doing so his team managed to create another and even severer risk. What type of risk is the new risk?

A. Known risk

B. Secondary risk

C. Residual risk

D. Unknown risk

13 Pete, the product lead, is monitoring risks that have been mitigated but are still active just with reduced probability and/or impact. What is he really doing?
   A. Performing a variance analysis
   B. Monitoring impact against overall project risk exposure
   C. Monitoring residual risks
   D. Monitoring secondary risks

14 Anne is the project manager for a hybrid construction project. She is gathering and analyzing performance data. What task would support this endeavor?
   A. Reconciling performance data and reports from risk relevant work packages
   B. Assessing impact of residual and secondary risks on project objectives
   C. Aggregating and summarizing risk data
   D. Preparing reports for different stakeholders

15 Thomas is the project manager of a large healthcare project. He has been monitoring risk responses and residual risks. Where should these findings be updated?
   A. The risk management plan
   B. The risk management strategy
   C. The risk register
   D. The issue log

1.2 Pretest Knowledge Assessment Answers

The correct option is marked in bold, and all the possible options are discussed in the explanation following each question.

1 Pete, the product lead for an agile team, is having his first workshop with the key stakeholders. He has started working on the risk strategy and planning. Which of the following is the least important topic to discuss with the key stakeholders before the first iteration planning session with the team?
   A. How the preliminary document analysis should be conducted
   B. Input for the assessment of the project environment for threats and opportunities
   C. The key stakeholders' risk thresholds based on risk appetites
   D. **The approval of the risk management strategy**
   Explanation: Options A, B, and C are all valid tasks, but these options are all wrong as this is a question about least importance. Option D is correct. The risk management strategy has not yet been finalized so approval is not possible.

2 Anne is the project manager for a hybrid construction project. During the work documenting the risk management plan, the team lead for the agile team asked which risk management activities should be conducted next. What is the best approach for Anne to take?

A. Anne will plan the predictive risk management activities, while others facilitate the agile activities, and when both are done, they will align all activities.

B. First, we need to reconsider which project methodology is needed (e.g., agile, waterfall, hybrid).

C. **We need to list the key risk management activities (e.g., who, what, when, where, how).**

D. We need to develop a common risk breakdown structure (RBS) that can support everyone on the project.

Explanation: Option A is wrong. Dividing the tasks would not work now. Option B is wrong. This decision has been made, and before working on the risk management plan, this should have been settled and any concerns discussed. Option C is correct. Thy need to figure out what to do. Option D is wrong. The RBS should have been developed within the company and be able to support all teams.

3 Thomas is the project manager of a large healthcare project. Currently he is analyzing the different environmental factors to be considered in the planning phase. Which of the following tools and techniques would be most valued for this task?

A. Force field analysis

B. **PESTLE**

C. Decision trees

D. Benchmarking

Explanation: Options A, C, and D are all wrong. These are PMI tools and techniques but just not for analyzing the external environment. Option B is correct. PESTLE, PEST, SWOT analysis, and similar tools and techniques would do the trick here.

4 Pete, the product lead, is working with his Scrum master on a concept for his team where the team members need to brainstorm risks, then draw them and explain them to the other team members. The next steps have yet to be finalized. All are very excited about this kind of workshop. What is really the purpose of the workshop?

A. **Conduct risk identification exercises**

B. Examine assumptions and constraints

C. Recognize the relationship between assumptions and/or constraints, and project objectives

D. Assess and document risk triggers

Explanation: Option A is correct. The technique is called my worst nightmare and is just an example of risk identification like brainstorming, which is also used. Options B, C, and D are all wrong. These are valid tasks but do not fit the context of the described workshop.

5 Anne is the project manager for a hybrid construction project and is planning the first risk identification workshop with the key stakeholders. When planning, she and her team need to identify some initial risks. Which of the following would be the least applied tool or technique for that task?

A. Conduct meetings

B. Interviews

C. Focus groups

D. **Conduct the qualitative assessment**

Explanation: Options A, B, and C are all valid tools and techniques for risk identification. These options are all wrong, as this is a question about the least applied tool or technique. Option D is correct as it is not for risk identification. The qualitative assessment is conducted after the risk identification.

6 Thomas is the project manager of a large healthcare project. Currently he is examining assumptions and constraints. He has identified these four tasks. What is the best sequence of these tasks?

1. Leverage the results of the assumption and constraint analysis
2. Categorize assumptions and constraints
3. Assess the risk associated with each assumption and/or constraint
4. Recognize the relationship between assumptions and/or constraints, and project objectives

The best sequence is

A. **1, 2, 3, and 4**

B. 4, 3, 2, and 1

C. 2, 1, 3, and 4

D. 2, 1, 4, and 3

Explanation: Option A is correct. This is the best sequence. Options B, C, and D are all wrong. These sequences are not optimal.

7 Pete, the product lead, is performing a qualitative analysis with some key stakeholders. When measuring impact, what is the most relevant project constraint for his agile team?

A. **Time**

B. Cost

C. Scope

D. Quality

Explanation: Option A is correct. Time is most relevant for the team as it may affect days lost during the iteration. Option B is wrong. Cost is fixed and not a major concern for the team during an iteration. Option C is wrong. Scope is flexible. Agile works well with change of scope. This is not a major concern for the team. Option D is wrong. Quality is a concern, but quality issues are often translated into time or costs.

8 Anne is the project manager for a hybrid construction project. She has performed the qualitative assessment and is now on her way to perform the quantitative assessment. However, her stakeholders need the risk budget, which covers monetary values for the main risks. Which tool or technique could support this work?

A. Monte Carlo

B. Decision trees

C. Critical path

D. **Expected monetary value**

Explanation: Options A, B, and C are all wrong. These are tools and techniques for quantitative assessment, but they may not support the context. Option D is correct. This technique measures monetary values of all the main risks in the risk register.

9 Thomas is the project manager of a large healthcare project. He and his team have just finished identifying threats and opportunities. Next, they need to assess project risk complexity, but what tool should they use?

A. Monte Carlo simulation

B. **Ishikawa diagram**

C. Sensitivity analysis

D. Benchmarking

Explanation: Options A, C, and D are all PMI tools and techniques, however, they do not assess project risk complexity. Option B is correct. It is for assessing project risk complexity, just like SWOT analysis, tree diagrams, and similar tools.

10 Pete, the product lead, and his team have managed to remove a negative risk from the risk board due to technical expertise. The risk response was a major success. What strategy was applied?

A. Exploit

B. **Avoid**

C. Mitigate

D. Contingency planning

Explanation: Option A is wrong. This strategy works for positive risks. Option B is correct. The risk was avoided as it was removed. Option C is wrong. Mitigate would reduce probability and/or impact, which was not the case. Option D is wrong. This is not a risk response.

11 Anne is the project manager for a hybrid construction project and has just encountered a risk. The risk response was triggered, but it failed greatly. She has no other responses left. The risk is still severe. What should she do next?

A. Activate the risk response plan

B. **Execute the contingency plan**

C. Execute the fallback plan

D. Escalate to the steering committee

Explanation: Option A is wrong. She has no other plans so this is not an option. Option B is correct. This is the next step after the risk responses. Option C is wrong. This is after the risk contingency plan. Option D is wrong. This is not a valid option.

12 Thomas is the project manager of a large healthcare project. He mitigated a risk, but by doing so his team managed to create another and even severer risk. What type of risk is the new risk?

A. Known risk

B. **Secondary risk**

C. Residual risk

D. Unknown risk

Explanation: Option A is wrong. Risk categorization is not relevant here. Option B is correct. This is a secondary risk created due to the risk response. Option C is wrong. This is not a residual risk. Option D is wrong. Risk categorization is not relevant here.

13 Pete, the product lead, is monitoring risks that have been mitigated but are still active just with reduced probability and/or impact. What is he really doing?

A. Performing a variance analysis

B. Monitoring impact against overall project risk exposure

C. **Monitoring residual risks**

D. Monitoring secondary risks

Explanation: Option A is wrong. This is not a variance analysis. Option B is wrong. He is not monitoring impact against overall project risk exposure. Option C is correct. Active risk with probability and/or impact left is a residual risk. Option D is wrong. A secondary risk is a new risk due to a response, which is not the case.

14 Anne is the project manager for a hybrid construction project. She is gathering and analyzing performance data. What task would support this endeavor?

A. **Reconciling performance data and reports from risk relevant work packages**

B. Assessing impact of residual and secondary risks on project objectives

C. Aggregating and summarizing risk data

D. Preparing reports for different stakeholders

Explanation: Option A is correct. This is the next step of the work. Options B, C, and D are all risk management activities, but are not relevant next steps in this case.

15 Thomas is the project manager of a large healthcare project. He has been monitoring risk responses and residual risks. Where should these findings be updated?

A. The risk management plan

B. The risk management strategy

C. **The risk register**

D. The issue log

Explanation: Option A is wrong. The plan has been developed and should not be updated with these findings. Option B is wrong. The strategy has been developed and should not be updated with these findings. Option C is correct. Risk data should be included in the risk register. Option D is wrong. The question is risk related not issues related.

Chapter 2

PMI-RMP Certification Overview

2.1 Certification

This chapter will answer the who, what, when, where, why, and how questions regarding the PMI Risk Management Professional (PMI-RMP) certification. Some of these answers are derived from the core of Project Management Institute (PMI) publications, which is freely available on the PMI global website.

- *PMI Risk Management Professional (PMI-RMP) Exam Content Outline and Specifications* (updated March 2022)
- *PMI Certification Handbook* (English or Arabic)
- *PMI Continuing Certification Requirements (CCR) Handbook*

A Role Delineation Study (RDS) is a research study that is conducted to serve as the basis for the creation of the examination. The result was a new and improved Examination Content Outline and Specifications November 2021 with new domains, tasks, enablers, and broadening of the approaches to also include hybrid and agile. This was tested and evolved into the *PMI Risk Management Professional (PMI-RMP) Exam Content Outline and Specifications* (updated March 2022).

2.2 Why Become Certified?

Risk management is a topic of growing importance in project management. PMI market research from the Pulse of the Profession series, i.e., "Capturing the Value of Project Management Through Decision Making" (2015) and "Beyond Agility" (2021), and research in general show the importance of risk management for successfully managing projects. The amount and sheer size of the projects we do require more risk management than ever to be successful. Just think about how risk management affects your work.

2.2.1 Why You Should Become Certified Now

I meet a lot of participants who complete a PMI-RMP course but end up not taking the PMI-RMP exam because they do not think they have the time, do not see the need for the certification, or are afraid of not passing the exam. All valid reasons, but I think you should consider going the extra mile and take the PMI-RMP when you have started this journey. Completing a decent PMI-RMP course means most of the content has been covered to some degree, so you are already halfway done. You have earned your diplomas of attendance; however the real PMI certificate holds much higher value and recognition. The certification is a great way of documenting your extensive knowledge of project risk management. If you take a PMI-RMP course and it includes the opportunity to take an exam, but you do not do it, then people may notice and think about the certifications as the extra icing on the cake. You need to know when the certification will come in handy. I do my share of consulting, and before a job I need to send my resume, including certifications, to the firm. But I never really know what the customer is looking for, so I rather have or include too much than too little. I used to remove my BA degree in Chinese from my IT resume, but for some reason it is always a great talking point and a way to differentiate myself. The PMI-RMP certification can also help build credibility (demonstrate knowledge) that you know something about risk management (demonstrate dedication to the profession). For me certifications can determine whether I land the job (and advance career potential) or not. For some consulting jobs, various certifications are mandatory requirements for considerations for the job. In other organizations, I experience increased competences like certifications as a route to obtain a higher salary. In some industries, the risk management maturity is high. However, I often see agile and hybrid risk management knowledge is more scarce, so now you can bring something extra to the table. Completing a certification requires extra effort, and by doing so you learn a lot, and the key takeaway is a common vocabulary and toolbox that may come in handy in many projects. Taking one step back, I see risk management as one of the key amplifiers for better project management (participants may apply the knowledge and skills to a higher degree than non-certified professionals), which is important due to the amount and sheer size of projects changing organizations these days.

Being a certified risk management practitioner includes a wide range of benefits for the individual. However, it also results in increased value for the organization that employs certified risk management practitioners. Some of the key benefits for the organizations are highlighted in the following list:

- Certifications acknowledge the competency of individuals who perform a role, which is increasingly recognized as a vital component of any successful project.
- Certifications can demonstrate the ability to transfer knowledge across the organization.
- Certifications indicate global knowledge of the working methods and standards of the organizations.
- Certifications can identify individuals with an advanced level of knowledge and qualifications.
- Certifications demonstrate a commitment to quality and may increase the effectiveness of working for the organization.
- Certifications obtain a relatively high value as the effort to pass the certification or costs associated are worth the gains from passing.
- Certifications produce reliable, quality results with increased efficiency and consistency.
- The value of certifications makes risk management indispensable for business results.

2.3 Who Certifies?

Project Management Institute is the world's leading not-for-profit professional membership association for the project, program and portfolio management profession. Founded in 1969, PMI delivers value for more than 2.9 million professionals working in nearly every country in the world through global advocacy, collaboration, education and research.

(PMI, 2022)

The Project Management Institute (PMI) delivers a wide range of certifications, with corresponding frameworks including processes, tools, and techniques to deliver for project as well as program and portfolio management:

- Certified Associate in Project Management (CAPM)
- Project Management Professional (PMP)
- PMI Risk Management Professional (PMI-RMP)
- PMI Agile Certified Professional (PMI-ACP)
- PMI Scheduling Professional (PMI-SP)
- PMI Professional in Business Analysis (PMI-PBA)
- Program Management Professional (PgMP)
- Portfolio Management Professional (PfMP)
- PMI Project Management Ready
- Agile Certifications (Disciplined Agile)
- Micro-Credentials (AHPP, CDP, and such)

To fully comprehend the value of a risk management certification, it is imperative to examine some questions that many justifiably ask. Before taking on a certification, one should research the organization, company, or group that has created the certification. This enables you to know the quality that certification might hold based upon the development, material, and the use of the certification. The value of a certification tends to increase with the amount of people being certified and demand from the industry.

Currently, more than 9070 professionals hold active PMI-RMP certifications and numbers are increasing as we speak. This book is closely aligned with certifications from PMI. PMI is an entity that is well known and trusted by organizations and their hiring managers for its credential standards. PMI is a global organization and recognized in more than 221 countries. There are more than 680,000 active individual members globally. This creates a solid foundation for a highly valued certification.

Other companies develop different kinds of certifications in the form of products. In most cases, look for international standards and similar recognitions when judging value. Of course, if the company is a recognized world leader, like Microsoft, Amazon, and SAP, the product speaks for itself.

The second and third questions you should ask are "What is in it?" and "What is in it for me?" A certification is a diploma showing competencies within an area, so it is highly important that the content is of some value. This means that the content of the certification ought to cover best practices from an industry and academic viewpoint.

The more comprehensive and advanced the content is the better. For example, the PMI-RMP certification is created by specialist risk management practitioners and aligned with the ISO standard and the various PMI publications. As a result, the PMI-RMP certification is well positioned to become, if it is not already, the new standard of knowledge for risk management professionals. This is enhanced with the recent changes of including predictive, hybrid, and agile approaches, which makes it even more valuable. When content is the best practice, it can provide the certification with an increased value if thought leaders have been part of the development. This is a mark of quality and may create wide recognition in the industry.

2.4 Who Becomes Certified?

To some degree, who becomes certified follows the same patterns as adopting risk management practices. Predictive risk management has been a focus of larger enterprises running major infrastructure and construction projects. These are the big firms you all know and trade with. This group may be new to agile and hybrid risk management, as they have firm best practices, data, and years of experience. The software industry knows agile but may be less mature when it comes to risk management. It can learn a lot from the predictive content or hybrid, as going predictive would be too much for the industry. Hybrid risk management is new to many practitioners, as many come from working predictive or agile. Another group that gets certified is all the project managers or business analysts who need more knowledge of risk management to deliver successful results no matter how the project is specified, planned, and delivered.

2.5 How to Become Certified

The PMI-RMP credential process is conducted online at the PMI website (http://www.pmi.org) and is highlighted by the timeline (see Table 2.1) of the PMI-RMP credential process. The *PMI Certification Handbook* explains this process, rules and regulations, costs, and more in detail. The process includes steps toward approval for taking the exam and processes for renewing certification after 3 years.

Table 2.1   PMI-RMP Credential Process

Process	Step	Explanation
Application process	1	Application submission (fill in the application)
	2	Application completeness review (5 working days)
	3	Application payment process
	4	Audit process (audit or not)
	5	Multiple-choice examination eligibility (application approved; now you can schedule the exam)
Certification renewable process	1	Certification cycle (certification renewable process)
	2	Certification maintenance
	3	Certification renewal
	4	Certification suspension
	5	Credential expiration

On your journey toward PMI-RMP certification, you need to fulfill the PMI-RMP eligibility requirements. These are found in Table 2.2 and contain requirements related to your degree, risk management experience, and education. You need to fulfill the requirements described in either option 1 or 2 to be able to sit for the exam.

Table 2.2 PMI-RMP Eligibility Requirements

	Option 1	*Option 2*
Degree	Secondary degree (high school diploma, associate's degree, or the global equivalent)	Four-year degree (bachelor's degree or the global equivalent)
Risk management experience	36 months of project risk management experience within the last consecutive 5 years	24 months of project risk management experience within the last 5 consecutive years
Risk management education	40 hours of project risk management education	30 hours of project risk management education

Tip: Most PMI-RMP training courses (PMI Authorized Training Partners, ATPs) may provide you with 30 or 40 hours of project risk management education. Alternatively, you can use non-PMI risk management education.

You can satisfy the project risk management education requirements by demonstrating the successful completion of courses, workshops, and training sessions offered by one or more of the following types of education providers:

A. PMI Authorized Training Partners (ATPs)
B. Employer-/company-sponsored programs
C. Training companies or consultants (e.g., training schools)
D. Distance-learning companies, including an end-of-course assessment
E. University/college academic and continuing education programs

2.5.1 Documenting the PMI-RMP Eligibility Requirements

The documentation of your educational degree and risk management education is fast. You just need to describe it, and if you are pulled out for audit, then share a copy of the transcripts. The risk management experience is written in the application as a combination of drop-down boxes and a project description of 200 to 500 words for each project. Consider the following guidelines:

■ The description should represent professional project risk management work experience only.
■ All the projects should be listed individually.
■ You need to include the true title of the project or basic descriptor of the project purpose, not your role on the project, in the title field.
■ Each project description should be a high-level summary of the project in total.

- The project risk management entries do not include routine, operational, or administrative tasks and responsibilities.
- The number of team members who participated in this project and the budget for the project should be accurately indicated.
- If selected for the PMI audit process, proper verification for the project risk management experience listed in the application can be obtained.

Applications do vary and different applications are approved, but illustrated next is an example of a structure of an application that tends to work fine for most applicants.

Tip: Make sure someone reviews your final application before filing it.

Also, if you have completed a PMI-RMP training course, it is likely the training company can provide guidance on the application.

Project title – Implementation of speech recognition software solution in the public sector

Objective: To tailor and roll-out speech recognition software from Nuance Communications to the hospitals in Region Zealand. The goal was 1500 active users within the first year of rollouts.

Role: I was a risk manager with full responsibilities for the risk management activities where I initially took part in the development of the business case before start of the project. During initiating (IN) I developed the risk management section of the project charter, found the project sponsor with the Project Manager, got approval from the project sponsor, and started working on the project. During planning (PL) I planned the various risk management workshops which I facilitated. The workshops were held with various groups of key stakeholders and subject matter experts with the purpose of identifying and assessing risk based upon the current data and risk breakdown structures and handover documents. In addition, I took part in risk-related activities in terms of planning and budgeting (EX). I collaborated with a team of five Project Managers, which was done with weekly meetings and ongoing follow-ups one on one. The Project Managers and I worked together on the risk register where each provided status and updates where I facilitated the process and was responsible for various risks and issues (MC). I worked on collecting work performance data to understand the risk and how the project was doing. It resulted in several minor changes to the schedule and budget as roll-out was delayed a few times. During closing (CL) I completed the lesson learned register section on risk management and gave overall feedback, which I have worked on since the start of the project and the project report which was presented for the PMO.

Outcome: The project managed 1200 active users within the first year, and the project was prolonged by one year to ensure implementation and minor updates to the system. The risk management activities were managed within the contingency allocated. The project delivered a full working solution, training, hardware, and adaption of the system to the various clinical workflows.

2.5.2 Continuing Certification Requirements (CCR)

Passing the PMI-RMP eligibility requirements and the actual exam is one thing; another aspect is the continuing certification requirements program. The continuing certification requirements program is an online application created to enhance ongoing professional development and foster learning opportunities and sustain the global recognition and value of certification. This is managed by collecting 30 professional development units (PDUs) within a 3-year cycle. The continuing certification requirements program includes "education" and "giving back to the profession" activities. Table 2.3 and Table 2.4 describe the activities and the maximum professional development units obtained within each category.

Table 2.3   Education

Education	Maximum PDU within the Category in a 3-Year Cycle
Courses offered by PMI Authorized Training Partners, chapters, and communities	None
Continuing education	None
Self-directed learning	30 PDUs
No maximum PDUs within a 3-year cycle. 18 point minimum is needed where 4 PDUs are in technical, leadership, and business/strategic.	

Table 2.4   Giving Back to the Profession

Giving Back to the Profession	Maximum PDU within the Category in a 3-Year Cycle
Creating knowledge	12 PDUs
Volunteering	12 PDUs
Work as a professional in project management	4 PDUs
Maximum is 12 PDUs within a 3-year cycle.	

Please keep in mind that some categories may have a maximum of 4 professional development units. In general, 1 PDU is awarded for 1 hour.

Exercise 2.1 Which of the following activities are accepted by PMI as professional development units (PDUs) and how many PDUs can one expect from these activities?

1. Attending a conference on IT practices
2. A work meeting on risk management
3. Reading a book on risk management practices
4. Taking part in a free online webinar
5. E-learning from IEEE or ACM
6. Traditional risk management 2-day course
7. Doing extra work on a project as a risks manager

_____

_____

_____

Answer: All activities in this exercise are provided as professional development units. However, the amount of professional development units may vary depending on the actual activity. This also stresses the fact that professional development units are not necessarily costly or bound to the PMI. It's all about ongoing professional development and fostering learning opportunities to sustain the global recognition and value of the certification.

Tip: Don't worry about PDUs before passing the exam. Some renew their certifications; others don't. If you renew your certification it comes with a minor cost and a new diploma.

2.6 When to Become Certified

During the PMI-RMP credential process (see Table 2.1), once the audit process is completed, you have earned eligibility for the multiple-choice examination, which enables you to schedule your examination at Pearson Vue, a globally recognized test center near you (computer-based testing), or schedule an online exam (online-proctored testing). At this stage you can select an appointment that fits your training and readiness. Most practitioners schedule a time as early as possible to have a fixed point for completing the certification; however, the actual exam is often a few months out in time. When you are approved for the exam, you have 1 year to take the actual exam, so plenty of time. The 1-year exam approval does count toward active certification, so in case the examination content outline changes, the exam approval does not allow you to take the old exam but the active one. In most cases any changes to the exam are informed 6 months in advance, which provide you with time to schedule the exam in case of changes.

2.7 Where to Become Certified

Pearson Vue test centers are located worldwide and found in most capitals and major cities, which should limit your traveling, if you want to sit for the exam (computer-based testing) or you can take the exam at your home or office as online-proctored testing (OPT). The online-proctored testing exam has more options for time and dates than the test center, where spots may be limited due to limitations or demands.

2.8 What Is PMI-RMP Certification?

The PMI Risk Management Professional (PMI-RMP) certification from the Project Management Institute (PMI) is described and publicly available in the *PMI Risk Management Professional (PMI-RMP) Exam Content Outline and Specifications* (updated March 2022). Before going into detail about the actual certification, let us look at the development of the certification, as it demonstrates the magnitude of the content and the approach, which varies from normal practice. The typical PMI certification, e.g., the Project Management Professional (PMP), is based upon a large framework, best practices, and academics in its approach to project management. Academic institutions and large US companies, like NASA, GE, and the Department of Defense, have provided input to the framework.

The PMI-RMP certification was formulated by a PMI supplier, the Alpine Testing Solution, and to some degree based upon the work by risk management specialists throughout the years and existing PMI publications. However, the PMI-RMP is so much more.

Exam candidates should be aware that the PMI-RMP exam is not written according to any single text or singularly supported by any specific reference. PMI does not endorse specific review courses, resources, references, or other materials for certification preparation. The references in the following list are not inclusive of all resources that may be utilized and should not be interpreted as a guaranteed means of passing the exam. As the PMI-RMP is a competency-based credential that assesses the integrated set of knowledge, skills, and abilities as gained from both practical and learned experiences, it should also be noted that the references identified herewith are but one element of a broader set of educational resources and texts that might possibly be utilized for exam study and preparation.

Tip: When updating the PMI website for the April 1, 2022, exam, the list of references was removed, and currently the 2019 standard is the only reference. However, these sources and the 2009 standard are all still relevant.

- *The Standard for Risk Management in Portfolios, Programs, and Projects* (2019) by Project Management Institute
- *A Guide to the Project Management Body of Knowledge (PMBOK Guide)*, Sixth Edition, by Project Management Institute
- *Practical Project Risk Management: The ATOM Methodology*, 3rd edition, by David Hillson and Peter Simon
- *Identifying and Managing Project Risk*, 3rd edition, by Tom Kendrick
- *Enterprise Risk Management: Today's Leading Research and Best Practices for Tomorrow's Executives*, 2nd edition, by John Fraser, Rob Quail, and Betty Simkins
- *Project Risk Management: A Practical Implementation Approach* by Michael M. Bissonette

This handbook has identified what you need to read in the PMI publications, which are mostly available as part of your PMI membership, which also gives you a discount on the exam. The additional books found in the PMI-RMP examination reference list are all included in this work, which should save you a significant amount of time/money, and at the same time present the ideas and concepts in a cohesive manner, which will increase your under-standing significantly and the likelihood of passing the PMI-RMP certification exam with flying colors.

Tip: Consider reading the *Agile Practice Guide* from the Project Management Institute and Agile Alliance.

2.9 What Is a Certification Blueprint?

The PMI-RMP certification exam consists of 115 questions, in which 100 questions are scored, while 15 questions are unscored. The questions are randomly mixed. The time allocated for the exam is 2 hours and 30 minutes, not including the online tutorial before the actual exam and the survey after completing the exam. The details are accumulated in Table 2.5. This gives you a little more than a minute per question which may sound like very little. However, after completing this book, it will become enough time for you. The number of correct answers needed for passing the PMI-RMP certifica-tion exam is not published by the PMI. However, the passing score for all PMI exams is determined by sound psychometric analysis. Most test takers estimate the needed score in the range of 63% to 67%. However, this is not verified by the PMI or any other sources.

Table 2.5   Exam Questions and Time Allocated

Number of Scored Questions	Number of Unscored Questions	Number of Questions in Total	Time Allocated
100	15	115	2 hours and 30 minutes

The content of the PMI-RMP certification is described in the *PMI-RMP Exam Content Outline and Specifications* (updated March 2022.) The PMI-RMP exam consists of five domains. Each domain includes two to six tasks, which have enablers. Enablers are illustrative examples of the work associated with the task. Please note that enablers are not meant to be an exhaustive list but rather offer a few examples to help demonstrate what the task encompasses. Chapters 4 to 8 explain the domains, tasks, and enablers in detail. The overall blueprint is found in Table 2.6, which divides the questions within the domains.

Table 2.6   PMI-RMP Exam Blueprint

Domain	Tasks in the Domain	Percentage of Items on Test
Risk Strategy and Planning	6	22
Risk Identification	4	23
Risk Analysis	3	23
Risk Response	2	13
Monitor and Close Risks	4	19

The pretest knowledge assessment (Chapter 1) and the two full sample exams (Chapters 9 and 10) follow the PMI-RMP exam blueprint. Appendices E and F both provide useful tools you can consider before completing the sample exams.

Chapter 3

Study Tips (What to Read and Do) and How to Pass the Exam

This chapter will explain the exam basics, from how to learn quickly and effectively to how to handle the actual PMI-RMP exam. The first section contains a detailed study plan to be applied and how to tailor it, so it is perfect for you. The following sections cover the details of the exam and what to do before and during the exam.

3.1 Step-by-Step Study Plan

The following is a step-by-step study plan for passing a PMI certification. Feel free to make adjustments until it perfectly fits your way of working.

1. Go to the PMI global website to download the following:
   a. *Exam Content Outline and Specifications* (updated March 2022)
   b. *PMI Certification Handbook*
   c. *PMI Continuing Certification Requirements (CCR) Handbook*

2. Go to the PMI global website, log in (requires membership), and download the following:
   a. *The Standard for Risk Management in Portfolios, Programs, and Projects* (2019)
   b. *Practice Standard for Project Risk Management* (2009)
   c. *A Guide to the Project Management Body of Knowledge (PMBOK Guide)*, Sixth Edition
   d. Optional – *A Guide to the Project Management Body of Knowledge (PMBOK Guide)*, Seventh Edition (It is not mandatory for the PMI-RMP exam; however it provides good fundamental knowledge.)
   e. Optional – *The Agile Practice Guide* from PMI and the Agile Alliance

3. Flip through the literature (in step 2); look at the organization, figures, tables, and such to get familiar with the flow and style.

4. Flip through this book; look at the organization, figures, tables, and such to get familiar with the flow and style.

5. Read Chapters 2 and 3.

6. Start with the pretest knowledge assessment test (Chapter 1).

7. The pretest will help identify your strengths and weakness.

8. Sign up for the PMI-RMP exam, so you have a goal/target.

9. Read Appendix A.

10. Appendix A – Complete all assignments.

11. Read Appendix B.

12. Appendix B – Complete all assignments.

13. Read Appendix C.

14. Appendix C – Complete all assignments.

15. Read Appendix D.

16. Appendix D - Complete all assignments.

17. Read Chapter 4, Section 4.4 for the first time.

18. Read the relevant sections in the literature.

19. Complete reading Chapter 5.

20. Do the pretest.

21. Read and understand the core content.

22. Complete all assignments.

23. Test yourself with the end-of-chapter practice questions.

24. Rinse and repeat (steps 18–23) for Chapters 5, 6, 7, and 8.

25. Complete the assessment test in Chapter 1 again and try to comprehend why the answers are right or wrong.

26. Read Appendix E.

27. Read Appendix F.

28. Take the full sample practice exam in Chapter 9.

29. Ensure that you understand why the answers are right or wrong.

30. Repeat selected sections if you have wrong answers on that topic.

31. Rinse and repeat steps 29 and 30 with the practice exam in Chapter 10.

32. Read the study tips in Chapter 3, Section 3.4 "During the Exam."

33. Apply some of the study tips. Discuss the content with other test takers.

34. Feel free to join a PMI-RMP prep course; however, you won't be needing it!

35. If you want flashcards for remembering, find an app or go online.

36. Pass the PMI-RMP exam with success on the first attempt.

37. Go out and apply the content; if possible, do this before the actual exam.

3.2 Exam Basics

The PMI-RMP examination contains 100 multiple-choice questions with 2 hours and 30 minutes allocated for answers – that is just a little more than 1 minute to answer each question. During the actual exam, the testing aides are calculators that are built into the software, scrap paper/pencils or markers, and note boards.

The PMI-RMP certification exam consists of 100 scored questions. Basically, the 100 questions may be decomposed into three equal-sized chunks of questions: easier questions, which have an emphasis on factual topics; medium questions, which may probe your understandings; and the harder questions with obscure practices and nuances.

This book is structured around Bloom's (1956) taxonomy of educational objectives, where the lowest level of knowledge is remembering, which, to some degree, may help you answer the easier questions. The second level of Bloom's taxonomy is based on understanding, which may help solve the medium difficulty questions. The more difficult questions is where you need to analyze and evaluate content.

The structure of this book is based upon an approach that makes it easy to remember and understand, enhanced by assignments to test this, and enables you to apply the content. If possible, apply the content in your day-to-day work and you will do wonders on the exam. Following the step-by-step study guide ensures that you come through all the steps to reach a high level of learning in a fast and easy manner.

The exam will test your knowledge of risk management domains and tasks documented in the *PMI Exam Content Outline and Specifications* (updated March 2022) and covered in detail throughout Chapters 4–8. This implies that you need to understand the many terms that are used to describe the work of a risk manager on a project or a project manager working with risk management activities on a project. In addition, you will be tested on your ability to apply established risk management practices in a variety of hypothetical situations. This also implies demonstrating a comprehensive understanding of certain project management, predictive, hybrid, and agile methodologies. If you are no expert on agile, make sure to read Appendices A and B.

At the exam, you will encounter 100 well-written multiple-choice questions with these attributes:

- Most of the wording should be in the question stem.
- Answer choices should be brief and parallel.
- Each question should address a single topic.
- Have four answer choices. Of those:
  - One choice should be the unambiguous correct answer.
  - One choice should be almost correct. The intent is to distinguish between those who truly know the content from those whose knowledge is more superficial.
  - A third choice can be like the previous one, or it can be less correct but sound plausible to the uninformed.
  - One choice should be clearly wrong (but in the same context).

The full practice exams in Chapters 9 and 10, the Chapter 1 pretest, and the end-of-chapter practice sample exam questions will illustrate and test you on this.

3.3 Before the Exam

The certification exams are, in most cases, passed or failed before attending the exam, which is highlighted by the alteration of a passage from Sun Tzu, a famous 6th century BC Chinese military strategist. The reason for this is that one aspect is the actual exam content; another aspect is mastering the exam from preparing for the actual exam. *You need both to do well every time.*

- It is said that if you know your *Exam Content Outline and Specifications* content and know how you learn, memorize, and perform at the exams, you will not be imperiled in a hundred exams;
- if you do not know your *Exam Content Outline and Specifications* content but do know how you learn, memorize and perform at the exams, you will win one and lose one;
- if you do not know your *Exam Content Outline and Specifications* content nor how you learn, memorize and perform at the exams, you will be imperiled in every single exam.

The following sections will provide you with some tips on how to learn, memorize, and perform at the exam. Commonsense guidance, like underline text with color pens, use Post-its, and other similar tips, is not included, as every individual is unique, so what works for you, may not work for others. But the following techniques and methods have been tried and tested by many risk professionals in the past.

Tip: A certification exam is a "special" case for many. It comes down to content and how to handle the exam. Being good at taking multiple-choice exams will come a long way.

Basically, if you follow these techniques while reading this book, you will most likely pass the PMI-RMP exam. The content of the PMI exam is structured around the application of risk management theory, practice, and reflection. A multichoice exam requires that you know your terminology/glossary and have completed as many sample exam questions and exams as possible, as it will help you to learn the content and the exam format. This is the reason that most chapters in this book include a pretest, posttest, and exercises. In addition, the book has a 15-question pretest and two full practice exams with 100 sample exam questions in each to prepare for the actual exam as best as possible. The two full practice exams can be found in Chapters 9 and 10. So follow the chapter outlined, do the exams and exercises, and consider the practice of "rinse and repeat" when you have read and completed all the material. Read Section 3.1 if you prefer a step-by-step study plan that really works for most test takers.

Table 3.1 explains some of the general study tips applied for passing the exams. These tips are all things you should consider before the exam and while preparing to maximize the results of your training.

Table 3.1   Study Tips

Study Tip	Explanation
Pair up	Explain it to someone, have someone explaining it to you, and discuss the content and application.
Read, reread, re-reread	Practice makes perfect.
Explain it to someone	Challenge your understanding. Even better, use it at work.
Don't book yourself solid	Apply the content.
Build skills in the right order	Don't jump around in the content before you have completed it all, unless you already know it all.
Success spirals	Complete one chapter and have success with the posttest before moving on.
Set realistic expectations	Think Pareto – With 20 % effort, you can master 80% of the content and you will pass the exam. However, if you want the last 20% correct, it as well would require that you learn all the content of the book by heart, which would require 80% more effort.
Time management	Before and during the exam.
Memorize all formulas and definitions	Check the glossary and chapter exercises.
Practice takes time	Take at least 2 months for the whole preparation. Do not try to attempt the exam without proper preparation.
Freeze your exam date well in advance	Do this at least 2 months before. The preferable exam dates may not be available, as there is always high demand for the exams. However, online options should always be available.
Read the *PMBOK Guide* – Sixth Edition	This is key content covered on the exam.
Read the PMI *Standard for Risk Management in Portfolios, Programs, and Projects* (2019)	This is key content covered on the exam.
Read the *PMI Practice Standard for Project Risk Management* (2009)	This is key content covered on the exam.
Read Appendices A and B on agile if you are not familiar with this topic	This is key content covered on the exam.

(*Continued*)

Table 3.1 (Continued)   Study Tips

Study Tip	Explanation
Don't read additional literature, as you only need to be an expert on the actual exam syllabus	Just read the PMI reference list if in need of additional literature. However, it's not needed as all is covered here.
Self-test	Test yourself, if you want to know how you are doing, what to improve, and when you are ready.
Write it out	Some prefer to talk about the content; others prefer to write it out.
Use mnemonics	Use memorization techniques like mnemonics.
The five senses	Some learn more effectively if all senses are applied.
Find out what you already know	You don't need to memorize what you already know.
Play around	Use games, apps, or whatever to make it fun.
Link and story	Link what you learn to a story to make it easier to remember.

You can complicate how you learn, memorize, and perform at the exams, and we can talk about the 3 R's of remembering (*record*, *retain*, and *retrieve*) or I can just explain it bluntly. What your read is important. You need to store (remember) what your read so you can recall it during the exam. To really make this work you need to understand the content and not forget it again. This is the science of forgetting and why repetition is fantastic. To expand upon this, the content you learn needs to be really understood, so it provides meaning (meaningfulness) to you. When storing the content in your mind it can help organize it. It could be categories like the five domains. Many test takers use association or link the content to something, like practice or something else, so it becomes easier to remember. Moreover, you can consider if virtualization could help, as it does for many test takers.

Some risk professionals find it useful to learn some techniques for remembering/memorizing while working with the content. Three techniques that have been proven useful for passing certifications exams, and at world memory championships, are *mnemonics*, *journey methods*, and *mind maps*. The techniques are explained next, and exercises have been developed for you to test yourself.

Tip: Learning a memorization technique can prove extremely useful for the exam, but it takes time and effort to master a learning technique worth something, so make sure you have the time and energy for it. You can still learn without a proven technique.

Mnemonics are commonly used for lists, numerical sequences, knowledge, skills, and techniques. Table 3.2 is an example of estimating techniques with the mnemonic of BIRDS, which makes it easier to remember. The reality is that mnemonics works best if you create your own.

Table 3.2   BIRDS Mnemonic

Mnemonic	Tool
B	Brainstorming
I	Interview
R	Root-cause
D	Delphi
S	SWOT-analyze

Exercise 3.1 What do you think this "International Space Station Crew Quickly Responded (when) Chemical Reaction Produced Smoke" mnemonic stands for?

_____

_____

_____

_____

Answer: These are the 10 knowledge areas found in the *PMBOK Guide* – Sixth Edition: Integration, Scope, Schedule, Cost, Quality, Resource, Communication, Risks, Procurement, and Stakeholders.

Exercise 3.2 Develop a mnemonic of your own.

_____

_____

_____

Answer: No right or wrong answers.

Another technique for memorizing is the journey method, which is a powerful, flexible, and effective mnemonic based on the idea of remembering landmarks on a well-known journey. I learned this technique from Oddbjørn By, a Norwegian, who at that time was taking part in the memory championships. He wrote a book called *Memo*. The idea in this case is to remember 10 things. The journey method works by connecting the 10 things to 10 rooms in a house.

Table 3.3   Journey Map

Room	Thing
At the front door	Vladimir Putin
Hallway	Maple leaf
Small Toilet	Mickey Mouse
Games room	Dragon
Bedroom	Carnival
Bathroom	Kangaroo
Kitchen	Curry
Living room	Maradona
Utility	Casserole
Cellar	Sultan

Exercise 3.3 Read Table 3.3 then see if you can memorize the 10 things by using the journey method.

_____

_____

_____

_____

Exercise 3.4 What are the 10 largest countries in the world?

_____

_____

_____

_____

Answer: Table 3.4 contains the answer. You need to translate the 10 things into countries like Mickey Mouse meaning USA and so on.

Table 3.4 Journey Map

Room	Country
At the front door	Russia
Hallway	Canada
Small toilet	USA
Games room	China
Bedroom	Brazil
Bathroom	Australia
Kitchen	India
Living room	Argentina
Utility	Kazakhstan
Cellar	Sudan

The journey method virtualizes the countries in the rooms. After a few minutes of memorizing this, you should be able to recall the countries by walking through the house in your memory. At the front door, I see a Russian, meaning Russia. Something else meaning Russia may also be useful if it is easier to remember. If you need bigger or smaller journeys, you can simply add more to them. Please keep in mind that you cannot add content to the rooms in your memory if you do not understand it properly.

Exercise 3.5 Try the journey method on another topic selected in this book and include your own landmarks.

_____
_____
_____
_____

Answer: No right or wrong answers.

Another technique for memorizing is the well-known mind map, which is a tool to remember key terms and concepts by the use of visualization. A mind map could include the five domains, some processes, tasks, enablers, and such. Figure 3.1 is an example of a mind map from the 2011 conference paper "Mind Map Generator Software Model with Text Mining Algorithm" by R. Kudelic, Mladen Konecki, and Mirko Maleković.

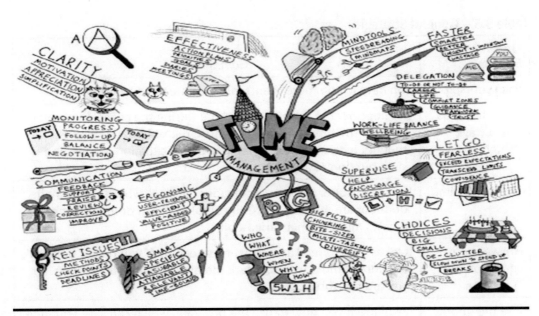

Figure 3.1   Mind map.

Exercise 3.6 Develop a mind map on another topic selected in this book.

_____

_____

_____

_____

Answer: No right or wrong answers.

3.4   During the Exam

The previous section covers various tools, techniques, and good ideas to do before the exam, that is while you are preparing. This section also covers various tools, techniques, and good ideas, but these are to be used during the actual exam. Table 3.5 highlights the general strategies.

Table 3.5   General Strategies

General Strategy	Comments
Pace yourself.	You have a little more than 1 minute for each question.
First questions are always tough.	It is important to keep your spirit up during the exam. As you get into the rhythm it will become more relaxed but it is always tougher in the beginning being in a new situation, nerves and such but don't keep.
Use *all* the time.	If you are done, go back to consider the once where you were in doubt or are missing. If are all completed, just double-check, and enjoy. Online format varies a bit.
Answer each question the first time.	It takes time to read and answer a question. If you read it but don't answer it, time is wasted. Mark the question after answering it if you are not sure.
Use the tutorial.	It will teach you how to use the program, which can save you time during the exam, and it is important to know how to mark answers when you what to go back and examine them again.
Use the mark question feature.	After answering the question, mark it so if you have time, you can go back and examine it again. Otherwise, you have already applied it in case of lack of time.
Take a break or two (test center only).	Take a break if you are answering the questions a little bit too fast, can't concentrate, or when you have completed all the questions the first time. A lot of wrong answers are not due to lack of knowledge but lack of clear mind. You will find time for a break of two during the onsite exam.
Online exams.	The break is free (10 minutes after approximately 58 questions), however, you can't go back to content turned in before the break.

Answering the questions should follow the process as illustrated in Figure 3.2.

Figure 3.2   Answering the questions.

To answer the questions, as in Figure 3.2, activity 3 in the process, you should consider the advice for handling questions, given in Table 3.6.

Table 3.6   Strategies for Answering the Exam Questions

Strategy for Questions	*Comments*
Read the question.	A critical step to passing the exam is to read and understand each question.
Read *all* the choices.	Reading each of the four answers is just as important as carefully reading the questions.
Use a process of elimination.	Remove the clearly wrong answers first so you can use the time on the two likely answers.
A guessing strategy.	You are well prepared, have read the material, and completed the book, so trust your instincts. It is not there by chance.
Remember that you're looking for the best answer.	One or two answers might do. However, you need to pick the best one according to PMI.
There are certain questions that contain extra information.	This information is irrelevant, and it does not relate to the correct answer. Beware of such questions, and remember it isn't necessary to use all the information provided to answer the question.
Each question has only one correct answer.	You need to select the most appropriate answer.
You need to answer the questions from a PMI perspective – not from your own perspective, which you acquired through experience.	Remember that PMI is trying to present an ideal environment for project managers that might be different from your own experience.
Beware of answer choices that represent generalizations, which may be characterized by words such as always, never, must, or completely.	These are often the incorrect choices.
Look out for choices that represent special cases. These choices tend to be correct and are characterized by words such as often, sometimes, may, generally, and perhaps.	The correct answer may not be grammatically correct.

Tip: The onsite exam gives you the opportunity to go back to revisit old questions. The online exam includes a free break. You need to decide what is best for you. I know online is easier to plan, but don't let that cloud your decision.

Exercise 3.7 What is your plan for preparing for the exam?

_____

_____
_____
_____

_____

Answer: No right or wrong answers.

Chapter 4

Domain I: Risk Strategy and Planning

Risk Strategy and Planning is the first domain and includes six tasks. The key definitions include a pretest. Make sure to use the *PMBOK Guide* – Sixth Edition references to check any new words or uncertainties. The introduction gives a short intro to the domain and underlying responsibilities (tasks) of the project risk manager within each domain to ease the understanding of the content. When covering a lot of content, it is important to understand where the tasks are performed; this is the risk management life cycle section. Section 4.4 gives a detailed description of the readings, and the mapping section in this chapter gives page references to the actual content. Keep in mind these references refer to the PMI *Standard for Risk Management in Portfolios, Programs, and Projects* (2019); the PMI *Practice Standard for Project Risk Management* (2009); and the *PMBOK Guide* – Sixth Edition. The focus in these publications is on the predictive content. Next, the underlying responsibilities (tasks) are shortly introduced. Following the tasks is the explanation of the predictive, agile, and hybrid approaches. The predictive approach you can read about, however, agile and hybrid content are included in the exam but not part of the PMI publications, so read these sections carefully.

DOI: 10.4324/9781003304012-4

Appendices A, B, and C include a more comprehensive explanation of the agile and hybrid content. At the end of this chapter you will find five practice questions that relate to the tasks covered and test various approaches, just like the real PMI-RMP exam.

Exercise 4.1 Starting from zero or a lot – What do you know about Risk Strategy and Planning? Write it down or share it with the people in the room.

_____

_____

_____

_____

_____

Answer: No right or wrong answers.

4.1 Domain I: Key Terms

In the beginning of each chapter are highlighted the key terms required by the Project Management Institute (PMI) for the PMI-RMP exam. Hence, you should start with these terms. If you already have a solid knowledge of them, you may consider skipping the chapter. However, once you have finished reading the chapter, you can refer to this list and test your knowledge. In Table 4.1, the terminology of the pretest is highlighted.

Table 4.1 Risk Strategy and Planning Terminology

Term	Source	Page
Assumption log	*PMBOK Guide* – Sixth Edition	699
Benchmarking	Missing reference information	Generic
Conflict resolutions	Missing reference information	Generic
Constraints	*PMBOK Guide* – Sixth Edition	701
Development approach	*PMBOK Guide* – Sixth Edition	704
Document review	*PMBOK Guide* – Sixth Edition	705
Enterprise environmental factors	*PMBOK Guide* – Sixth Edition	706
Historical information	*PMBOK Guide* – Sixth Edition	708
Issue log	*PMBOK Guide* – Sixth Edition	709
Lessons learned	*PMBOK Guide* – Sixth Edition	709
Lessons learned register	*PMBOK Guide* – Sixth Edition	709
Opportunity	*PMBOK Guide* – Sixth Edition	712
Organizational process assets	*PMBOK Guide* – Sixth Edition	712
PESTLE	Missing reference information	Generic
Project charter	*PMBOK Guide* – Sixth Edition	715
Project communication management	*PMBOK Guide* – Sixth Edition	715
Project management information system	*PMBOK Guide* – Sixth Edition	716
Project management plan	*PMBOK Guide* – Sixth Edition	716
RACI chart	*PMBOK Guide* – Sixth Edition	718
Responsibility assignment matrix (RAM)	*PMBOK Guide* – Sixth Edition	720
Risk appetite	*PMBOK Guide* – Sixth Edition	720
Risk breakdown structure	*PMBOK Guide* – Sixth Edition	720
Risk categories	*PMBOK Guide* – Sixth Edition	720
Risk management plan	*PMBOK Guide* – Sixth Edition	721
Risk management strategy	Missing reference information	Generic
Risk principles	The Standard for Risk Management in Portfolios, Programs, and Projects (2019) Practice Standard for Project Risk Management (2009)	Generic

(Continued)

Table 4.1 (Continued)   Risk Strategy and Planning Terminology

Term	Source	Page
Risk register	*PMBOK Guide* – Sixth Edition	721
Risk report	*PMBOK Guide* – Sixth Edition	721
Risk thresholds	*PMBOK Guide* – Sixth Edition	721
Servant leadership	Missing reference information	Generic
Stakeholder analysis	*PMBOK Guide* – Sixth Edition	723
Stakeholder engagement plan	*PMBOK Guide* – Sixth Edition	723
SWOT analysis	*PMBOK Guide* – Sixth Edition	724
Threat	*PMBOK Guide* – Sixth Edition	724

Exercise 4.2 Pretest terminology – Make sure you fully understand all terms in Table 4.1. If you are completing this exercise in a room with more people, then explain all the terms pairwise.

_____

_____

_____

_____

_____

Answer: Check definitions if needed.

4.2 Domain I: Brief Introduction – Risk Strategy and Planning

Risk Strategy and Planning aims at creating the risk management plan with input from the risk management strategy, the risk threshold of the stakeholders based upon the willingness to take risks, the assessment of the project environment, preliminary document analysis, and so on. This focus on creating a strong fundament for the projects risk management activities is planned with the key stakeholders and require ongoing engagement.

The Risk Strategy and Planning domain is heavily influenced by the *PMBOK Guide* – Sixth Edition, where its section 11.1 "Plan Risk Management" explains the process, tools, and techniques in great detail. This is a must read.

The PMI *Practice Standard for Project Risk Management* (2009) is important to read as it provides the building block for understanding the critical success factors and the tools and techniques for risk management planning. Read its chapter 4 on plan risk management, chapter 2 on principles and concepts, and chapter 3 introduction to project risk management, supported by appendix D1, which includes techniques, examples, and templates.

The Standard for Risk Management in Portfolios, Programs, and Projects (2019) supports this, and the PMI *Practice Standard for Project Risk Management* (2009) adds to it with key success factors and principles you need to fully comprehend. Its chapter 4.3 "Key Success Factors" gives insight into the processes and some of the tools and techniques, while supporting materials are found in chapter 7, chapter 2 has context and key concepts, and appendix X6 has tools and techniques.

Exercise 4.3 Know the terminology – List the name of the term described: "a component of the project, program or portfolio management plan that describes how risk management activities will be structured and performed."

_____

_____

_____

_____

Answer: Risk management plan

4.3 Domain I: Risk Management Life Cycle

The Risk Management Life Cycle is a structured approach to the comprehensive view of risks. It is important to have a structured approach when working with risks, and for the PMI-RMP exam it is important to know where we are in the life cycle/process and by doing so what tools, techniques, or underlying responsibilities the exam question context is referring to. The Risk Management Life Cycle gives you a guiding star. You can read about the Risk Management Life Cycle in the PMI *Standard for Risk Management in Portfolios, Programs, and Projects* (2019), section 4.1, pages 28–29; and the *PMBOK Guide* – Sixth Edition, chapter 11 on project risk management. The processes are detailed in sections 11.1 to 11.7 of the *PMBOK Guide* – Sixth Edition. Table 4.2 has the overview.

Table 4.2 Risk Management Life Cycle Overview

Domain/PLC	Plan Risk Management	Identify Risks	Perform Qualitative Risk Analysis	Perform Quantitative Risk Analysis	Plan Risk Responses	Implement Risk Responses	Monitor Risks
Risk Strategy and Planning	Tasks						

📋 **Exercise 4.4 Risk Strategy and Planning crossword**

				3. & 8.		6.			
	7.		5.						
1.		4.							
			2.						

Across: 1. Approach to solve conflicts, without the ending -*s*; 2. Negative risk; 3. Risk structure

Down: 4. Style of leadership; 5. Important review; 6. External environment assessment; 7. Analysis of internal and external factors; 8. Chart that includes people to keep informed among others

_____

_____

_____

_____

Answers: 1. Resolution, 2. Threat, 3. RBS, 4. Servant, 5. Document, 6. PESTLE, 7. SWOT, 8. RACI

4.4 Domain I: Mapping the PMI-RMP Exam Content Outline to the Readings

Obtaining PMI-RMP certification requires candidates to pass the PMI-RMP certification exam. The *PMI Risk Management Professional (PMI-RMP) Exam Content Outline and Specifications* (updated March 2022) documents the domains, tasks, and enablers that are addressed on the PMI-RMP certification exam, as well as the percentages of questions allocated to each of the exam domains.

To assist you in your preparation for the exam, Table 4.3 indicates where the material from the *Exam Content Outline* is covered in the readings. Content not covered by the readings is included in this chapter, or see Appendices A, B, and C for detailed content on agile and hybrid.

Table 4.3 Risk Strategy and Planning Readings

	Domain I: Risk Strategy and Planning (22%)	*Standard (2019) #1*	*Standard (2009) #2*	*PMBOK (6th ed.) #3*
Task 1	Perform a preliminary document analysis	132		
	• Gather and review documents; give examples of preliminary documents to review prior to risk identification; includes industry benchmarks (if available), previous lessons learned, historical data, and the sources of the above information	133	28	409–418
	• Determine and assign who is responsible for the preliminary document analysis (e.g., project manager, risk manager, financial controller)	24	12	317
	• Establish documents relevant to the risk process	57–60	14–18	395–458
Task 2	Assess project environment for threats and opportunities	8		
	• Determine which OPA/EEF/project methodology is needed (e.g., agile, waterfall, hybrid)			37–41, 135
	• Analyze the different environmental factors to be considered in the planning phase (e.g., PESTLE, SWOT analysis)	135		415
	• Determine the organizational and cultural risk appetite; analyze environment for risk culture maturity			720
	• Evaluate the project management information system process and data			95
	• Conduct a stakeholder analysis			512
	• Analyze constraints to risk management; government, market laws/rules, organizational, environmental, and technical risks			
	• Focus stakeholders on creating a culture of risk awareness	4		
	• Determine business driver of project, including key assumptions, benefits, and materialization of project			4-9

(Continued)

Table 4.3 (Continued) Risk Strategy and Planning Readings

	Domain I: Risk Strategy and Planning (22%)	*Standard (2019) #1*	*Standard (2009) #2*	*PMBOK (6th ed.) #3*
Task 3	Confirm risk thresholds based on risk appetites			
	• Align project risk thresholds to organizational risk appetite	8–10	10	407
	• Calculate the risk the organization can absorb (e.g., financial, scope, environmental, technical, legal, schedule, quality, contract)			
	• Discuss risk thresholds	8–10	10	407
	• Lead conflict resolutions between stakeholders in agreeing on risk appetite		10	
Task 4	Establish risk management strategy			
	• Establish risk processes and tools	57–60	14–18	395–458
	• Provide risk management templates/forms			
	• Determine risk metrics			
	• Identify risk categories			425
	• Coach/mentor team on risk management best practices (servant leadership)			
	• Lead stakeholders to adopt the risk strategy			
Task 5	Document the risk management plan			401–408
	• Define organizational risk roles and responsibilities; align roles and responsibilities with a project RAM (e.g., RACI) chart			317
	• Prepare a list of the key artifacts/resources that will be used to compile a risk management plan			
	• Outline the list of key risk management activities (e.g., who, what, when, where, how)			
	• Explain how the risk breakdown structure (RBS) can be used to support the risk management plan	148		425

(Continued)

Table 4.3 (Continued)   Risk Strategy and Planning Readings

	Domain I: Risk Strategy and Planning (22%)	*Standard (2019) #1*	*Standard (2009) #2*	*PMBOK (6th ed.) #3*
	• Define a risk communication plan			366–378
	• Define risk prioritization criteria			
	• Define stakeholder empowerment and education strategy			
Task 6	Plan and lead risk management activities with stakeholders		22	516–522
	• Collaborate with the team that will conduct the risk planning on the project			
	• Leverage stakeholder analysis done by the project manager			
	• Manage stakeholder risk appetite and attitudes			
	• Engage stakeholders in the risk prioritization process			
	• Set appropriate expectations with stakeholders on the rules of engagement			
	• Tailor risk communication for stakeholders			
	• Lead stakeholder empowerment for risk strategies in the risk management plan			
	• Train, coach, and educate stakeholders in risk principles and processes in order to create shared understanding of principles and processes, and foster engagement in risk management			

#1 Standard (2019) refers to *The Standard for Risk Management in Portfolios, Programs, and Projects* (2019), Project Management Institute.
#2 Standard (2009) refers to the *Practice Standard for Project Risk Management* (2009), Project Management Institute.
#3 PMBOK 6th ed. refers to *A Guide to the Project Management Body of Knowledge (PMBOK Guide)*, Sixth Edition, Project Management Institute.

4.5 Domain I: Task 1 – Perform a Preliminary Document Analysis

The purpose of the first task is to perform a preliminary document analysis or document review prior to risk identification and development of the risk management strategy and risk management plan. This work is conducted early in the planning. Documentation is gathered and reviewed for relevant information prior to risk identification and risk planning. Sometimes this document review is supported by meetings or interviews with subject matter experts, and participants from similar projects and such to add details to the preliminary document analysis. The preliminary documents review prior to risk identification could include industry benchmarks, previous lessons learned from the repository, and historical information/data. The roles and responsibilities of the participants involved need to be planned, to which a responsibility assignment matrix (RAM) or similar item may prove useful. The common participants would include project managers, risk managers, sales, financial controllers, and such. The aim here is to establish explicit documentation, learn from others, and gather tacit knowledge previously relevant to the project's risk process. The findings can also provide input to the creating of the risk register, risk report, assumption log, and issue log.

4.6 Domain I: Task 2 – Assess Project Environment for Threats and Opportunities

The purpose of this task is to assess the project environment for risks, whether it is negative risks/threats or positive risks/opportunities. To complete this project environment assessment, several activities could be conducted. One activity determines which enterprise environmental factors (EEFs) and organizational process assets (OPAs) are to be included and how the development approach, that is agile, waterfall, or hybrid, would impact the assessment. An analysis of the different environmental factors to be considered in the planning phase should be conducted. The common analyses are PESTLE or just PEST, MOST/VMOST analysis, Porter's Five Forces, Resource Audit, Boston Box, SWOT analysis, and similar external market scans. The project needs to set the risk appetite right for the assessment. To support the decision, the project should analyze the environment for the risk culture maturity to determine the organizational risk appetite and cultural risk appetite, which should be taken into consideration for the project's risk appetite. Assessing the project environment for threats and opportunities include an evaluation of the project management information system process and data, as processes and data can provide valuable input. The project environment includes the various project stakeholders who affect or are affected by the project. To take the stakeholders into account, a stakeholder identification and analysis should be conducted. The identified and assessed project stakeholders are engaged to create a project culture of risk awareness. The project environment assessment needs to consider and analyze constraints to the risk management effort, which may include constraints within government; market laws/rules;

and organizational, environmental, and technical risks. Last, the project needs to determine the business drivers of the project, including key assumptions, benefits, and materialization of the project, which give valuable insights into the purpose of the project and the driving benefits that may help identify threats and opportunities.

Exercise 4.5 Know the terminology – List the name of the term described: "a philosophy and set of practices that enriches the lives of individuals, builds better organizations and ultimately creates a more just and caring world."

_____
_____
_____
_____
_____

Answer: Servant leadership

4.7 Domain I: Task 3 – Confirm Risk Thresholds Based on Risk Appetites

It is important for a project to discuss and agree with the key stakeholders on how much risk the project should take. How much risk to take is the risk threshold (the measure of acceptable variation around an objective); however, it is influenced by other factors. One factor is the risk appetite (the degree of uncertainty an organization is willing to accept in anticipation of a reward) or the tendency to take risks, which may vary from project to project, from one project stakeholder to another. The project stakeholders need to agree upon the risk appetite or tendency to take risk as it serves as the basis for the project risk threshold. If the project stakeholders cannot discuss and agree, then the project team needs to lead conflict resolutions to reach a conclusion. Another factor is the organizational risk appetite. The organizational risk appetite should be considered by the project so it aligns the project risk thresholds to the organizational risk appetite. How much risk a project should take may depend on how much risk the organization can absorb. A large international organization may absorb more risks than a smaller domestic firm. The calculation of how much risk an organization can absorb is commonly labeled as risk tolerance or risk capacity. This should include financial, scope, environmental, technical, legal, schedule, quality, contract, etc. Last, the risk attitude, which is the disposition toward uncertainty, could also affect the risk thresholds.

4.8 Domain I: Task 4 – Establish Risk Management Strategy

The fourth task is the establishment of the project's risk management strategy. The risk management strategy is the general approach to how risk management should be managed and one of the main components of the risk management plan. The risk management strategy describes the risk processes and tools, risk management templates/forms, risk metrics, and the risk categories that can be applied in the Risk Breakdown Structure. The risk management strategy should be adopted by the project stakeholders and team. The team should apply the risk management activities and best practices described in the risk management strategy and risk management plan. The project has a task to coach and mentor the team on risk management best practices, where servant leadership may prove useful in hybrid or agile environments. Keep in mind the risk management strategy is not a PMI-defined term so some ambiguity may exist.

4.9 Domain I: Task 5 – Document the Risk Management Plan

The risk management plan defines how the project should conduct the risk management activities. This ensures that the degree, type, and visibility of risk management are proportionate to both the risks and the importance of the project to the organization. The risk management plan includes;

- the risk strategy (see Task 4)
- methodology
- risk prioritization criteria
- outlines the key risk management activities (e.g., who, what, when, where, how)
- defines organizational roles and responsibilities, which should be aligned with the project's roles and responsibilities [apply a project responsibility assignment matrix (RAM), e.g., RACI chart]
- funding, timing
- risk categories or how the risk breakdown structure (RBS) can be used to support the risk management plan
- the project's stakeholder risk appetite (see Task 3)
- definitions of risk probability and impact
- reporting formats
- tracking.

To document the risk management plan, the project charter and all components of the project management plans are required. These inputs serve to prepare a list of the key artifacts/resources that will be used to compile the risk management plan. Documenting the risk management plan for the project supports the definition of the risk communication plan and the project stakeholder empowerment and education strategy.

4.10 Domain I: Task 6 – Plan and Lead Risk Management Activities with Stakeholders

The final task of the Risk Strategy and Planning domain involves planning and leading the project stakeholders in the various risk management activities. The risk management activities conducted with the project stakeholders leverage the project stakeholder analysis done by the project manager. The project team that would conduct the risk planning on the project should collaborate with the project stakeholders. The project team should manage the project stakeholder risk appetite and risk attitudes, and engage the project stakeholders in the ongoing risk prioritization process. The risk management plan should set the appropriate expectations with stakeholders on the rules of engagement and tailor the project risk communication for the project stakeholders. The risk management plan includes the risk management strategy in which the project stakeholders should be empowered. Last, the project should train, coach, and educate the project stakeholders in risk principles [the PMI *Standard for Risk Management in Portfolios, Programs, and Projects* (2019) and the PMI *Practice Standard for Project Risk Management* (2009)] and processes to create a shared understanding of the risk principles and risk processes, and foster project stakeholders' engagement in risk management.

4.11 Domain I: Predictive Approaches

The tasks in Sections 4.5 to 4.10 describe the predictive approach to risk management. Read Section 4.4 for the required readings. This approach should be used when there is a high level of risk that requires constant review, control, and planning. Risks can be defined early on and are relatively stable. The upfront planning and analysis may reduce the risks.

Tip: Various models do exist if in doubt about when to use one development approach over the other and the reasons for the choices like well-defined scope and requirements. Consider the Cynefin framework, Stacey matrix, and similar models.

Exercise 4.6 Know the terminology – List the name of the term described: "plan, processes, policies, procedures, and knowledge bases that are specific to and used by the performing organization."

_____

_____

_____

_____

_____

Answer: Organization process assets

4.12 Domain I: Agile Approaches

The Risk Strategy and Planning domain is based upon predictive thinking where the risk effort should be analyzed, the environment assessed, stakeholders involved, the risk threshold defined and planned, and the risk management strategy and risk management plan documented. This is not the agile way of working. The agile way of working is without a plan, that is, organic throughout the process. In a Scrum-based environment, the product owner should engage with the key stakeholders and ensure the product backlog is refined to affect the risk thresholds and contains relevant considerations for the upcoming work. Analyses, spikes, and experiments can be conducted when needed, and the product owner and key stakeholders should assess the project environment to some degree. The risk threshold should be settled by the product owner with the key stakeholders, while the need to document the strategy and plan is often kept to a minimum of documentation. In predictive environments, strategy and planning is done up front, however, in agile the how-to approach is completed iteratively when needed and part of the organic process with Scrum rituals/meetings and tasks already divided between the core Scrum roles. Read Appendices A and B for a more detailed description.

Tip: Consider reading the *Agile Practice Guide* from the Project Management Institute and Agile Alliance.

4.13 Domain I: Hybrid Approaches

The hybrid approaches are a combination of the predictive and agile approaches, in which the approach to the project is based upon the context. Risk strategy and planning tend to have a predictive focus; however, the agile approaches open the opportunity to reduce the upfront planning, trusting the process and limiting the documentation, which may increase the value delivery of the project. Hybrid approaches could imply fewer agile concepts, but it could also imply going with the best from both approaches. That could mean a strong emphasis on analysis, environment scan, risk management strategy, and risk management planning, while basing the work on the agile processes with time-boxed meetings, clear roles and responsibilities, limited documentation, and such. Read Appendix C for a more detailed description.

Tip: Hybrid is (1) an agile or predictive approach followed by an agile or predictive approach, (2) a combined agile and predictive approach used simultaneously, or (3) largely agile or predictive with agile or predictive components.

Exercise 4.7 Beat the clock –

Take 5 minutes and collect your thoughts, then recap the whole chapter in a 1-minute speech. If you are alone, then talk loudly or take notes.

_____

_____

_____

_____

_____

Answer: No right or wrong answers.

4.14 Domain I: Sample PMI-RMP Exam Questions on Risk Strategy and Planning

This section contains five short exam questions in the PMI-RMP format for you to check your knowledge of the content presented in this chapter and to check your readiness for the PMI-RMP exam. The answers are provided (in boldface) following the questions section. If you make mistakes, you should go back and learn why mistakes were made. Do not learn the questions and answers; learn the content.

4.14.1 Questions

1 Pete, the project manager, is working with key stakeholders to assess the project environment. Which of the following is the best example of a threat or opportunity?
   A. The project is expected to base its deliverables upon product line XZY.
   B. The project needs to be completed before the end of summer 2022.
   C. The head of design has left the project.
   D. It might be possible to reduce the costs of labor with virtual teams.

2 Mary, the product owner of a Scrum team, works with key stakehold-
ers to confirm risk thresholds based on risk appetites. How should these
findings be included in the next sprint?
   A. Risk and opportunities should be included in the product backlog.
   B. The product owner should allocate more funds for risk contingency.
   C. Do nothing. The process will handle it.
   D. Include the findings in the sprint backlog and update during the
      sprint retrospective.

3 A business is working to establish a project's risk management strategy.
How can the strategy be applied in the project?
   A. It should be included in the business case.
   B. It should be included in the risk management plan.
   C. It should be included in the project charter.
   D. It is a separate document and not included in other documents.

4 John, the PMO staff member, is working on a company template for proj-
ects to use to document the risk management plan. Which of the follow-
ing should not be included?
   A. The risk management strategy
   B. Roles and responsibilities
   C. Timing
   D. The categories of the WBS

5 Mary and Brett are working with the project manager to plan various risk
management activities to be conducted with the key stakeholders. Which
is the following is the least effective approach?
   A. Knowledge sharing workshop for project managers
   B. Risk identification and assessment workshop for technicians
   C. Interviews with key stakeholders
   D. WBS breakdown session

4.14.2 Answers

1 Pete, the project manager, is working with key stakeholders to assess the project environment. Which of the following is the best example of a threat or opportunity?
  A. The project is expected to base its deliverables upon product line XZY.
  B. The project needs to be completed before the end of summer 2022.
  C. The head of design has left the project.
  D. **It might be possible to reduce the costs of labor with virtual teams.**
  Explanation: Option A is an assumption, which is not a risk. Option B is a constraint, which is not a risk. Option C is an issue, not a risk. Option D is an opportunity and the best example.

2 Mary, the product owner of a Scrum team, works with key stakeholders to confirm risk thresholds based on risk appetites. How should these findings be included in the next sprint?
  A. **Risk and opportunities should be included in the product backlog.**
  B. The product owner should allocate more funds for risk contingency.
  C. Do nothing. The process will handle it.
  D. Include the findings in the sprint backlog and update during the sprint retrospective.
  Explanation: Option A is correct. Option B is incorrect as costs are fixed. Option C would not help the next sprint. Option D is wrong as it should not be included in the sprint backlog, and it is not up to the team to update the risk threshold during a sprint retrospective.

3 A business is working on establishing a project's risk management strategy. How can the strategy be applied in the project?
  A. It should be included in the business case.
  B. **It should be included in the risk management plan.**
  C. It should be included in the project charter.
  D. It is a separate document and not included in other documents.
  Explanation: Option A is not correct as the risk management strategy is not included in the business case. Risk is included but not the strategy. Option B is correct as the risk management strategy is included in the risk management plan. Option C is not correct. The project charter does contain high-level risks but not the risk management strategy. Option D is not correct as the risk management strategy is a component of the risk management plan.

4 John, the PMO staff member, is working on a company template for projects to use to document the risk management plan. Which of the following should not be included?

A. The risk management strategy

B. Roles and responsibilities

C. Timing

D. **The categories of the WBS**

Explanation: Options A, B, and C are all incorrect as these elements are included in the risk management plan. Option D is correct as the categories of the WBS are not included; however, categories of the RBS are. Make sure to read this question carefully.

5 Mary and Brett are working with the project manager to plan various risk management activities to be conducted with the key stakeholders. Which is the following is the least effective approach?

A. Knowledge sharing workshop for project managers

B. Risk identification and assessment workshop for technicians

C. Interviews with key stakeholders

D. **WBS breakdown session**

Explanation: Options A, B, and C are incorrect, as they are fine risk management activities. Option D is a planning activity and the least effective for risk management.

4.15 Domain I: Summary of the Content – Somewhat Sequential

Domain 1: Risk Strategy and Planning

- Perform a preliminary document analysis
- Assess project environment for threats and opportunities
- Confirm risk thresholds based on risk appetites
- Establish risk management strategy
- Document the risk management plan
- Plan and lead risk management activities with stakeholders

Domain 2: Risk Identification

- Conduct risk identification exercises
- Examine assumption and constraint analyses
- Document risk triggers and thresholds based on context/environment
- Develop risk register

Domain 3: Risk Analysis

- Perform qualitative analysis
- Perform quantitative analysis
- Identify threats and opportunities

Domain 4: Risk Response

- Plan risk response
- Implement risk response

Domain 5: Monitor and Close Risks

- Gather and analyze performance data
- Monitor residual & secondary risks
- Provide information required to update relevant project documents
- Monitor project risk levels

Development approaches

- Predictive
- Hybrid
- Agile

Chapter 5

Domain II: Risk Identification

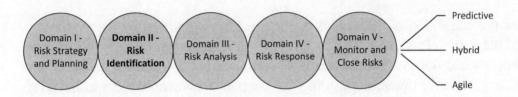

Risk Identification is the second domain and includes four tasks. The key definitions include a pretest. Make sure to use the *PMBOK Guide* – Sixth Edition references to check any new words or uncertainties. The introduction gives a short intro to the domain and underlying responsibilities (tasks) of the project risk manager within each domain to ease the understanding of the content. When covering a lot of content, it is important to understand where the tasks are performed; this is the risk management life cycle section. Section 5.4 gives a detailed description of the readings, however, the mapping section in this chapter gives page references to the actual content. Keep in mind these references refer to the PMI *Standard for Risk Management in Portfolios, Programs, and Projects* (2019); the PMI *Practice Standard for Project Risk Management* (2009)l and the *PMBOK Guide* – Sixth Edition. The focus of these publications is on predictive content. Next, the underlying responsibilities (tasks) are shortly introduced. Following the tasks is the explanation of the predictive, agile, and hybrid approaches. The predictive approach you can read about, however, agile and hybrid content is included in the exam but are not part of the PMI publications, so read these sections carefully. Appendices A, B, and C include more comprehensive explanations of the agile and hybrid content. At the end of this chapter, you will find five practice questions that relate to the tasks covered and test various approaches, just like the real PMI-RMP exam.

DOI: 10.4324/9781003304012-5

Exercise 5.1 Think it, ink it – It is time to read about Risk Identification. What do you already know? Think about it, and then write it down.

_____

_____

_____

_____

_____

Answer: No right or wrong answers.

5.1 Domain II: Key Terms

At the beginning of each chapter, the key terms required by the Project Management Institute (PMI) for the PMI-RMP exam are highlighted. Hence, you should start with these terms. If you already have a solid knowledge of them, you may consider skipping the chapter. However, once you have finished reading the chapter, you can refer to this list and test your knowledge. In Table 5.1, the terminology of the pretest is highlighted.

Table 5.1 Risk Identification Terminology

Term	Source	Page
Assumption	*PMBOK Guide* – Sixth Edition	699
Assumption and constraint analysis	*PMBOK Guide* – Sixth Edition	Generic
Constraint	*PMBOK Guide* – Sixth Edition	701
Impact	PMI Practice Standard for Project Risk Management (2009)	110
Interviews	*PMBOK Guide* – Sixth Edition	709
Opportunity	*PMBOK Guide* – Sixth Edition	712
Probability	PMI Practice Standard for Project Risk Management (2009)	110
Risk attributes	*PMBOK Guide* – Sixth Edition	Generic
Risk register	*PMBOK Guide* – Sixth Edition	720
Risk thresholds	*PMBOK Guide* – Sixth Edition	721
Threats	*PMBOK Guide* – Sixth Edition	724
Trigger condition	*PMBOK Guide* – Sixth Edition	725

Exercise 5.2 Pretest terminology – Make sure you fully understand all terms in Table 5.1. If you are completing this exercise in a room with more people, then explain all the terms pairwise.

_____

_____

_____

_____

_____

Answer: Check definitions if needed.

5.2 Domain II: Brief Introduction – Risk Identification

The domain of risk identification consists of four tasks. The first task focuses on conducting risk identification exercises, the documentation, and assessment of the findings. The second task has an emphasis on assumptions and constraints. The risks associated with each assumption and/or constraint need to be assessed. Assumptions and constraints may also be converted into a risk, which illustrates the importance of the understanding these. The risks identified and assessed should be documented in the risk register, and each identified risk should have a risk trigger, so it is clear when the risk action owner should initiate the risk response. In addition, the project should document the risk thresholds based on the unique context/environment of the project.

The risk identification domain is heavily influenced by the *PMBOK Guide* – Sixth Edition, where chapter 11.2 "Identify Risks" explains these processes and tools and techniques in great detail. This is a must-read.

The PMI *Practice Standard for Project Risk Management* (2009) is important to help understand the critical success factors and the tools and techniques for risk identification. Read its section 5.2 on risk identification and section 5.3 on perspectives, supported by appendix D.2, which includes techniques, examples, and templates.

The *Standard for Risk Management in Portfolios, Programs, and Projects* (2019) supports this and adds the key success factors and principles you need to fully comprehend. Its section 4.3 "Key Success Factors" gives insight into the processes and some of the tools and techniques, while supporting materials are found in chapter 7.1.1 on risk identification, and appendix X6.2.1 on assumption and constraint analysis, and X6.2.10 on interviews.

Exercise 5.3 Know the terminology – List the name of the term described: "an uncertain event or condition that, if it occurs, has a positive or negative effect on one or more project objectives."

_____

_____

_____

_____

_____

Answer: Risk

5.3 Domain II: Risk Management Life Cycle

The Risk Management Life Cycle is a structured approach to the comprehensive view of risks. It is important to have a structured approach when working with risks, and for the exam it is important to know where we are in the life cycle/process and by doing so what tools and techniques the exam question context is referring to. The Risk Management Life Cycle gives you a guiding star. You can read about the Risk Management Life Cycle in the PMI *Standard for Risk Management in Portfolios, Programs, and Projects* (2019), chapter 4.1, pages 28–29; and the *PMBOK Guide* – Sixth Edition, chapter 11 on project risk management, with the processes described in sections 11.1 to 11.7. Table 5.2 has the overview.

Table 5.2   Risk Management Life Cycle Overview

Domain/PLC	Plan Risk Management	Identify Risks	Perform Qualitative Risk Analysis	Perform Quantitative Risk Analysis	Plan Risk Responses	Implement Risk Responses	Monitor Risks
Risk Identification		Tasks					

Exercise 5.4 Risk Identification crossword

2.		4.					6.			
3.		5.								
1.										

Across: 1. Element of an important analysis; 3. Positive risk, without the first letter

Down: 2. Probability; 4. Another word for likelihood, without *-ty*; 5. Risk; 6. Important condition

_____

_____

_____

Answers: 1. Constraint, 2. Impact, 3. (O)pportunity, 4. (Pr)obability, 5. Register, 6. Trigger

5.4 Domain II: Mapping the PMI-RMP Exam Content Outline to the Readings

Obtaining PMI-RMP certification requires candidates to pass the PMI-RMP certification exam. The *PMI Risk Management Professional (PMI-RMP) Exam Content Outline and Specifications* (updated March 2022) documents the domains, tasks, and enablers that are addressed on the PMI-RMP certification exam, as well as the percentages of questions allocated to each of the exam domains.

To assist you in your preparation for the exam, Table 5.3 indicates where the material from the *Exam Content Outline* is covered in the readings. Content not covered by the readings is included in this chapter.

Table 5.3 Risk Identification Readings

	Domain II: Risk Identification (23%)	Standard (2019) #1	Standard (2009) #2	PMBOK (6th ed.) #3
Task 1	Conduct risk identification exercises	58	25–30	409–418
	• Conduct meetings, interviews, focus groups, and other SME support activities			
	• Perform detailed analyses of risk identification exercise results			
	• Analyze documents, audio transcripts, telemetry data, etc., and understand the business context of information			
	• Indicate risks as threats or opportunities			
Task 2	Examine assumption and constraint analyses	130	28	415,521
	• Leverage the results of the assumption and constraint analysis			
	• Categorize assumptions and constraints			
	• Assess the risk associated with each assumption and/or constraint			
	• Recognize the relationship between assumptions and/or constraints, and project objectives (e.g., predict the cascade effect of project stakeholder holiday schedules on project timelines)			
	• Encourage stakeholders to challenge assumptions and constraints			
Task 3	Document risk triggers and thresholds based on context/environment		54–55	417, 448
	• Assess, confirm, and document risk compliance thresholds, and categories against updated risk data	8		398
	• Assess and document risk triggers, causes, and timing			
	• Assess and document risk consequences and/or impact			
	• Empower stakeholders to challenge existing thresholds			

(*Continued*)

Table 5.3 (Continued)   Risk Identification Readings

		Domain II: Risk Identification (23%)	*Standard (2019) #1*	*Standard (2009) #2*	*PMBOK (6th ed.) #3*
Task 4		Develop risk register		29	417
		• Analyze the validity of identified risks and triggers			
		• Examine the risk attributes, like probability, impact, urgency		32	
		• Establish risk origin and ownership, e.g., internal/external			
		• Classify risks as threats or opportunities	7–8		

#1 Standard (2019) refers to *The Standard for Risk Management in Portfolios, Programs, and Projects* (2019), Project Management Institute.
#2 Standard (2009) refers to the *Practice Standard for Project Risk Management* (2009), Project Management Institute.
#3 PMBOK 6th ed. refers to *A Guide to the Project Management Body of Knowledge (PMBOK Guide)*, Sixth Edition, Project Management Institute.

5.5 Domain II: Task 1 – Conduct Risk Identification Exercises

The first task, conduct risk identification exercises, is the process of risk identification and the initial analysis of the results. Risk identification is an ongoing exercise, which is conducted during various data gathering activities such as meetings, structured or semi-structured interviews, focus groups, and other subject matter experts support activities. Risks are identified in these exercises, and to some degree each risk is assigned a risk probability and impact. The team then performs a detailed analysis of the risk identification exercise results by analyzing the findings in terms of examining the documents, audio transcripts, telemetry data, and the like to understand the risks identified and the business context of the information.

Tip: Learn the tools and techniques in the *PMBOK Guide* – Sixth Edition and try to remember the BIRDS mnemonic.

5.6 Domain II: Task 2 – Examine Assumption and Constraint Analyses

The purpose of the second task is to conduct the assumption and constraint analysis, which is a data analysis technique that involves analyzing assumptions and constraints on the project for the purposes of identifying risks. Each project has a group of assumptions and constraints, such as assumptions that work can be conducted all year and a constraint stating that work needs to be completed by the end of the year. When examining the assumptions and constraints, some may turn out to be false and have an impact on the project objective (e.g., predict the cascade effect of project stakeholder holiday schedules on project timelines). In these circumstances the assumptions and constraints may be converted into a risk, which may be a threat or an opportunity. The results should be leveraged and categorized, and the risk associated with each assumption or constraint should be assessed in terms of probability and impact. The project should have all participants, subject matter experts, and stakeholders challenge the assumptions and constraints to test them and, when needed, convert them into threats or opportunities. Some may argue that a risk with a high probability is an assumption, so these concepts can be argued from different perspectives.

Tip: Be sure to understand the differences between assumptions and constraints.

5.7 Domain II: Task 3 – Document Risk Triggers and Thresholds Based on Context/Environment

This task involves the documentation of the risk triggers and risk thresholds. These two concepts are important to understand when the risk action owner should act to what degree risks should be managed. The risk triggers are unique for each risk, and the risk threshold is unique for each project as it is based on the context/environment. The risk register holds a description and analysis of all the identified risks. Each risk includes a column with the risk trigger, which is the timing when the risk response should be activated. The risk trigger could be caused by various factors, such as the amount of errors, complaints, and bad weather multiple days in a row. When the risk trigger occurs, the risk response is activated with the purpose of obtaining the expected consequence and/or impact. The second part of the task involves assessing, confirming, and documenting the risk compliance thresholds, and categorizes it against the updated risk data. It is expected that the key stakeholders, subject matter experts, and others are empowered to challenge existing risks thresholds to ensure the projects aims for the right exposure.

5.8 Domain II: Task 4 – Develop Risk Register

The fourth task is the development of the risk register and assessment of other risk parameters. Tables 5.4–5.6 illustrate various types of risk registers and common content to be included. The development of the risk register also involves the analysis of the validity of identified risks and triggers; various other risk parameters, like probability, impact, urgency, the risk origins, and ownership (e.g., internal or external); and classification of the risks as threats or opportunities.

Table 5.4   Risk Register

Component	Description of the Component	Example of the Component
ID	Unique identification of the risk	2
Creator	Who identified the risk	Klaus Nielsen
Date	Date of risk identification	2014/05/05
Category	Category from RBS	Business
Description	Wording on the risk	Lack of management buy-in
Risk owner	Responsible for handling the risk	CFO
Probability	Probability of occurrence	High (3)
Impact	Impact of risk	Extreme (5)
Expected monetary value (EMV)	Probability, i.e., 10% × Impact of $2,500,000	$250,000
Risk detection	Detection rate	Extreme (5)
Risk matrix	The qualitative assessment	Risk matrix
Risk score of P × I × D	Multiply probability, impact, and detection	75
Proximity	Time of occurrence	Within the next 14 days
Triggers	What initiates a response	Extraordinary board meeting
Response category	Risk strategies	Transfer
Action/contingency	Action based upon our strategy	Meet with CEO
Residual rating	Exposure to loss after mitigation	24
Actionee	Who will take action	My boss
Status	Open or closed	Open
Last review	Date of last review	2014/06/06
Next review	Date for next review	2014/07/07

In some circumstances, to develop a risk register with emphasis on the controls and actions planned, the simplified version presented in Table 5.5 may be useful.

Table 5.5   Risk Register with Controls

Risk	Probability	Impact	Controls	Probability	Impact	Action Planned	Target Date	Owner
Increased costs	5	4	Audit	4	3	Weekly budget controls	11.11.2014	Me
...								

Alternatively, if the risk register is too complicated, it may become difficult to work with and implement within the organization. Then, a much simpler approach may be used, where just main risks and their countermeasures are documented, as illustrated in Table 5.6.

Table 5.6   Main Risks

Main Risk	Countermeasure
Development	Monthly reviews
Implementing	Retrospectives or frequent lesson learn

5.9 Domain II: Predictive Approaches

The tasks in Sections 5.5, 5.6, 5.7, and 5.8 describe the predictive approach to risk management. Read Section 5.4 for the required readings.

5.10 Domain II: Agile Approaches

This domain has a focus on risk identification and associated factors. Risk identification is conducted in agile as an iterative/ongoing effort for the whole team that is supported by the process that gives multiple opportunities to identify risks during the process, whether they are part of the iteration planning, daily standups, iteration review, or iteration retrospective. The risks identified are documented informally in the impediment log, the product backlog, or on a risk "register" board in a highly visible area, such as the war room, where the team spend most of its time. The agile team needs to make assumptions and constraints into account, and some teams would apply an assumption and constraints analysis. In agile, each risk still needs to be identified and agreed upon as a risk trigger so the team members, Scrum master, or product owner, and so forth know when to initiate the agreed-upon risk response. The risk threshold is decided by the product owner in close collaboration with the key stakeholders. The team and Scrum master may provide input to the risk threshold for the team's work, but it is still the final decision of the product owner. The risk register can be applied informally and/or part of the risk board; however, it is rarely as detailed as applied in the predictive environment. Read Appendices A and B for a more detailed description.

Exercise 5.5 Know your agile process keywords – Match the keywords, 1 to 4, to their descriptions, A to D.

1. Iteration planning
2. Daily standup
3. Iteration review
4. Iteration retrospective
A. A 15-minute meeting with emphasis on three questions
B. Meeting divided into two sections: first, examines user stories; second, creates tasks and estimate tasks
C. Last ceremony of the sprint and time to reflect
D. The big exam, what has been produced during the sprint

_____
_____
_____
_____
_____

Answers: 1B, 2A, 3D, and 4C.

Tip: Consider reading the *Agile Practice Guide* from the Project Management Institute and Agile Alliance.

5.11 Domain II: Hybrid Approaches

Hybrid approaches may combine, tailor, and use the more relevant processes, tools, techniques, and ideas from Sections 5.9 and 5.10 to make the perfect fit with their project and unique context. Initially, risk identification can be conducted at risk management exercises or iterative parts of the process. The tasks can be given to individual team members or be shared with the whole team. Both approaches use assumptions and constraint analysis to some degree, so it needs to be considered, as many projects might experience assumptions and constraints that may lead to opportunities or threats. Every project needs a risk threshold; whether it is decided by one person, the product owner, the steering committee or set by the company governance is not vital, just that it is set and considered, so the project can act accordingly. All risks identified, unless just on the watchlist, should have a risk trigger so the team or risk action owners know when to launch the risk response. Risk documentation may be formal in a risk register, less formal on a risk board, or combined with the product backlog and such. It is important to have considered the need and use of risk documentation. Read Appendix C for a more detailed description.

Tip: Hybrid is (1) an agile or predictive approach followed by an agile or predictive approach, (2) a combined agile and predictive approach used simultaneously, or (3) largely agile or predictive with agile or predictive components.

Exercise 5.6 Stand, stretch, and speak – It is time to recap and articulate what you have learned in this chapter, so get up, stretch, and then articulate what you have learned from this chapter.

_____

_____

_____

_____

_____

Answer: No right or wrong answers.

5.12 Domain II: Sample PMI-RMP Exam Questions on Risk Identification

This section contains five short exam questions in the PMI-RMP format for you to check your knowledge of the content presented in this chapter and to check your readiness for the PMI-RMP exam. The answers are provided (in boldface) following the questions section. If you make mistakes, you should go back and learn why mistakes were made. Do not learn the questions and answers; learn the content.

5.12.1 Questions

1 The project has just been initiated, and the project manager works with key stakeholders to build a project chapter. Which of the following would not be a good approach to the identification of the risk section?
   A. Set up meetings with key subject matter experts
   B. Ask the business to develop a risk breakdown structure
   C. Conduct semi-structured interviews with management
   D. Have the business analyst do structured interviews with key subject matter experts

2 The new haven project is defining assumptions and the risks associated with them. Which of the following four is the best example of an assumption?

A. The project needs to be completed end of year X.
B. It is expected that the project may encounter bad weather (when work must be stopped) one week each month during the winter.
C. The project plans on using product X and product Z for the basement construction.
D. Earlier this week, two team members left the project.

3 The new haven project is defining constraints and the risks associated with them. Which of the following four is the best example of a constraint?

A. The technical requirements are not clear.
B. It is expected to be closed for business in December.
C. The project must only use UK-based skilled resources.
D. The project is not going to obtain the final funding.

4 The risk manager of the project has been assigned five risks to which he needs to do something at certain points in time. These points in time are unique for each risk. What are these action points associated with the risks called?

A. Risk description
B. Probability and impact
C. Risk trigger
D. Risk register

5 What is the best place for an agile Scrum product owner to keep track, refine, and prioritize the risk to be handled by the agile Scrum team?

A. Product backlog
B. Iteration backlog
C. Risk register
D. Risk board

5.12.2 Answers

1 The project has just been initiated, and the project manager works with key stakeholders to build a project chapter. Which of the following would not be a good approach to the identification of the risk section?
   A. Set up meetings with key subject matter experts
   B. **Ask the business to develop a risk breakdown structure**
   C. Conduct semi-structured interviews with management
   D. Have the business analyst do structured interviews with key subject matter experts
   Explanation: This is a "not" question. Meetings (option A), semi-structured interviews (option B), and structured interviews (option D) are all valid ways of identifying risks. Option D is the correct answer option. The RBS is important, however, it should have been developed based upon historical data and not developed by the business.

2 The new haven project is defining assumptions and the risks associated with them. Which of the following four is the best example of an assumption?
   A. The project needs to be completed end of year X.
   B. It is expected that the project may encounter bad weather (when work must be stopped) one week each month during the winter.
   C. **The project plans on using product X and product Z for the basement construction.**
   D. Earlier this week, two team members left the project.
   Explanation: Option A is wrong as it is a constraint. Option B could be an assumption; however, it is a bit unclear, so option C is a better example of an assumption. Option D is wrong as it is an issue.

3 The new haven project is just defining constraints and the risks associated with them. Which of the following four is the best example of a constraint?
   A. The technical requirements are not clear.
   B. It is expected to be closed for business in December.
   C. **The project must only use UK based skilled resources.**
   D. The project is not going to obtain the final funding.
   Explanation: Option A is wrong. It is an issue. Option B is wrong, as it is an assumption. Option C is a constraint on the use of resources. Option D is wrong, as it is an issue.

4 The risk manager of the project has been assigned five risks to which he needs to do something at certain points in time. These points in time are unique for each risk. What are these action points associated with the risks called?

A. Risk description

B. Probability and impact

C. **Risk trigger**

D. Risk register

Explanation: Option A is wrong as the risk description describes the risk, not what to do and when to act. Option B is wrong as probability and impact are part of the qualitative risk analysis but will not provide any information about when to act. Option C is correct as the risk trigger explains what triggers the risk response. Option D is wrong as the risk register contains the information, but if the risk trigger is part of the risk register then that would be a more precise option.

5 What is the best place for an agile Scrum product owner to keep track, refine, and prioritize the risk to be handled by the agile Scrum team?

A. **Product backlog**

B. Iteration backlog

C. Risk register

D. Risk board

Explanation: Option A is the best option as risks for the team are included in the product backlog and managed, prioritized, and refined by the product owner, like other work for the Scrum team. Option B is wrong as the team breaks user stories, risks, and such into tasks that are included in the iteration backlog. Option C is wrong as management of risk in a risk register is the predictive approach. Option D is wrong as risk can be posted on the risk board, but refinement and prioritization should have been done in the backlog.

5.13 Domain II: Summary of the Content – Somewhat Sequential

Domain 1: Risk Strategy and Planning

- Perform a preliminary document analysis
- Assess project environment for threats and opportunities
- Confirm risk thresholds based on risk appetites
- Establish risk management strategy
- Document the risk management plan
- Plan and lead risk management activities with stakeholders

Domain 2: Risk Identification

- Conduct risk identification exercises
- Examine assumption and constraint analyses
- Document risk triggers and thresholds based on context/environment
- Develop risk register

Domain 3: Risk Analysis

- Perform qualitative analysis
- Perform quantitative analysis
- Identify threats and opportunities

Domain 4: Risk Response

- Plan risk response
- Implement risk response

Domain 5: Monitor and Close Risks

- Gather and analyze performance data
- Monitor residual & secondary risks
- Provide information required to update relevant project documents
- Monitor project risk levels

Development approaches

- Predictive
- Hybrid
- Agile

Chapter 6

Domain III: Risk Analysis

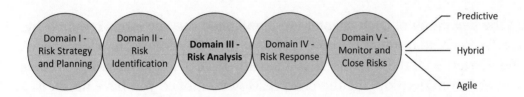

Risk Analysis is the third domain and includes three tasks. The key definitions include a pretest. Make sure to use the *PMBOK Guide* – Sixth Edition references to check any new words or uncertainties. The introduction gives a short intro to the domain and underlying responsibilities (tasks) of the project risk manager within each domain to ease the understanding of the content. When covering a lot of content, it is important to understand where the tasks are performed; this is the risk management life cycle section. Section 6.4 gives the detailed description of the readings, however, the mapping section in this chapter gives page references to the actual content. Keep in mind these references refer to the PMI *Standard for Risk Management in Portfolios, Programs, and Projects* (2019); the PMI *Practice Standard for Project Risk Management* (2009); and the *PMBOK Guide* – Sixth Edition. The focus in these publications is on the predictive content. Next, the underlying responsibilities (tasks) are shortly introduced. Following the tasks is the explanation of the predictive, agile, and hybrid approaches. The predictive approach you can read about; however, agile and hybrid content are included in the exam but not part of the PMI publications, so read these sections carefully. Appendices A, B, and C include a more comprehensive explanation of the agile and hybrid content. At the end of this chapter, you will find five practice questions that relate to the tasks covered and test various approaches, just like the real PMI-RMP exam.

DOI: 10.4324/9781003304012-6

**Exercise 6.1 Where do you stand on Risk Analysis? –
Get up and articulate what you know about Risk Analysis
and its influences on the development approach?**

_____

_____

_____

_____

_____

Answer: No right or wrong answers.

6.1 Domain III: Key Terms

At the beginning of each chapter are highlighted the key terms required by
the Project Management Institute (PMI) for the PMI-RMP exam. Hence, you
should start with these terms. If you already have a solid knowledge of them,
you may consider skipping the chapter. However, once you have finished
reading the chapter, you can refer to this list and test your knowledge. In
Table 6.1 the terminology of the pretest is highlighted.

Table 6.1 Risk Analysis Terminology

Term	Source	Page
Assumption and constraint analysis	The Standard for Risk Management in Portfolios, Programs, and Projects (2019)	131
Brainstorming	The Standard for Risk Management in Portfolios, Programs, and Projects (2019)	131
Checklists	The Standard for Risk Management in Portfolios, Programs, and Projects (2019)	131
Critical path	*PMBOK Guide* – Sixth Edition	704
Decision tree analysis	*PMBOK Guide* – Sixth Edition	704
Document analysis/review	The Standard for Risk Management in Portfolios, Programs, and Projects (2019)	132
Expected monetary value	*PMBOK Guide* – Sixth Edition	Generic
Hierarchical charts	*PMBOK Guide* – Sixth Edition	Generic
Impact	Practice Standard for Project Risk Management (2009)	110
Influence diagrams	*PMBOK Guide* – Sixth Edition	708
Interviews	*PMBOK Guide* – Sixth Edition	709
Monte Carlo analysis	Practice Standard for Project Risk Management (2009)	110
Opportunity	*PMBOK Guide* – Sixth Edition	712
Probability	Practice Standard for Project Risk Management (2009)	109
Probability and impact matrix	*PMBOK Guide* – Sixth Edition	714
Prompt lists	*PMBOK Guide* – Sixth Edition	Generic
Risk breakdown structure	*PMBOK Guide* – Sixth Edition	720
Risk category	*PMBOK Guide* – Sixth Edition	702
Risk management plan	*PMBOK Guide* – Sixth Edition	721
Risk rating	*PMBOK Guide* – Sixth Edition	Generic
Risk register	*PMBOK Guide* – Sixth Edition	721
Risk report	*PMBOK Guide* – Sixth Edition	721
Root-cause analysis	*PMBOK Guide* – Sixth Edition	721
Sensitivity analysis	*PMBOK Guide* – Sixth Edition	722
Simulations	*PMBOK Guide* – Sixth Edition	723
SWOT analysis	*PMBOK Guide* – Sixth Edition	724
Treat	*PMBOK Guide* – Sixth Edition	724

Exercise 6.2 Pretest terminology – Make sure you fully understand all the terms in Table 6.1. If you are completing this exercise in a room with more people, then explain all the terms pairwise.

_____

_____

_____

_____

_____

Answer: Check definitions if needed.

6.2 Domain III: Brief Introduction – Risk Analysis

The risk analysis is essential in risk management activities. The risk management activities should have been described in the risk management plan, and this domain executes the qualitative and quantitative risk analysis. The qualitative risk analysis begins with a risk categorization or framework like the risk breakdown structure or prompt lists. The categorizations contain best practices and historical data on risks. This means the project team is already familiar with the common risks within their domain and it can also help them planning the risk management activities, so all categorized risks are assessed with various key stakeholders and subject matter experts. The qualitative risk management is a matter of assessing probability and impact to all the identified risks which will guide the prioritization. In the qualitative risk analysis, probability and impact are multiplied, resulting in a risk score or risk rating which gives the prioritization. The prioritization can be mapped to a data representation such as a probability and impact matrix or hierarchical charts, and documented in the risk register. After the qualitative assessment of the individual risks, the quantitative assessment examines the risks toward the project objectives, and more advanced tools and techniques can be applied. Some of the most common tools and techniques are sensitivity analysis, simulations such as the Monte Carlo analysis, decision tree analysis, expected monetary value, and influence diagrams, which can be documented in the risk register and/or supplemented with a risk report. The third task in this domain involves the engagement of the stakeholders who can support the project with the identification of threats and opportunities from data gatherings such as brainstorming, checklists, and interviews, and analyzing the findings using tools and techniques such as SWOT analysis, root cause analysis, assumption and constraint analysis, and document analysis/review.

The risk analysis domain is heavily influenced by the *PMBOK Guide –* Sixth Edition, where the qualitative risk analysis (section 11.3), quantitative risk analysis (section 11.4), and identifying risks (section 11.2) processes and tools and techniques are explained in great detail. This is a must read.

From the PMI *Practice Standard for Project Risk Management* (2009) it is important to understand the critical success factors and the tools and techniques for qualitative and quantitative risk analysis. Read its chapters 5, 6, and 7, supported by appendices D, D.2, D.3, and D.4, which include techniques, examples, and templates.

The *Standard for Risk Management in Portfolios, Programs, and Projects* (2019) supports this and adds to it with key success factors and principles you need to fully comprehend. Its sections 4.3, 4.4, and 4.5 give insight into the processes and some of the tools and techniques, while supporting materials are found in appendices X6.2, X6.3, X6.4, and X8 (risk classification).

Exercise 6.3 Know the terminology – List the name of the term described: "a document in which the result of risk analysis and risk response planning are recorded."

_____

_____

_____

_____

_____

Answer: Risk register

6.3 Domain III: Risk Management Life Cycle

The Risk Management Life Cycle is a structured approach to the comprehensive view of risks. It is important to have a structured approach when working with risks, and for the exam it is important to know where we are in the life cycle/process and, by doing so, what tools and techniques the exam question context is referring to. The Risk Management Life Cycle gives you a guiding star. You can read about the Risk Management Life Cycle in *The Standard for Risk Management in Portfolios, Programs, and Projects* (2019), section 4.1, pages 28–29; and the *PMBOK Guide* – Sixth Edition, chapter 11 on project risk management. The processes are in section 11.1 on plan risk management to section 11.7 on monitor risks. Table 6.2 has the overview.

Table 6.2   Risk Management Life Cycle Overview

Domain/PLC	Plan Risk Management	Identify Risks	Perform Qualitative Risk Analysis	Perform Quantitative Risk Analysis	Plan Risk Responses	Implement Risk Responses	Monitor Risks
Risk Analysis		Task 3	Task 1	Task 2			

Exercise 6.4 Risk Analysis crossword

			1.						
	3.								
									4.
5.									
				2.					
	6.								

Across: 1. Type of storm, 3. Type of tree, 5. List of important things, 6. Type of analysis

Down: 2. Most important way of a project, 4. Monetary value

_____

_____

_____

Answers: 1. Brain(storming) 2. Critical (path), 3. Decision (tree analysis), 4. Expected (monetary value), 5. Prompt, 6. Root cause (analysis)

6.4 Domain III: Mapping the PMI-RMP Exam Content Outline to the Readings

Obtaining PMI-RMP certification requires candidates to pass the PMI-RMP certification exam. The *PMI Risk Management Professional (PMI-RMP) Exam Content Outline and Specifications* (updated March 2022) documents the domains, tasks, and enablers that are addressed on the PMI-RMP certification exam, as well as the percentages of questions allocated to each of the exam domains.

To assist you in your preparation for the exam, Table 6.3 indicates where the material from the *Exam Content Outline* is covered in the readings. Content not covered by the readings is included in this chapter.

Table 6.3 Risk Analysis Readings

	Domain III: Risk Analysis (23%)	*Standard (2019) #1*	*Standard (2009) #2*	*PMBOK (6th ed.) #3*
Task 1	Perform qualitative analysis	33–34	31–36	419–427
	• Perform a nominal classification or risks in the RBS using classifications from the risk management plan (e.g., environment, organizational, project management, technical, etc.)			406
	• Estimate the impact of risk on project schedule, budget, resources, and scope			
	• Prioritize the risk based on impact, and urgency			
	• Apply the risk matrices; agreed-upon assessment approach, historical information, definitions of probability and impact, risk categories, preestablished criteria			
	• Perform an ordinal classification			
	• Coach stakeholders on risk categorization strategies			
Task 2	Perform quantitative analysis	34–35	37–42	428–436
	• Analyze risk data and process performance information against established metrics			
	• Analyze a project's general risks			
	• Perform a forecast and trend analysis on new and historical information			
	• Perform sensitivity analysis; Monte Carlo, decision trees, critical path, expected monetary value, etc.			
	• Perform risk weighting and calculate risk priority			
Task 3	Identify threats and opportunities	32–33	25–30	409–418
	• Assess project risk complexity; SWOT analysis, Ishikawa diagram, tree diagram			

(Continued)

Table 6.3 (Continued)   Risk Analysis Readings

	Domain III: Risk Analysis (23%)	*Standard (2019) #1*	*Standard (2009) #2*	*PMBOK (6th ed.) #3*
	• Perform an impact analysis on project objectives; project scopes, schedule cost, and resources, quality, and stakeholders			
	• Assess project compliance objectives against organizational strategic objectives; procedures, project plans, corporate, and project governance, regulatory governance			
	• Empower stakeholders to independently identify threats and opportunities			

#1 Standard (2019) refers to *The Standard for Risk Management in Portfolios, Programs, and Projects* (2019), Project Management Institute.
#2 Standard (2009) refers to the *Practice Standard for Project Risk Management* (2009), Project Management Institute.
#3 PMBOK 6th ed. refers to *A Guide to the Project Management Body of Knowledge (PMBOK Guide)*, Sixth Edition, Project Management Institute.

6.5 Domain III: Task 1 – Perform Qualitative Analysis

The purpose of task 1 is to perform a qualitative analysis of the identified risks. This task is like the process "perform qualitative risk analysis," which is described in the *PMBOK Guide* – Sixth Edition, section 7.3, pages 419–427. At this point in time the project has identified risks, and an assessment is needed to perform the first prioritization. The nominal classification, ordinal classification, and classification based upon a risk breakdown structure or prompt list are described in the risk management plan, and the results are documented in the risk register. The risk management plan sets the stage for how the project should perform the qualitative analysis whether it is based upon historical information, definitions of probability and impact, risk categories, preestablished criteria, or an agreed-upon assessment approach. Many projects would choose a combination that is summarized in a classification. A classification or risk breakdown structure would include various categories of relevant risks for the project, like environment, organizational, project management, and technical, which can guide the project's assessment of the risks. With the categorization settled, each risk needs to be assessed. The qualitative analysis analyzes the risks, one by one, and sets a value to the probability and impact of each risk. This assessment could be based upon a scale of 1 to 5. So, a risk could have a probability of 3 and impact of 4. The analysis of the impact of the risk is on project objectives such as schedule, budget, resources, and scope. When all the risks have been qualitatively assessed, the project may map (data representation) them to the probability and impact matrix to obtain an overview and have a tool for communication. Besides probability and impact, the risk register may also include a column called risk score or risk rating, which is the probability multiplied with impact, so a probability of 3 and impact of 4 would result is a risk rating of 12, which may be higher or lower than the risk tolerance. The qualitative analysis gives projects the means to prioritize risks. This qualitative assessment may be supplemented with urgency, dormancy, or other risk parameters. This task also includes the engagement of stakeholders and subject matter experts, so they have knowledge of the risk categorization strategies to take part and be reassured.

Tip: The qualitative risk analysis is just about probability and impact while all the other and more advanced techniques are for quantitative risks analysis.

6.6 Domain III: Task 2 – Perform Quantitative Analysis

The purpose of task 2 is to perform a qualitative analysis of the identified risks. This task is like the process "perform quantitative risk analysis," which is described in the *PMBOK Guide* – Sixth Edition, section 11.4, pages 428–436. At this point in time the project has identified the risks and performed the qualitative analysis, which have resulted in the prioritization of the identified risks. Some projects take the next step and perform the quantitative analysis, which analyzes the project's general risk data with more advanced tools and techniques. The quantitative analysis can be performed for various purposes. One purpose would be to analyze risk data and work performance information against established metrics. This analysis can be supported by performing a forecast and trend analysis on new and historical information. Quantitative analyses are often tool-supported as they are more complicated to perform than qualitative analyses. Some of the commonly applied tools and techniques for quantitative analysis are simulations, i.e., Monte Carlo analysis, decision tree analysis, critical path, expected monetary value, sensitivity analysis, and influence diagrams. The PMI *Practice Standard for Project Risk Management* (2009) includes a detailed description with the pros, cons, and critical success factors of the tools and techniques. The results, which are documented in the risk register and risk report, from the quantitative analysis can support risk weighting and risk priority.

Tip: Understand the differences between qualitative and quantitative risk assessment, not just the tools and techniques. The PMI *Practice Standard for Project Risk Management* (2009) has a good explanation.

6.7 Domain III: Task 3 – Identify Threats and Opportunities

Task 3 seems to include a combination of processes as the project continues the identification of risks and conducts a more detailed analysis that supplements the qualitative and quantitative assessments. One part of the task is empowering the key stakeholders to independently identify threats/negative risks and opportunities/positive risks. This is described in section 11.2 "Identify Risks" process in the *PMBOK Guide* – Sixth Edition, and the supporting tools would be labelled data gathering. Data gathering for identification of risks could include brainstorming, checklists, and interviews. The full and comprehensive list of tools and techniques for risk identification is found in the PMI *Practice Standard for Project Risk Management (*2009). The other part of the task involves a more detailed data analysis of the identified risks. One approach is to assess the project risk complexity, which can be performed using a SWOT analysis, Ishikawa diagram/root-cause analysis, various tree diagrams, assumption and constraint analysis, or document analysis/review. Another approach would be to perform an impact analysis of the identified risks on project objectives such as scope, schedule, cost, resources, quality, or stakeholders. Like the first two approaches for some projects, it could be of importance to assess project compliance objectives against organizational strategic objectives such as procedures, project plans, corporate, project governance, and regulatory governance. This task broadens the identification of risks to highlight the empowerment of the stakeholders and the supportive approaches to the assessment of the identified risks.

6.8 Domain III: Predictive Approaches

Sections 6.5, 6.6, and 6.7 described the predictive approach to the domain. Read Section 6.4 for the required readings.

Exercise 6.5 Know the terminology – List the name of the term described: "the sequence of activities that represent the longest part through a project, which determines the shortest possible duration."

_____

_____

_____

_____

_____

Answer: Critical path

6.9 Domain III: Agile Approaches

The agile approach to this domain has an emphasis on some of the same differences as seen in some of the other domains. If we begin an agile Scrum process, then the identification and assessment of risks is conducted iteratively during the process. Risks can be identified and qualitative and quantitative assessed during any meeting whether it is iterative planning, daily standup, iterative review, or the iterative retrospective. This gives the agile team a wide range of opportunities to continuously identify, assess, and, for that matter, respond to risks. The predictive approach highlights the importance of assigned roles and responsibilities, like the risk action owner. However, in an agile context, the whole team identifies, assesses, and responds on an iterative basis during the process to the various risk management activities. In the predictive approach, risks are formally documented in the risk register and risk report, while the agile approach favors more informal documentation of the risks and use of a risk board or similar methods that support transparency. In agile, the identification of risks may be based upon a risk breakdown structure, prompt list, but some may claim that is not agile. The challenge with these categorizations in agile is the nature of work varies often so the organization may not have historical information/data to build the categorizations for the agile teams to use. The product owner may coach and empower the key stakeholders on the risk categorization strategies and ask them to identify treats and opportunities, so they can provide the product owner with their feedback. However, its often the core Scrum team – that is, the product owner, Scrum master, and Scrum team – that manages the risk management activities. An agile team could do a qualitative assessment using probability and impact for the prioritization, however, it may be conducted in bigger chunks like small, medium, or large. The prioritization helps the product owner refine the product backlog, which contains the risks for the team. The other risks are managed outside the product backlog by the product owner and the Scrum master. The Scrum master may document these in the impediment log. When it comes to quantitative risk assessment in agile, the opinions vary. Some practitioners may argue it is not applied, while others would use them. In agile, the tools and techniques are often simple, and foster communication and interaction. That means tools and techniques like simulations and decisions trees are rarely applied, however, expected monetary value and sensitivity analyses are often used. An expected monetary analysis works well on the information radiator to illustrate the risks exposed over time with probability in percentages and impact in days. In the predictive approach, projects may do forecasts, analyze trends, examine complexity, do an impact analysis, or compliance objective; but in agile, risk analysis is used if it provides value to the work, otherwise risk management activities are conducted as part of the process. Read Appendices A and B for a more detailed description.

Tip: Consider reading the *Agile Practice Guide* from the Project Management Institute and Agile Alliance.

6.10 Domain III: Hybrid Approaches

If the project is using a hybrid approach, a qualitative and quantitative analysis is still needed. However, the project has some choices to make. Should roles and responsibilities be tied to individual people or should the whole team share ownership to some degree? Should the project apply the agile approach as the structure for the ongoing iterative qualitative and quantitative assessment, or follow the predictive approach? The predictive approach tends to be formal, while agile is more informal. Should the project go for one or the other, or is it possible to choose a part in the middle, perhaps use a risk register for documentation, but skip the risk report but apply information radiators for the team risks? Both agile and predictive have an emphasis on qualitative assessments, while many of the tools and techniques for quantitative assessments are typically applied in a predictive environment. But some tools like expected monetary values work well in both approaches, so that might be a good choice. Both approaches emphasize applying risk matrices, however, do whatever makes sense in agile so waste is not created, and apply some that work for both approaches like historical data. Involving key stakeholders is important no matter which approach is being applied, however, it might be useful to have the project manager act as a product owner to streamline communication and protect the team. Read Appendix C for a more detailed description.

Tip: Hybrid is (1) an agile or predictive approach followed by an agile or predictive approach, (2) a combined agile and predictive approach used simultaneously, or (3) largely agile or predictive with agile or predictive components.

Exercise 6.6 Build in body breaks – Time for a short break, but quickly recap what you just have learned before taking a well-deserved break.

_____
_____
_____
_____
_____

Answer: No right or wrong answers.

6.11 Domain III: Sample PMI-RMP Exam Questions on Risk Analysis

This section contains five short exam questions in the PMI-RMP format for you to check your knowledge of the content presented in this chapter and to check your readiness for the PMI-RMP exam. The answers will be provided in boldface following the question section. If you make mistakes, you should go back and learn why mistakes were made. Do not learn the questions and answers, learn the content.

6.11.1 Questions

1 The project manager is managing various risk workshops with key stakeholders and subject matter experts. The workshops often have discussions about whether the probability or impact of a certain risk is one number or the other, i.e., 2 or 3 based upon a scale of 1 to 5. What should the project manager have done to avoid these debates?
   A. It is a matter of involving the right people in the right workshops.
   B. Apply large chunks like small, medium, or large.
   C. Use wordings, examples, and numbers to describe the scale of 1 to 5, which should limit the debates.
   D. This cannot be avoided as we are dealing with people.

2 You are working as a product owner for an agile team and one of your key stakeholders, a management representative, comes back to you with several identified risks. What additional information would you like to know?
   A. Who helped with the identification?
   B. When do you think the risk may occur?
   C. How sure are you about the identified risks?
   D. Is the impact of the risk more than X amount of dollars?

3 You, as the project manager for a big construction project, are really concerned that some risks would have a larger range of possible outcome than others. Which tool would help you assess this?
   A. Influence diagram
   B. Monte Carlo simulation
   C. Expected monetary value
   D. Sensitivity analysis

4 With your agile team you have created an information radiator including an expected monetary analysis so the risk exposure is clear, and at this point everyone can see that the risk exposure is dropping with each iteration as risks are iteratively being mitigated or avoided. The probability for each risk has been assessed by the team in percentages. However, team members disagree on how to assess the impact. What would be the best solution?

A. Assess impacts in monetary terms like $10,000.
B. Assess impacts in time like lost days.
C. Assess impact in scope like a task not completed during the iteration.
D. Do not assess impact, just probability.

5 You are working as the project manager on a project where you have a project team and two agile development teams. The agile teams are struggling with delivering the tasks that support the project's compliance objectives. More assessment is needed or the project will be closed. Which of the following would not be applied or assess project compliance objective against?

A. Organizational strategic objectives
B. Procedures
C. Project plans
D. Budget

6.11.2 Answers

1 The project manager is managing various risk workshops with key stakeholders and subject matter experts. The workshops often have discussions about whether the probability or impact of a certain risk is one number or the other, i.e., 2 or 3 based upon a scale of 1 to 5. What should the project manager have done to avoid these debates?

A. It is a matter of involving the right people in the right workshops.
B. Apply large chunks like small, medium, or large.
C. **Use wordings, examples, and numbers to describe the scale of 1 to 5, which should limit the debates.**
D. This cannot be avoided as we are dealing with people.

Explanation: Option A is wrong as it is too simple to state it is a matter of involving the right people and with unclear guidelines everyone may have the discussions. Option B sounds like an agile approach, but this is predictive and does not solve the issue. Option C is the best one as you need to help the people doing the assessment with the best possible guidance. Option D is wrong as it can be avoided to some degree with guidance.

2 You are working as product owner for an agile team and one of your key stakeholders, a management representative, comes back to you with several identified risks. What additional information would you like to know?
A. Who helped with the identification?
B. **When do you think the risk may occur?**
C. How sure are you about the identified risks?
D. Is the impact of the risk more than X amount of dollars?
Explanation: It is not relevant who helped with the identification, which makes Option A wrong. Option B is relevant and the best choice as proximity is a useful risk parameter. Option C touches upon certainty where all risks are expected to have certainty, otherwise, they should not be included. Option D is wrong as impact can be assessed during the quantitative assessment and whether a risk has a large or small impact should not be the guiding criteria for including it.

3 You, as the project manager for a big construction project, are really concerned that some risks would have a larger range of possible outcome than others. Which tool would help you assess this?
A. Influence diagram
B. Monte Carlo simulation
C. Expected monetary value
D. **Sensitivity analysis**
Explanation: A large range of possible outcomes is different wording for sensitivity. The best technique and option would be option D, while the other quantitative techniques would not be the best choice in this context.

4 With your agile team you have created an information radiator including an expected monetary analysis so the risk exposure is clear, and at this point everyone can see that the risk exposure is dropping with each iteration as risks are iteratively being mitigated or avoided. The probability for each risk has been assessed by the team in percentages. However, team members disagree on how to assess the impact. What would be the best solution?
A. Assess impacts in monetary terms like $10,000.
B. **Assess impacts in time like lost days.**
C. Assess impact in scope like a task not completed during the iteration.
D. Do not assess impact, just probability.
Explanation: Option A is not the best option because costs are fixed and information on increased cost would not help the Scrum team. Option B is the best option as lost days as an iteration is of great importance. Option C is not correct as tasks not being complete is measured at the end of the iteration during the iteration review. Option D is wrong as it is important to also assess the impact.

5 You are working as the project manager on a project where you have a project team and two agile development teams. The agile teams are struggling with delivering the tasks that support the project's compliance objectives. More assessment is needed, or the project will be closed. Which of the following would not be applied or assess project compliance objective against?

A. Organizational strategic objectives

B. Procedures

C. Project plans

D. **Budget**

Explanation: Options A, B, and C are all possible project compliance objectives and described in the *Exam Content Outline*, while option D is not. As this is a "not" question, option D is the correct answer.

6.12 Domain III: Summary of the Content – Somewhat Sequential

Domain 1: Risk Strategy and Planning

- Perform a preliminary document analysis
- Assess project environment for threats and opportunities
- Confirm risk thresholds based on risk appetites
- Establish risk management strategy
- Document the risk management plan
- Plan and lead risk management activities with stakeholders

Domain 2: Risk Identification

- Conduct risk identification exercises
- Examine assumption and constraint analyses
- Document risk triggers and thresholds based on context/environment
- Develop risk register

Domain 3: Risk Analysis

- Perform qualitative analysis
- Perform quantitative analysis
- Identify threats and opportunities

Domain 4: Risk Response

- Plan risk response
- Implement risk response

Domain 5: Monitor and Close Risks

- Gather and analyze performance data
- Monitor residual & secondary risks
- Provide information required to update relevant project documents
- Monitor project risk levels

Development approaches

- Predictive
- Hybrid
- Agile

Chapter 7

Domain IV: Risk Response

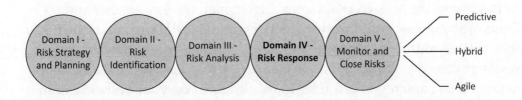

Risk Response is the fourth domain and includes two tasks. The key definitions include a pretest. Make sure to use the *PMBOK Guide* – Sixth Edition references to check any new words or uncertainties. The introduction gives a short intro to the domain and underlying responsibilities (tasks) of the project risk manager within each domain to ease the understanding of the content. When covering a lot of content, it is important to understand where the tasks are performed; this is the risk management life cycle section. Section 7.4 gives a detailed description of the readings; however, the mapping section in this chapter gives page references to the actual content. Keep in mind these references refer to the PMI *Standard for Risk Management in Portfolios, Programs, and Projects* (2019); the PMI *Practice Standard for Project Risk Management* (2009); and the *PMBOK Guide* – Sixth Edition. The focus of these publications is on predictive content. Next the underlying responsibilities (tasks) are shortly introduced. Following the tasks are the explanations of the predictive, agile, and hybrid approaches. The predictive approach you can read about; however, agile and hybrid content are included in the exam but not part of the PMI publications, so read these sections carefully. Appendices A, B, and C include a more comprehensive explanation of the agile and hybrid content. At the end of this chapter, you will five practice questions that relate to the tasks covered and test various approaches, just like the real PMI-RMP exam.

DOI: 10.4324/9781003304012-7

Exercise 7.1 Starting from zero or a lot – What do you know about Risk Response? Write it down or share it with the people in the room.

_____
_____
_____
_____
_____

Answers: No right or wrong answers.

7.1 Domain IV: Key Terms

At the beginning of each chapter are highlighted the key terms required by the Project Management Institute (PMI) for the PMI-RMP exam. Hence, you should start with these terms. If you already have a solid knowledge of them, you may consider skipping the chapter. However, once you have finished reading the chapter, you can refer to this list and test your knowledge. In Table 7.1, the terminology of the pretest is highlighted.

Table 7.1   Risk Response Terminology

Term	Source	Page
Alternative analysis	*PMBOK Guide* – Sixth Edition	699
Assumption log	*PMBOK Guide* – Sixth Edition	699
Contingency plan	Practice Standard for Project Risk Management (2009)	109
Cost-benefit analysis	*PMBOK Guide* – Sixth Edition	703
Fallback plans	*PMBOK Guide* – Sixth Edition	706
Lessons learned register	*PMBOK Guide* – Sixth Edition	709
Multicriteria decision analysis	*PMBOK Guide* – Sixth Edition	711
Plan risk response	*PMBOK Guide* – Sixth Edition	713
Project team assignments	*PMBOK Guide* – Sixth Edition	Generic
Residual risks	*PMBOK Guide* – Sixth Edition	719
Responsibility assignment matrix	*PMBOK Guide* – Sixth Edition	720
Risk acceptance	*PMBOK Guide* – Sixth Edition	720
Risk action	The Standard for Risk Management in Portfolios, Programs, and Projects (2019)	166
Risk action owner	The Standard for Risk Management in Portfolios, Programs, and Projects (2019)	167
Risk avoidance	*PMBOK Guide* – Sixth Edition	720
Risk escalation	*PMBOK Guide* – Sixth Edition	720
Risk exploiting	*PMBOK Guide* – Sixth Edition	721
Risk mitigation	*PMBOK Guide* – Sixth Edition	721
Risk owner	*PMBOK Guide* – Sixth Edition	721
Risk register	*PMBOK Guide* – Sixth Edition	721
Risk report	*PMBOK Guide* – Sixth Edition	721
Risk sharing	*PMBOK Guide* – Sixth Edition	721
Risk transference	*PMBOK Guide* – Sixth Edition	721
Secondary risks	*PMBOK Guide* – Sixth Edition	722

Exercise 7.2 Pretest terminology – Make sure you fully understand all terms in Table 7.1. If you are completing this exercise in a room with more people, then explain all the terms pairwise.

_____

_____

_____

_____

_____

Answers: Check definitions if needed.

7.2 Domain IV: Brief Introduction – Risk Response

Hopefully the relevant positive and negative risks have been identified and documented in the risk register. The risks have been qualitatively analyzed by including the probability and impact of each risk, which would help prioritize the risk register. The quantitative analysis might have been conducted on all the risks and the relationship to the project objectives. At this point the project should plan the relevant risk response strategies for the risks, assign roles and responsibilities, and let others know when (trigger condition) to do what (execute the agreed-upon risk response strategy). If the risk response strategy results in residual or secondary risks, these need to be handled. When all risk response strategies for the risk have been applied, the contingency plans come into play. If the impact is high, a fallback plan might have been developed.

Risk response planning and implementation are explained in detail in the *PMBOK Guide* – Sixth Edition; read "Plan Risk Response" (section 11.5) and "Implement Risk Reponses" (section 11.6). From the PMI *Practice Standard for Project Risk Management* (2009) it is important to understand the critical success factors (People, Planning and Analysis) and the tools and techniques for "Plan Risk Responses Process" (chapter 8; also see appendix D5, which includes techniques, examples, and templates). *The Standard for Risk Management in Portfolios, Programs, and Projects* (2019) supports this and adds to it with key success factors and principles you need to fully comprehend. Its sections 4.6 and 4.7 give insight into the processes, while supporting materials are found in appendices X6.5 and X6.6 of the standard.

Exercise 7.3 Know the terminology – List the name of the term described: "the degree of uncertainty an entity is willing to take on, in anticipation of a reward."

_____

_____

_____

_____

_____

Answers: Risk appetite

7.3 Domain IV: Risk Management Life Cycle

The Risk Management Life Cycle is a structured approach to the comprehensive view of risks. It is important to have a structured approach when working with risks, and for the exam, it is important to know where we are in the life cycle/process and by doing so what tools and techniques the exam question context is referring to. The Risk Management Life Cycle gives you a guiding star. You can read about the Risk Management Life Cycle in *The PMI Standard for Risk Management in Portfolios, Programs, and Projects* (2019), section 4.1, pages 28–29; and the *PMBOK Guide* – Sixth Edition, chapter 11 on project risk management. The processes are in section 11.1 "Plan Risk Management" to section 11.7 "Monitor Risks." Table 7.2 has the overview.

Table 7.2 Risk Management Life Cycle Overview

Domain/PLC	Plan Risk Management	Identify Risks	Perform Qualitative Risk Analysis	Perform Quantitative Risk Analysis	Plan Risk Responses	Implement Risk Responses	Monitor Risks
Risk Response		Task 1	Task 2				

Exercise 7.4 Risk Response crossword

1.				4.						
3.										
	5.									
		6.								
										2.

Across: 1. Type of analysis, without the last "e"; 3. Last resort; 5. Negative risk response strategy; 6. Positive risk response strategy

Down: 2. Place to document assumptions; 4. Type of risks due to other responses

_____

_____

_____

Answers: 1. Alternativ(e) (analysis), 2. (Assumption) log, 3. Fallback (plans), 4. Residual (risks), 5. (Risk) Mitigation, 6. (Risk) Sharing

7.4 Domain IV: Mapping the PMI-RMP Exam Content Outline to the Readings

Obtaining PMI-RMP certification requires candidates to pass the PMI-RMP certification exam. The *PMI Risk Management Professional (PMI-RMP) Exam Content Outline and Specifications* (updated March 2022) documents the domains, tasks, and enablers that are addressed on the PMI-RMP certification exam, as well as the percentages of questions allocated to each of the exam domains.

To assist you in your preparation for the exam, Table 7.3 indicates where the material from the *Exam Content Outline* is covered in the readings. Content not covered by the readings is included in this chapter.

Table 7.3 Risk Response Readings

	Domain IV: Risk Response (13%)	*Standard (2019) #1*	*Standard (2009) #2*	*PMBOK (6th ed.) #3*
Task 1	Plan risk response	35–38	43–50	437–448
	• Determine appropriate risk response strategy: avoid, accept, mitigate, enhance, contingency planning, etc.			
	• Decide the risk response actions (time bound) based on the risk response strategies and identify action owners			
	• Assess the effectiveness of the risk response actions against the identified strategy and the project objectives impact; cost/schedule/ environment, etc., effect of the action on the probability or the risk impact			
	• Illustrate and communicate effectiveness of the risk response strategies; risk burndown chart, dot plots			
	• Determine the workaround			
	• Allocate responsibilities			
	• Outline an appropriate responsibility matrix for a metricized project environment			
	• Reevaluate organizational risks			
Task 2	Implement risk response	38–39	N/A	449–452
	• Execute the risk response plan(s)			
	• Execute the contingency plan(s)			
	• Encourage stakeholders to provide feedback on the risk response			
	• Evaluate and react to secondary and residual risks from the response implementation; improvise as needed			

#1 Standard (2019) refers to *The Standard for Risk Management in Portfolios, Programs, and Projects* (2019), Project Management Institute.

#2 Standard (2009) refers to *Practice Standard for Project Risk Management* (2009), Project Management Institute.

#3 PMBOK 6th ed. refers to *A Guide to the Project Management Body of Knowledge (PMBOK Guide)*, Sixth Edition, Project Management Institute.

7.5 Domain IV: Task 1 – Plan Risk Response

This task seems to be like the "Plan Risk Response" process described in the *PMBOK Guide* – Sixth Edition (section 11.5). The purpose of this task is to determine the appropriate risk response strategy for the relevant risks. The various risk response strategies are split into risk response strategies for positive and negative risks. The risk response strategies for negative risks are avoid, mitigate, transfer, accept, and escalate, while the risk response strategies for positive risks are exploit, enhance, share, accept, and escalate. If in doubt about which strategy to apply, an alternative analysis, cost-benefit analysis, or similar process can be conducted, while the multicriteria decision analysis can support the decision-making. Each risk should have been allocated an assigned risk owner and risk action owner with responsibility to initiate the risk response strategy based upon the identified risk trigger. To ensure clear governance, it is recommended to create a responsibility assignment matrix or RACI chart and project team assignments. The risk response strategies are assessed for the effectiveness of the risk response actions against the identified strategy and the project objectives' impact such as cost, schedule, and scope. The risk response strategy may result in a secondary risk or residual risks if the effectiveness of the strategy leaves some of the risk to be handled. The risk register will include probability and impact assessment of the risks before and after the effect of the risk response strategy. The assessment of the effectiveness of the risk response strategies should be illustrated and communicated in the form of a risk burndown chart, dot plots, and so forth. The risk should be associated with a contingency plan; in some cases also a fallback plan. If the strategies fail, the project needs to determine the workaround.

Tip: Make sure you understand the positive and negative risk responses, and which are similar or just opposite.

7.6 Domain IV: Task 2 – Implement Risk Response

This task seems to be like the "Implement Risk Response" process described in the *PMBOK Guide* – Sixth Edition (section 11.6). The purpose of this task is for the risk action owner to execute the risk response plan(s) that are assigned for the individual risks when the risk trigger happens. Part of the process is to encourage stakeholders to provide feedback on the risk response strategies. If the risk response strategies do not provide the expected result, the contingency plan(s) must be executed. In case this fails the fallback plan as well should be executed by the risk action owner. After implementing the initial risk response, it is important to evaluate and react to secondary and residual risks from the response implementation.

7.7 Domain IV: Predictive Approaches

The predictive approach to the planning and implementation of risk responses is as described in Sections 7.5 and 7.6. At this point in the Risk Management Life Cycle, risks have been identified, analyzed, and documented in the risk register. Now the probability and impact of each risk has been assessed. Not all risks should be handled whether they are positive or negative. With the assessment in place the project needs to figure out what to do with them; this is called risk response strategies. The *PMBOK Guide –* Sixth Edition includes a set of risk response strategies for positive and negative risks. Depending on the importance of the risk, a risk response strategy is decided, risk trigger conditions are agreed upon, and a responsible risk owner and risk action owner are selected, so if a certain condition happens, then the owner will act with the agreed-upon response and the project would have allocated resources. Risk response strategies are applied to the risk of importance. If probability and impact are analyzed to be above our risk tolerance, the risk response strategies are applied to bring the risk below the risk tolerance. After selecting a risk response strategy, the risk's probability and impact are reassessed, so the risk response strategy would reduce the probability and/or impact from this level to this level. The remaining probability and impact are the residual risk, which may be dealt with. If still too high or if low, it can be placed on the watchlist. In addition to the risk response strategy, a contingency plan should be developed, and if important a plan B or fallback plan should be developed. If these do not provide the expected result, the project may end up with a workaround.

Implementing or executing a risk response means that the risk action owner will act when the risk trigger condition is reached. The risk response strategy may work perfectly or not; if not, then the risk action owner executes the next step, which is the contingency plan. The contingency plan may work perfectly or not; if not, then the risk action owner may have a fallback plan or initiate the workaround. The risk response strategies executed may leave some risks left: the residual risk or, in case of a new risk due to the response, the so-called secondary risk. Both risks need to be documented and handled.

Whether the project is planning or implementing a risk response it is important to engage the stakeholders to provide feedback and keep them informed. See Section 7.4 for the required readings.

7.8 Domain IV: Agile Approaches

The agile approaches to the planning and implementation of risk responses are both similar and different from the predictive approaches. The predictive approach would include clear governance and responsibilities, while the agile approaches would focus on the entire team participating. In the predictive environment, risk response planning is conducted during the planning and reassessment during the project, while in agile this is conducted more frequently as part of the process and exit meetings. One of the many strengths of the agile approaches is also the opportunities for ongoing improvements, which could be an iteration retrospective or just part of the continuous improvements. Agile approaches vary in how they approach the planning and implementation of risk responses, so let's illustrate this using the Scrum framework. All work performed by the Scrum team is prioritized by the product owner with the prioritization of the product backlog, which is committed to as part of the sprint planning meeting. In Scrum, the product backlog would also include risks that the Scrum team needs to handle, meaning selecting a risk response strategy and being the risk action owners. Some risks are handled by the Scrum team; others by the Scrum master or product owner, depending on the risks. The product owner is the risk owner of all the risks, but the risk action owners vary in the Scrum core team. The risk action owners are the ones to execute the risk responses when needed. In the agile approach, there is a strong focus on transparency, which means the risk register could be translated into a risk board where the Scrum team's risk and risk responses are visible to all Scrum team members. This helps focus on the risk responses and guides identifications of new risks. Another great agile tool is the agile burndown chart, where the risk exposure is illustrated based upon an expected monetary analysis. The risk response strategies could be the same as for the predictive approaches; however, some argue that the agile approaches could use avoid, mitigate, contain, and evade. Avoid and mitigate are like the PMI strategies, while contain is a contingency like setting aside some funds, and evade is another word for accept. In agile, residual risks and secondary risks are treated like all other risks. During this process the product owner keeps the key stakeholders informed and engaged. If a workaround is needed due to the lack of effectiveness of the risk response, the workaround is decided by the product owner in cooperation with the key stakeholders. Read Appendices A and B for a more detailed description.

Tip: Consider reading the *Agile Practice Guide* from the Project Management Institute and Agile Alliance.

Exercise 7.5 Know your agile role keywords – Match the keywords, 1 to 4, to their descriptions, A to D.

    1. Product owner
    2. Scrum master
    3. Scrum team
    4. Scrum guidance body
    A. The overall risk owner
    B. Provides advice and regulations for many agile teams
    C. Performs the work and does some risk mitigation, if prioritized
    D. Facilitates the process and fosters an environment where risk responses
       are conducted

_____

_____

_____

_____

Answers: 1A, 2D, 3C, and 4B

7.9 Domain IV: Hybrid Approaches

Planning and implementing risk response in a hybrid approach can be applied in many ways as the predictive and agile approaches are so similar yet different, with emphasis on the entire team, frequency, and transparency. Read Appendix C for a more detailed description.

Tip: Hybrid is (1) an agile or predictive approach followed by an agile or predictive approach, (2) a combined agile and predictive approach used simultaneously, or (3) largely agile or predictive with agile or predictive components.

Exercise 7.6 Stand and deliver – Get up and recap what you have learned in this chapter and how you are going to apply it.

_____

_____

_____

_____

Answer: No right or wrong answers.

7.10 Domain IV: Sample PMI-RMP Exam Questions on Risk Responses

This section contains five short exam questions in the PMI-RMP format for you to check your knowledge of the content presented in this chapter and to check your readiness for the PMI-RMP exam. The answers will be provided in boldface following the questions section. If you make mistakes, you should go back and learn why mistakes were made. Do not learn the questions and answers; learn the content.

7.10.1 Questions

1 The product owner has a long list of identified risks in the product development project and is now in the process of refining the product backlog to ensure the risks included can be mitigated by the Scrum team. Which of the following would be a good candidate to be included in the product backlog?
   A. Two designers have left the team
   B. The funding might be pulled
   C. The design phase may take 3 months instead of the planned 2 months
   D. Requirements are unclear

2 The agile team is struggling with a risk and has conducted a deep dive by developing a prototype that has helped in managing the risk, so the probability and impact are much lower than before. Which risk response strategy is being applied?
   A. Enhance
   B. Mitigate
   C. Avoid
   D. Manage

3 The risk response strategy has just been triggered by the risk action owner. The risk response is not working out as expected. The risk action owner has reached out to the project manager to figure out what to do. What would be the best next action?
   A. Execute the contingency plan
   B. Execute the fallback plan
   C. Create a workaround
   D. Execute the following risk responses

4 Your agile Scrum team is using DevOps for continuous integration and
   delivery. A risk in the toolchain has been identified that could have a
   major impact on the time to market for the team's development. Which
   of the following should have the responsibility to act on this risk?
   A. The product owner
   B. The Scrum master
   C. The Scrum team
   D. The shared service team that manages the toolchain for all teams

5 You are working as project manager on a major construction project, and
   due to a lack of stakeholder engagement you decide with the board to
   do more to encourage the stakeholders to provide feedback on the vari-
   ous risk response strategies. What would be a good next step?
   A. Arrange a workshop where you go through the risk register and
      encourage feedback
   B. Invite key stakeholders to participate in the team's iteration review
   C. Share access to the information radiator with the key stakeholders and
      allow them to take responsibility for one or more of the risks
   D. Include the key stakeholders in the risk-relevant communication from
      the team

7.10.2 Answers

1 The product owner has a long list of identified risks in the product
   development project and is now in the process of refining the product
   backlog to ensure the risks included can be mitigated by the Scrum
   team. Which of the following would be a good candidate to be included
   in the product backlog?
   A. Two designers have left the team
   B. The funding might be pulled
   C. **The design phase may take 3 months instead of the planned 2
      months**
   D. Requirements are unclear
   Explanation: Option A is an issue but not a risk as the designers have left
   the team. Option B is a risk; however, it is not likely it can be mitigated
   by the Scrum team. Option C is the best choice as the Scrum team can
   influence and mitigate a plan risk. Option D is an issue but not a risk as
   requirements are unclear.

2 The agile team is struggling with risk and has conducted a deep dive by developing a prototype that has helped in managing the risk, so the probability and impact are much lower than before. Which risk response strategy is being applied?

A. Enhance

B. **Mitigate**

C. Avoid

D. Manage

Explanation: Option A is wrong as the enhanced strategy is for positive risks and aims to increase probability and/or impact. That is not the case in this context. Option B is correct as it is a negative risk where the action has resulted in lower probability and impact. Option C is wrong as the avoid strategy would eliminate the risk, which is not the case here. Option D is a made-up term.

3 The risk response strategy has just been triggered by the risk action owner. The risk response is not working out as expected. The risk action owner has reached out to the project manager to figure out what to do what. What would be the best next action?

A. **Execute the contingency plan**

B. Execute the fallback plan

C. Create a workaround

D. Execute the following risk responses

Explanation: Option A is the best choice. If a risk response fails to deliver, then next is the contingency plan. Option B is wrong as the fallback plan is like a plan B that is executed after the contingency plan. Option C is wrong as the workaround is when all responses and plans have failed or been accepted. Option D is a bit tricky as a risk may include more than one risk response; however, in this case option A is a better choice with the limited information.

4 Your agile Scrum team is using DevOps for continuous integration and delivery. A risk in the toolchain has been identified that could have a major impact on the time to market for the team's development. Which of the following should have the responsibility to act on this risk?

A. The product owner

B. The Scrum master

C. The Scrum team

D. **The shared service team that manages the toolchain for all teams**

Explanation: Option A is not the best choice as the product owner would most likely not have the opportunity to manage the risk or have knowledge of it. Option B is not the best choice as the Scrum master would most likely not have the opportunity to manage the risk or have knowledge of it. Option C could work; however, option D is the best choice if a shared team is present.

5 You are working as project manager on a major construction project, and due to a lack of stakeholder engagement you decide with the board to do more to encourage the stakeholders to provide feedback on the various risk response strategies. What would be a good next step?

A. **Arrange a workshop where you go through the risk register and encourage feedback**

B. Invite key stakeholders to participate in the team's iteration review

C. Share access to the information radiator with the key stakeholders and allow them to take responsibility for one or more of the risks

D. Include the key stakeholders in the risk-relevant communication from the team

Explanation: Option A is the best choice as the workshop, and full risk register will give an opportunity to discuss the risks with the key stakeholders and have them provide feedback when they have something to bring to the table. Option B is wrong as the context is predictive, and the iteration review is the agile approach. Also, the iteration review is at the end of the iteration, so perhaps a bit late anyway. Option C is not the best choice as it sounds agile, but we do not want random stakeholders taking responsibility. Option D could work but is not the best choice as it is too passive and offers too little encouragement to the participants.

7.11 Domain IV: Summary of the Content – Somewhat Sequential

Domain 1: Risk Strategy and Planning

- Perform a preliminary document analysis
- Assess project environment for threats and opportunities
- Confirm risk thresholds based on risk appetites
- Establish risk management strategy
- Document the risk management plan
- Plan and lead risk management activities with stakeholders

Domain 2: Risk Identification

- Conduct risk identification exercises
- Examine assumption and constraint analyses
- Document risk triggers and thresholds based on context/environment
- Develop risk register

Domain 3: Risk Analysis

- Perform qualitative analysis
- Perform quantitative analysis
- Identify threats and opportunities

Domain 4: Risk Response

- Plan risk response
- Implement risk response

Domain 5: Monitor and Close Risks

- Gather and analyze performance data
- Monitor residual & secondary risks
- Provide information required to update relevant project documents
- Monitor project risk levels

Development approaches

- Predictive
- Hybrid
- Agile

Chapter 8

Domain V: Monitor and Close Risks

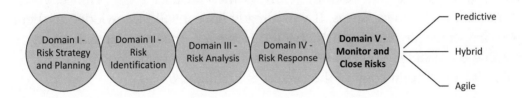

Monitor and Close Risks is the fifth domain and includes four tasks. The key definitions include a pretest. Make sure to use the *PMBOK Guide* – Sixth Edition references to check any new words or uncertainties. The introduction gives a short intro to the domain and underlying responsibilities (tasks) of the project risk manager within each domain to ease the understanding of the content. When covering a lot of content, it is important to understand where the tasks are performed; this is the Risk Management Life Cycle section. Section 8.4 gives a detailed description of the readings; however, the mapping section in this chapter gives page references to the actual content. Keep in mind these references refer to the PMI *Standard for Risk Management in Portfolios, Programs, and Projects* (2019); the PMI *Practice Standard for Project Risk Management* (2009); and the *PMBOK Guide* – Sixth Edition. The focus of these publications is on predictive content. Next, the underlying responsibilities (tasks) are shortly introduced. Following the tasks is the explanation of the predictive, agile, and hybrid approaches. The predictive approach you can read about; however, agile and hybrid content is included in the exam but not part of the PMI publications, so read these sections carefully. Appendices A, B, and C include a more comprehensive explanation of the agile and hybrid content. At the end of this chapter, you will find five practice questions that relate to the tasks covered and test various approaches, just like the real PMI-RMP exam.

DOI: 10.4324/9781003304012-8

Exercise 8.1 Where do you stand on Monitor and Close Risks? – Get up and articulate what you know about Monitor and Close Risks and its influence on development approaches.

_____

_____

_____

_____

_____

Answer: No right or wrong answers.

8.1 Domain V: Key Terms

At the beginning of each chapter are highlighted the key terms required by the Project Management Institute (PMI) for the PMI-RMP exam. Hence, you should start with these terms. If you already have a solid knowledge of them, you may consider skipping this chapter. However, once you have finished reading the chapter, you can refer to this list and test your knowledge. In Table 8.1 the terminology of the pretest is highlighted.

Table 8.1   Monitor and Control Risks Terminology

Term	Source	Page
Change logs	*PMBOK Guide* – Sixth Edition	700
Cost baseline	*PMBOK Guide* – Sixth Edition	703
Lessons learned	*PMBOK Guide* – Sixth Edition	709
Performance measurement baseline	*PMBOK Guide* – Sixth Edition	712
Project documents	*PMBOK Guide* – Sixth Edition	Generic
Project management plan	*PMBOK Guide* – Sixth Edition	716
Residual risk	*PMBOK Guide* – Sixth Edition	719
Risk audit	*PMBOK Guide* – Sixth Edition	720
Risk register	*PMBOK Guide* – Sixth Edition	721
Risk report	*PMBOK Guide* – Sixth Edition	721
Risk reassessment	PMI Practice Standard for Project Risk Management (2009)	102
Secondary risk	*PMBOK Guide* – Sixth Edition	722
Scope baseline	*PMBOK Guide* – Sixth Edition	722
Variance analysis	*PMBOK Guide* – Sixth Edition	725
Work package	*PMBOK Guide* – Sixth Edition	726
Work performance data	*PMBOK Guide* – Sixth Edition	726
Work performance information	*PMBOK Guide* – Sixth Edition	726
Work performance reports	*PMBOK Guide* – Sixth Edition	726

Exercise 8.2 Pretest terminology – Make sure you fully understand all the terms in Table 8.1. If you are completing this exercise in a room with more people, then explain all the terms pairwise.

_____

_____

_____

_____

_____

Answer: Check definitions if needed.

8.2 Domain V: Brief Introduction – Monitor and Close Risks

Monitor and Close Risks is the ongoing watching, evaluating/validation, reporting, identifying of new risks, and managing of all risks. The supporting tasks involve gathering and analyzing work performance data, managing residual and secondary risks, and in the process updating the relevant documentation and informing key stakeholders. During this work, the project needs to ensure the project risk levels are within tolerance and to monitor the impact on overall project risk exposure to the enterprise. Think of it as work performance data gathering, work performance analysis, and representation of the data. This is to some degree explained in the *PMBOK Guide* – Sixth Edition (see its section 11.7 "Monitor Risks"). However, in the PMI *Practice Standard for Project Risk Management* (2009) it is important to understand the critical success factors and the tools and techniques to monitor and control risks, i.e., the risk audit and risk reassessment. The overall emphasis is on the ongoing tracking, documentation, and awareness of risks. *The Standard for Risk Management in Portfolios, Programs, and Projects* (2019) supports this and adds to it with key success factors and principles you need to fully comprehend.

8.3 Domain V: Risk Management Life Cycle

The Risk Management Life Cycle is a structured approach to the comprehensive view of risks. It is important to have a structured approach when working with risks, and for the exam it is important to know where we are in the life cycle/process and by doing so what tools and techniques the exam question context is referring to. The Risk Management Life Cycle gives you a guiding star. You can read about the Risk Management Life Cycle in the PMI *Standard for Risk Management in Portfolios, Programs, and Projects* (2019), section 4.1, pages 28–29; and the *PMBOK Guide* – Sixth Edition, chapter 11 on project risk management. The processes are in sections 11.1 "Plan Risk Management" to 11.7 "Monitor Risks." Table 8.2 has the overview.

Table 8.2   Risk Management Life Cycle Overview

Domain/PLC	Plan Risk Management	Identify Risks	Perform Qualitative Risk Analysis	Perform Quantitative Risk Analysis	Plan Risk Responses	Implement Risk Responses	Monitor Risks
Monitor and Close Risk							Tasks

Exercise 8.3 Monitor and Close Risks crossword

										4.
		1.								
5.		6.				2.				
				3.						

Across: 1. Type of log, 3. Type of risk control of the process, 5. Type of analysis

Down: 2. Important baseline, 4. Type of risk, 6. Work performance data and information becomes

_____

_____

_____

Answers: 1. Change (Logs), 2. Cost (Baseline), 3. (Risk) Audit, 4. Secondary (Risk), 5. Variance (Analysis), 6. (Work Performance) Reports

8.4 Domain V: Mapping the PMI-RMP Exam Content Outline to the Readings

Obtaining PMI-RMP certification requires candidates to pass the PMI-RMP certification exam. *The PMI Risk Management Professional (PMI-RMP) Exam Content Outline and Specifications* (updated March 2022) documents the domains, tasks, and enablers that are addressed on the PMI-RMP certification exam, as well as the percentages of questions allocated to each of the exam domains.

To assist you in your preparation for the exam, Table 8.3 indicates where the material from the *Exam Content Outline* is covered in the readings. Content not covered by the readings is included in this chapter.

Table 8.3   Monitor and Control Risks Readings

	Domain V: Monitor and Close Risks (19%)	*Standard (2019) #1*	*Standard (2009) #2*	*PMBOK (6th ed.) #3*
Task 1	Gather and analyze performance data	39–40	34	
	• Reconcile performance data and reports from risk relevant work packages			95, 109, 112, 157
	• Analyze data to determine the completion status against the baseline		101–105	87, 161, 217, 254
	• Perform a variance analysis			111
	• Monitor impact against overall project risk exposure to enterprise	157–159		458
Task 2	Monitor residual and secondary risks			439, 446
	• Monitor risk response and document residual risk		49	419
	• Monitor risk response for secondary risks			422
	• Assess impact of residual and secondary risks on project objectives	147	26	425
	• Update and communicate impact of residual and secondary risks			417
Task 3	Provide information required to update relevant project documents		55	453
	• Aggregate and summarize risk data, and update project documents, i.e., risk register, lessons learned, project management plan, change logs, etc.		34	89, 456
	• Monitor and close out expired risks			453–458
Task 4	Monitor project risk levels	102–126	10, 51–52	397
	• Assess project risk level			
	• Prepare reports for different stakeholders			
	• Communicate risk levels to key stakeholders		11	

#1 Standard (2019) refers to *The Standard for Risk Management in Portfolios, Programs, and Projects* (2019), Project Management Institute.

#2 Standard (2009) refers to the *Practice Standard for Project Risk Management* (2009), Project Management Institute.

#3 PMBOK 6th ed. refers to *A Guide to the Project Management Body of Knowledge (PMBOK Guide)* – Sixth Edition, Project Management Institute.

8.5 Domain V: Task 1 – Gather and Analyze Performance Data

The purpose of this task is to gather and analyze performance data. The projects need to keep track of how the project is performing. This is done by reconciling work performance data into work performance information, which is used for work performance reports from risk-relevant work packages. The work performance data, which are raw observations, are applied to determine the completion status against the baseline. Keep in mind the overall baseline is the performance measurement baseline; read the *PMBOK Guide* – Sixth Edition definition on page 712, and it consists of the cost, schedule, and scope baseline. To ensure the project is progressing as planned, various analyses can be conducted, one being a variance analysis by examining where the project is and where it is supposed to be and if there is a variance. Other analyses could be a trend analysis and technical performance measurement. The purpose of gathering and analyzing work performance data is also to monitor the impact on overall project risk exposure to the enterprise, not just the project. The risk exposure to the enterprise can, with other risks, be part of the risk report.

8.6 Domain V: Task 2 – Monitor Residual and Secondary Risks

The purpose of this task is to monitor residual and secondary risks. The projects have risks and when risk responses take effect. Projects may have some risks left, which are called residual risks. Read the definition in the *PMBOK Guide* – Sixth Edition on page 719. Or the risk response may lead to another risk, called the secondary risk. Read the definition in the *PMBOK Guide* – Sixth Edition on page 722. It is important for a project to monitor residual and secondary risks, as there are risks that are left after the response or whole new risks arise due to the risk response. The *PMBOK Guide* – Seventh Edition also includes a section on "addressing opportunities and threats"; read section 3.10 for supplementary information. The project needs to document this, which is usually done in the risk register. This could also lead to the need to update relevant project documents, as discussed in the next task. Monitoring and documenting risk responses for residual and secondary risks is conducted with emphasis on assessing the impact on project objectives. Is the remaining risk (residual) going to affect the schedule? Is the secondary risk going to have an impact on the budget? The status of all risks – whether these are positive or negative risks, residual or secondary – needs to be communicated to the relevant key stakeholders and subject matter experts.

8.7 Domain V: Task 3 – Provide Information Required to Update Relevant Project Documents

The purpose of this task is to provide information required to update relevant project documents. The Monitor and Close Risk domain monitors progress by collecting data, and in that process the situation is analyzed. The results may require updating relevant project documents. The most common project documents would include the risk register, lessons learned, project management plan, and change logs. The *PMBOK Guide* – Sixth Edition holds the full list of the various project documents (read page 746). Collecting and analyzing data may be conducted as part of a risk audit and lessons learned session, which results in various findings that need to be documented. Keep in mind that updating the project management plan may also include updating one of the components of the project management plan, which includes the various other plans, like the schedule management plan and cost management plan. The *PMBOK Guide* – Seventh Edition holds the full list of plan artifacts; read section 4 on models, methods, and artifacts. Updates to relevant project documents may just be performed, changed as part of the change process (use of the change log) or simply close out the expired risks.

8.8 Domain V: Task 4 – Monitor Project Risk Levels

The purpose of this task is to monitor project risk levels after being set early in the project by the enterprise and/or key stakeholders. This sets the stage for what project risk levels are acceptable. The team lead or project manager needs to continually assess the project risk levels. The information on project risk levels should be documented and communicated to the different key stakeholders' parts of the plans for stakeholders' engagement and communication. An important technique highlighted in the PMI *Practice Standard for Project Risk Management* (2009) is the need to do a risk reassessment (page 102), which is conducted as part of the monitoring process.

8.9 Domain V: Predictive Approaches

If you read through the descriptions of the preceding tasks, you will see that they explain the predictive approach, as the *PMBOK Guide* – Sixth Edition, the PMI *Standard for Risk Management in Portfolios, Programs, and Projects* (2019), and the PMI *Practice Standard for Project Risk Management* (2009) have a strong emphasis on the predictive approach. In the predictive approach our focus is to keep track of the performance measurement baseline, which includes the scope, cost, and time. By doing so we can control the project. We gather data on how we are doing; in PMI language this is work performance data, work performance information, and work performance reports. With this information we can perform data analysis, like variance analysis or trend analysis, on how we are doing and where we are supposed to be. When it comes to risk management most of the relevant information is collected in a risk database and applied to the risk register. The risk register should contain information about residual and secondary risks and include roles like the risk owner to monitor them, so they can activate the risk response if the triggers happen. From a PMI perspective, the risk register and risk information are general input and are needed to update relevant project documents. This could include the various plans, contingency budget, communication, and stakeholder engagement. The project management needs to agree with the key stakeholders or the enterprise about what project risk levels they are aiming for and then make sure to monitor them throughout the project lifecycle. The project manager could monitor the risk register and have workshops with the subject matter experts and key stakeholders to ensure data is correct and that they are on the right risk levels. See Section 8.4 for the required readings.

8.10 Domain V: Agile Approaches

Working agile is a different mindset/culture and would require a different framework like Scrum to manage the governance of the delivery. However, the tasks are still relevant. Most agile frameworks consist of meetings/rituals, artifacts, and roles. At this point we want to monitor and close risks. The first task is to gather and analyze performance data. One of the key principles of agile is the widespread application of transparency, so if we want to see how we are performing, then look at the high visibility board, whether it is an information radiator, task board, Scrum board, and such. The board would tell us what needs to be done, what is in progress, and what has been completed so far in this iteration (sprint in Scrum). This performance information could include various charts like velocity, burndown/burnup chart, information on various metrics like cycle/lead time, throughputs, earned value management (EVM), risks, and such. Transparency also applied to the agile process, so watching or taking part in the process whether it's a daily standup meeting, iteration planning, iteration review, or iteration retrospective will clearly highlight how the team is performing. During any Scrum, ritual risks can be identified and analyzed. The sprint retrospective is a way of also including the risk audit or risk reassessment. Agile frameworks like Scrum have clearly defined roles in which the product owner, Scrum master, or Scrum team will all be able to provide information on how the work is progressing.

Monitoring residual and secondary risks does not play a major role in the literature of agile; however, it is still equally as important as other approaches. In agile, risks are identified during the process and then divided between the roles. The Scrum master may use an impediment log, while the product owner has a separate list. The work performed by the Scrum team must be prioritized by the product owner and included in the iteration/sprint as part of the iteration planning if the Scrum team needs to deal with the risks. This means that the various roles, like being risk owner, each have a responsibility of monitoring residual and secondary risks. The Scrum team may inform the product owner, thus handling the residual and secondary risks before part of the next iteration.

In agile, when providing the information required to update relevant project documents, we tend to think about the product backlog, our boards, changing a user story, personas, and so on, because we have a limited emphasis on creating various project documents as the artifacts are enough to support the process. Project documents are typically referred to as artifacts, but all kinds of agile artifacts do exist that could be updated.

The last task focuses on monitoring project risk levels. If you were using Scrum, then this task would be the product owner's to fulfill. The product owner is the overall decision maker and needs to ensure the project risks levels are just right. Too much could result in waste, while too little may be taking the risk of less business value. The Scrum team could apply a risk burndown chart based upon expected monetary values (Probability × Impact), i.e., a 10% probability of a 10-day delay. With this approach everyone can see how the risk exposure hopefully declines over time as risks are mitigated in the iterations. Some risks have a higher impact on business value than others, and in these cases you may want to choose the risk response called avoid. So making sure all the avoid responses are in place or have been conducted could also work to monitor the risk levels. Read Appendices A and B for a more detailed description.

Tip: Consider reading the *Agile Practice Guide* from the Project Management Institute and Agile Alliance.

8.11 Domain V: Hybrid Approaches

Hybrid approaches are a combination of predictive and agile. So based upon the context, you do what works, which makes good sense. However, this is not an exact science and what works well for some in one situation may not be the best solution in another situation, so it is about understanding the context and making the right choices. Let's say we do predictive project management with a project manager in charge and included in the project are a few Scrum teams. We should gather and analyze performance data as a combination of predictive and agile; that's using a task board for the agile teams for scope and progress and combining it with deliveries of other work packages and such. Some work packages might be including in the product backlog, while others are handled by other teams. The sum of all the risks identified could be managed in the overall risk register, and the risk owners could be found in any of the teams. The residual and secondary risks would be monitored in the risk register; however, the agile team might use the board or backlog, while other teams are fine with just the risk register. In Monitor and Close Risks, we also provide information required to update relevant project documents, which could include traditional project management plans and project documents and agile artifacts should as the product backlog. The monitoring of the project risk levels is the responsibility for the project manager; however, during the project execution the agile team should include this information on the information radiators, while the other teams include their information in the risk register. Read Appendix C for a more detailed description.

Tip: Hybrid is (1) an agile or predictive approach followed by agile or predictive approach, (2) a combined agile and predictive approach used simultaneously, or (3) largely agile or predictive with agile or predictive components.

Exercise 8.4 Visual notetaking – Turn your notes from this chapter into a visual representation.

_____
_____
_____
_____
_____

Answer: No right or wrong answers.

8.12 Domain V: Sample PMI-RMP Exam Questions on Monitor and Close Risks

This section contains five short exam questions in the PMI-RMP format for you to check your knowledge of the content presented in this chapter and check your readiness for the PMI-RMP exam. The answers will be provided in boldface following the questions section. If you make mistakes, you should go back and learn why mistakes were made. Do not learn the questions and answers; learn the content.

8.12.1 Questions

1 You are working as a project manager for a plan-based construction project. Your team is in the process of collecting performance data for the next big review at the end of the phase. Data are coming in, but there seems to be a problem with the schedule. The project might be delayed more than expected and approved by the key stakeholders. What action should be taken next?

A. Address this at the next daily standup meeting

B. Talk with the scheduler, as it is clear the CPI data from the EVM analysis is wrong

C. Reexamine the work performance data and if they are still wrong, conduct a variance analysis

D. Perform a change so the schedule baseline is updated to reflect the new data

2 During your agile transformation, key stakeholders express their concerns about the COVID situation, which may influence the Scrum team performance. The team has mitigated this risk by having all team members vaccinated. However, the stakeholders feel their concerns for the team are not being taken seriously. What action should be taken next?

A. The project manager should set up a meeting with the team and key stakeholders to see if they can find a common solution.

B. The product owner should label this a secondary risk on the risk board.

C. The Scrum core team should do nothing, as the stakeholders are overreacting and meddling in their personal affairs.

D. The Scrum master should document this in the risk register or impediment log as a residual risk.

3 The subject matter expert on the IT railroad project has mitigated a risk that has turned into a secondary risk. Which of the following best illustrates this?

A. The risk has been mitigated by having more skilled resources work on the work package; however, a part of the risk is still relevant.

B. The project has used new technology to quickly lay the rails. However, it turns out that it is damaging to the nature around the rails. The project needs to restore the nature.

C. The project manager was worried about a lack of skilled labor, but due to a partnership more resources are joining. Now the only concern is possible extra costs.

D. The project mitigated a risk by the use of new technology, so the risk is reduced in probability and impact to now be on the watchlist.

4 Your team is working on a hybrid healthcare project. The project manager is assigned from the business, while the team is from IT and running Scrumbot. The project manager is in the US, while the team is in Europe. The project manager is in the process of updating relevant project documents and has asked the team for an update on the top five risks for the status report. What would be the best approach for the team to document this information?

A. The team should update the information radiator located in the team's war room.

B. The project manager could set up a conference call with the team to discuss the risks.

C. The team should update the electronic Jira board, which should connect to the risk register.

D. The project manager should discuss the risks individually with the team members, so they don't influence other team members' opinions.

5 During your agile transformation, key stakeholders express their concerns about the project risk levels. What action should be taken next to address these concerns?

A. Give the key stakeholders access to the risk burndown chart illustrating risk exposure based upon the expected monetary analysis.

B. Have the project manager go through the risk register with the key stakeholders.

C. Make sure all risks with high probability and impact have an risk response strategy.

D. Arrange a conference call between the project manager and the key stakeholders to review the risk attitude, risk tolerance, and risk thresholds to ensure the right project risk levels.

8.12.2 Answers

1 You are working as a project manager for a plan-based construction project. Your team is in the process of collecting performance data for the next big review at the end of the phase. Data are coming in, but there seems to be a problem with the schedule. The project might be delayed more than expected and approved by the key stakeholders. What action should be taken next?

A. Address this at the next daily standup meeting

B. Talk with the scheduler as it is clear the CPI data from the EVM analysis is wrong

C. **Reexamine the work performance data and if they are still wrong, conduct a variance analysis**

D. Perform a change so the schedule baseline is updated to reflect the new data

Explanation: This question relates to task 1, and the context is a plan-based project. Option A is an agile ritual, and the problem is not part of the three questions covered. Option B is about EVM; however, CPI is cost performance index. SPI might have worked here. Option C is the best choice as data needs to be checked, and if verified, then a variance analysis could examine the possible differences. Option D creates a change; however, it is too early to access if a change is needed.

2 During your agile transformation, key stakeholders express their concerns about the COVID situation, which may influence the Scrum team performance. The team has mitigated this risk by having all team members vaccinated. However, the stakeholders feel their concerns for the team are not being taken seriously. What action should be taken next?

A. The project manager should set up a meeting with the team and key stakeholders to see if they can find a common solution.

B. The product owner should label this a secondary risk on the risk board.

C. The Scrum core team should do nothing, as the stakeholders are overreacting and meddling in their personal affairs.

D. **The Scrum master should document this in the risk register or impediment log as a residual risk.**

Explanation: This question relates to task 2, and the context is agile. Option A is a possible solution if the setup was predicted, which is not the case. Option B states it is a secondary risk, which is wrong as it is a residual risk. Option C tries to ignore it, which may not be the best solution. Option D is the best option as it is a residual risk discussed.

3 The subject matter expert on the IT railroad project has mitigated a risk that has turned into a secondary risk. Which of the following best illustrates this?

    A. The risk has been mitigated by having more skilled resource work on the work package; however, a part of the risk is still relevant.

    B. **The project has used new technology to quickly lay the rails; however, it turns out that it is damaging to the nature around the rails. The project needs to restore nature.**

    C. The project manager was worried about a lack of skilled labor, but due to a partnership more resources are joining. Now the only concern is possible extra costs.

    D. The project mitigated a risk by use of new technology, so the risk is reduced in probability and impact to now be on the watchlist.

Explanation: This question relates to task 2 and focuses on secondary risks. Option A is a residual risk. Option B is the best option as a new risk arises due to the action of the response. Option C is close. Option D is a risk being mitigated.

4 Your team is working on a hybrid healthcare project. The project manager is assigned from the business, while the team is from IT and running Scrumbot. The project manager is in the US, while the team is in Europe. The project manager is in the process of updating relevant project documents and has asked the team for an update on the top five risks for the status report. What would be the best approach for the team to document this information?

    A. The team should update the information radiator located in the team's war room.

    B. The project manager could set up a conference call with the team to discuss the risks.

    C. **The team should update the electronic Jira board, which should connect to the risk register.**

    D. The project manager should discuss the risks individually with the team members, so they don't influence other team members' opinions.

Explanation: This question relates to task 3 and is a hybrid environment. Option A does not work with people working distributed. The PM can't access the data on the board. Option B could work, but it is not the best option. Option C is the best option, as data are shared and no extra work is needed. Option D is almost a Delphi approach and requires a lot of time. It is not the best option.

5 During your agile transformation, key stakeholders express their concerns about the project risk levels. What action should be taken next to address these concerns?

A. **Give the key stakeholders access to the risk burndown chart illustrating risk exposures based upon the expected monetary analysis.**

B. Have the project manager go through the risk register with the key stakeholders.

C. Make sure all risks with high probability and impact have an risk response strategy.

D. Arrange a conference call between the project manager and the key stakeholders to review the risk attitude, risk tolerance, and risk thresholds to ensure the right project risk levels.

Explanation: This question relates to task 4 and is an agile environment. Option A is the best option and illustrates how this can be done. Option B is a plan-based approach and would not be the best choice in an agile context as we do not have a PM. Option C only focuses on high risk and does not solve the concerns. Option D is a possible plan-based solution, which may not be the best choice in an agile environment.

8.13 Domain V: Summary of the Content – Somewhat Sequential

Domain 1: Risk Strategy and Planning

- Perform a preliminary document analysis
- Assess project environment for threats and opportunities
- Confirm risk thresholds based on risk appetites
- Establish risk management strategy
- Document the risk management plan
- Plan and lead risk management activities with stakeholders

Domain 2: Risk Identification

- Conduct risk identification exercises
- Examine assumption and constraint analyses
- Document risk triggers and thresholds based on context/environment
- Develop risk register

Domain 3: Risk Analysis

- Perform qualitative analysis
- Perform quantitative analysis
- Identify threats and opportunities

Domain 4: Risk Response

- Plan risk response
- Implement risk response

Domain 5: Monitor and Close Risks

- Gather and analyze performance data
- Monitor residual & secondary risks
- Provide information required to update relevant project documents
- Monitor project risk levels

Development approaches

- Predictive
- Hybrid
- Agile

Chapter 9

Full Practice Exam 1

The PMI-RMP full practice exam 1 consists of 100 questions that should be completed in no more than 2.5 hours in total. The PMI exam contains 115 questions; however, 15 questions are not scored. Table 9.1 gives the overview of the PMI-RMP exam breakdown, which you should use if you need to go back and revisit a chapter and as confirmation that all content has been covered, understood, and mastered. All the test questions are split equally between the predictive, hybrid, and agile approaches as you will encounter at the actual exam.

Section 9.1 contains the questions. Each question includes four possible answers; however, only one is correct. Section 9.2 includes all the answers (in boldface) and explanations. At this stage you should have at least 70 correct questions before moving on to the actual certification exam.

Do not attempt to take the full practice exams before you are ready. You will not get the full benefit, and retaking the exam may result in flawed results. These are the last practice exams you should take before getting above average on the actual PMI exam.

DOI: 10.4324/9781003304012-9

Table 9.1   PMI-RMP Practice Exam 1 Breakdown

Domain	Split	Questions	Test Questions
Risk Strategy and Planning	22%	22	
Task 1 Perform a preliminary document analysis		3	1–3
Task 2 Assess project environment for threats and opportunities		3	4–6
Task 3 Confirm risk thresholds based on risk appetites		4	7–10
Task 4 Establish risk management strategy		4	11–14
Task 5 Document the risk management plan		4	15–18
Task 6 Plan and lead risk management activities with stakeholders		4	19–22
Risk Identification	23%	23	
Task 1 Conduct risk identification exercises		5	23–27
Task 2 Examine assumption and constraint analyses		6	28–33
Task 3 Document risk triggers and thresholds based on context/environment		6	34–39
Task 4 Develop risk register		6	40–45
Risk Analysis	23%	23	
Task 1 Perform qualitative analysis		7	46–52
Task 2 Perform quantitative analysis		8	53–60
Task 3 Identify threats and opportunities		8	61–68
Risk Response	13%	13	
Task 1 Plan risk response		7	69–75
Task 2 Implement risk response		6	76–81
Monitor and Close Risks	19%	19	
Task 1 Gather and analyze performance data		5	82–86
Task 2 Monitor residual and secondary risks		5	87–91
Task 3 Provide information required to update relevant project documents		5	92–96
Task 4 Monitor project risk levels		4	97–100
Summary	100%	100	1–100

9.1 Full Practice Exam 1 Questions

1 Murray, the project manager of a big healthcare project, is working on the preliminary document analysis. Which of the following documents should he review prior to the risk identification?
A. Risk management plan
B. Industry benchmarks
C. The lessons learned from his healthcare project
D. All of the above

2 Mary, the product owner of an agile software development team, is considering performing a preliminary document analysis. What does she need to do?
A. She needs to determine and assign who is responsible for the preliminary document analysis.
B. She needs to refine the product backlog and have the team working on the tasks.
C. She needs to do it herself as the PO.
D. She should discuss it with the Scrum master, who can facilitate the process.

3 Jimmy is working on a hybrid project where his task is to establish documents relevant to the risk process as part of the preliminary document analysis. Which of the following documents should he discard as least relevant for his work?
A. The company's risk procedures
B. The project charter
C. The benefit realization plan
D. The team charter

4 Pete has assessed the project environment for threats and opportunities. Several top opportunities were found that may have major impact on the realization of the business case benefits if delivered early. However, the project scope is not settled. Which project methodology is needed?
A. Agile
B. Waterfall
C. Hybrid
D. Waterfall with incremental deliverables

5 Pete has assessed the project environment for threats and opportunities. However, he failed to take the stakeholders into account. What should he do next?
   A. Talk with the steering committee
   B. Conduct a stakeholder analysis
   C. Get an interview with the sponsor
   D. Read lessons learned from previous projects

6 Pete has assessed the project environment and analyzed constraints to risk management. Which of the following is he least likely to include in his assessment?
   A. Market rules
   B. Market laws
   C. Technical risks
   D. Secondary risks

7 Otto, the project manager, is eager to ensure the risk threshold of the project is on the right level. What should it be aligned with to manage this?
   A. Risk tolerance
   B. Risk appetites
   C. Risk capacity
   D. Risk adverse

8 Otto, the project manager, aims at calculating the risk the organization can absorb. Which of the following is he least likely to consider?
   A. Financial
   B. Scope
   C. Legal
   D. Procurement

9 Otto, the project manager, wants to confirm the risk thresholds based on risk appetites. What would be a good topic for the next steering committee meeting?
   A. Calculate the risk appetite
   B. Discuss risk thresholds
   C. Discuss the calculations of the risk threshold based upon the risk budget
   D. Discuss the risk contingency

10 Otto, the project manager, is working on confirming the risk thresholds based on risk appetites. What should he expect?
   A. He should have it signed as soon as possible to avoid too many conflicts.
   B. He should invite the stakeholders for a review session so they are familiar with the content.
   C. He must lead conflict resolutions between stakeholders in agreeing on risk appetite.
   D. He should mentor and coach about risk appetite.

11 Jane is an agile product owner in a hybrid environment. She is considering whether or not her project/team should establish a risk management strategy. Which of the following would highlight the need for a risk management strategy?
   A. It is a mandatory section of the risk management plan
   B. To establish risk processes and tools
   C. An assumption for coaching the team on risk management best practices
   D. Support servant leadership

12 Jane, an agile product owner in a hybrid environment, has decided to establish a risk management strategy. The PMO informs her that the risk management strategy should determine risk metrics. Which of the following would be a good example of a risk metric for her team to use?
   A. Escaped defects
   B. Schedule performance index
   C. Cost variance
   D. Risk exposure based upon expected monetary value

13 Jane, an agile product owner in a hybrid environment, has decided to establish a risk management strategy. Her team wants to create an RBS. Which of the following would be a good approach to identify risk categories?
   A. Ask one of the project managers to share their RBS
   B. See if they can find some historical data to be used as a basis for the development of an RBS
   C. Forget it; risk categories are of little value in agile environments
   D. Have the Scrum master facilitate the development of the RBS by the team

14 Jane, an agile product owner in a hybrid environment, has decided to establish a risk management strategy. What approach could support the coaching/mentoring of the team on risk management best practices?
A. Resources for a training effort
B. Adaptive leadership
C. Servant leadership
D. Sessions by the Scrum master

15 When documenting the risk management plan, which tool and technique could help in defining organizational risk roles and responsibilities?
A. RACI
B. Responsibility assignment matrix
C. RASI
D. All of the above

16 When documenting the risk management plan, which question could outline the key risk management activities?
A. Who?
B. What?
C. When?
D. All of the above

17 How can the risk breakdown structure (RBS) support the risk management plan?
A. Highlights the key activities
B. Categories for risk identification
C. Mandatory for performing the qualitative risk assessment
D. Important input for most of the quantitative tools and techniques

18 When documenting the risk management plan other plans are needed. Which plan would provide the most value when documenting the risk management plan?
A. The risk communication plan
B. Project management plan
C. Project communication plan
D. Risk management approaches

19 The project team plans to engage the stakeholders in upcoming risk management activities. What would be an activity in which to engage the stakeholders?
A. Engage stakeholders in developing the RBS
B. Engage stakeholders in defining roles and responsibilities
C. Engage stakeholders in the risk prioritization process
D. Engage stakeholders in defining risk strategies

20 When planning risk management activities with the key stakeholders, how can the project tailor the risk communication for the stakeholders?
A. Ensure all stakeholders receive the full and comprehensive project communication all the time
B. Try to understand the need of the stakeholders and then adapt the communication to fit these needs
C. Follow company procedures on project risk communication
D. Limit risk communication to avoid information overload

21 When planning risk management activities with the key stakeholders, how can the project educate the stakeholders on risk management to foster engagement?
A. Provide project management training
B. Share understanding of risk principles
C. Invite the stakeholders to the team's daily standup meetings
D. Teach the stakeholders about risk management facilitation

22 When planning risk management activities with the key stakeholders, what is the goal of training, coaching, and educating the stakeholders in risk principles and processes?
A. General risk management awareness
B. To reduce conflicts with the team
C. To engage the stakeholders in performing activities
D. To foster engagement in risk management

23 Murray and Kim are both parts of an agile Scrum team. When would it be the most suitable time to identify risks?
A. Arrange a kickoff meeting before sprint 0
B. Only during sprint planning and sprint review
C. During the process
D. Include it in the sprint retrospective

24 John, the project manager of a plan-based construction project, is in the process of planning various activities for risk identification. John has identified several good activities, but one activity is probably not the most effective one. Which activity should John not include?
A. Meetings with various subject matter experts
B. Interviews with key stakeholders
C. Focus groups with industry representatives
D. Obtain lessons learned from the agile development teams

25 Pete is working in a hybrid environment and needs to come up with a good activity or process for risk identification that benefits the predictive and agile approach his project is combining. Which of the following would be the most valued activity or change of process?
A. Make sure risks are identified iteratively (all the time) like in Scrum
B. Make sure risks are identified before starting each phase
C. Make sure lessons learned are collected from all types of projects to cover the hybrid approach
D. Make sure risks are identified before reaching a milestone

26 The IT healthcare project has identified a bunch of risks that have been described in the risk register. However, many of the columns in the Excel sheet lack data. What could be the next step to increase the quality of the identified risks?
A. Assign risk owners
B. Examine the risks for possible secondary or residual risks
C. Perform detailed analyses of risk identification exercise results
D. Conduct a qualitative risk assessment

27 When conducting various risk identification exercises, it is important to understand the business context of the information. Which of these examples is not the best representation of this concept?
A. Documents
B. Audio transcripts
C. Telemetry data
D. Sprint retrospective

28 The project has spent a lot of time and resources on examining assumptions and constraints. How could the project proactively leverage the results of the assumption and constraint analysis?
A. Convert some assumptions and constraints into risks
B. Update the risk register with the new insights
C. Allocate risk contingency to fit with the findings
D. Update lessons learned based upon the results

29 The project has spent a lot of time and resources on examining assumptions and constraints. Now the project has a list of these. What could the team do next?
A. Convert all of them into risks
B. Categorize the assumptions and constraints
C. Conduct a qualitative analysis on the assumptions
D. Conduct a quantitative analysis on the constraints

30 The project has spent a lot of time and resources on examining assumptions and constraints. Some are converted, the rest have been categorized. What would be a good next step?
  A. Update the risk contingency budget
  B. Provide input to the planning of the risk activities
  C. Assess the risks associated with each assumption and/or constraint
  D. Perform an assessment of the probability and impact on monetary values of the risks associated with each assumption and/or constraint

31 When examining the assumption and constraint analysis, which is the best example to recognize the relationship between assumptions and/or constraints, and project objectives?
  A. The holiday season may have a cascade effect on the project timeline
  B. Investments in risk responses may influence the risk budget
  C. Lack of risk management may result in more issues
  D. Poor project management may influence the project deliveries

32 Which of the following assumptions and/or constraints may not have an impact on a project objective?
  A. Key stakeholders available during the Chinese New Year period
  B. Lack of skilled labor
  C. In July, no work is possible due to bad weather/windy conditions
  D. Funding not approved

33 Assumption and constraint analyses work best with the involvement of the stakeholders. Which of the following tasks would be a good use of the stakeholders' active engagement?
  A. Encourage stakeholders to convert assumptions and constraints to risks
  B. Encourage stakeholders to categorize assumptions and constraints
  C. Encourage stakeholders to challenge assumptions and constraints
  D. All of the above

34 Paul is updating the risk registers and finds various risk triggers. Which one of these should he ask the team to reassess and document?
  A. Structural failure of crane
  B. Incorrect loading
  C. Operator overextends load
  D. Dropped object

35 Paul is updating the risk registers and now has updated the various risk triggers. However, risk triggers are related to causes. He examines one trigger where a crane drops a heavy object. Which one of these causes should he ask the team to reassess and document?
A. Strong winds
B. Overload protection
C. Use lifting plan
D. Check safety manifest

36 Paul is updating the risk registers and now has updated the various risk triggers and causes. He examines one risk where a crane drops a heavy object. Which one of these risk consequences is valid?
A. Load too heavy
B. Pre-lift crane check
C. Use lifting plan
D. Object dropped in sea

37 Which of the following is not a good example of the risk impact where the risk is a crane drops a heavy object?
A. Personnel hit by object
B. Object may not be dropped
C. Object dropped in sea
D. Object impacts ground

38 Which quantitative analysis assesses and documents risk triggers, causes, consequences, and/or impact?
A. Decision tree
B. Bowtie analysis
C. Monte Carlo simulation
D. Analytical hierarchy process

39 When documenting risk triggers and thresholds based on the context/environment, which of the following tasks is the least important?
A. Assess, confirm, and document risk compliance thresholds and categories against updated risk data
B. Assess and document risk triggers, causes, and timing
C. Assess and document risk probabilities and/or impact
D. Empower stakeholders to challenge existing thresholds

40 When developing a risk register, it is important to analyze the validity of certain elements. What are these elements?
A. Identified risks and triggers
B. Probabilities and impacts
C. Risk attributes
D. Risk ownership

41 When developing a risk register, it is important to examine the relevant risk attributes. Which of the following do not fall into that category?
A. Probability
B. Impact
C. Urgency
D. Opportunity

42 Which of these risks should be classified as a threat in the risk register?
A. Probability of increased sales due to close ties with the customer
B. Increased costs due to bad weather
C. Increased savings due to effective production
D. Fewer team members leaving the team due to close cooperation

43 Which of these risks should not be classified as an opportunity in the risk register?
A. Reduced material use due to use of new technology
B. Happy stakeholders due to increased engagement
C. Increased stock rates due to good reputation
D. Increased resource use due to planning

44 When developing the risk register it is important to establish risk origin and ownership. Which of the following does not fit this statement?
A. Internal stakeholders
B. External subject matter expert
C. Increased probability and impact
D. Derived from the risk breakdown structure

45 John, the project manager of an IT project, is in the process of developing the risk register. Which of the following tasks is hardly relevant for this work?
A. Examine the risk attributes like probability, impact, urgency
B. Classify risks only as threats
C. Establish risk origin and ownership, e.g., internal/external
D. Analyze the validity of identified risks and triggers

46 Murray, the project manager of a large healthcare project, is in the process of performing the qualitative analysis where some of the risks are identified using the RBS. Which document provides the classification used in the RBS?
A. Risk management strategy
B. Project management plan
C. Risk management plan
D. Project charter

47 Which of the following is not an example of a commonly applied classification of risks in an RBS?
   A. Environment
   B. Organizational
   C. Project management
   D. Leadership

48 When performing the qualitative analysis, the estimate of the impact of risks may affect various project objectives. Which of the following is not one of them?
   A. Quality
   B. Project schedule
   C. Budget
   D. Scope

49 Pete is performing the qualitative analysis with his team. Which two parameters need to be assessed?
   A. Probability and likelihood
   B. Probability and impact
   C. Consequence and impact
   D. Time and materials

50 Ann, the product owner, wants to apply risk matrices as part of the core team qualitative analysis. She found several good resources; however, one of them is not the best resource. Which one?
   A. Agreed-upon assessment approach
   B. Historical information
   C. Preestablished criteria
   D. Definition of done from previous iterations

51 Jimmy, the project manager, has key stakeholders in his project with limited knowledge of the risk categorization strategies his project could apply. What would be the best approach to more engagement of the stakeholders?
   A. Coach the stakeholders on risk categorization strategies
   B. Provide formal training to all the stakeholders
   C. Find a mentor for the key stakeholders
   D. Allow the key stakeholders to participate in various risk management activities

52 When performing the qualitative analysis, which task should be included?
   A. Estimate the impact of risk on only project schedule, budget, and resources
   B. Prioritize the risk based on impact and detectability
   C. Apply only the risk matrices based upon historical information and preestablished criteria
   D. Perform an ordinal classification

53 Allan, the project manager, has completed the qualitative analysis and now wants to perform the quantitative analysis. Several techniques have been selected; however, one is not applied for quantitative analysis. Which one is it?
   A. Sensitivity analysis
   B. Decision tree
   C. Earned value management
   D. Expected monetary value

54 Paula, the business analyst, wants to see which risks and activities on the critical path have the highest standard deviation. Which technique can support this work?
   A. Monte Carlo simulation
   B. Benchmarking
   C. Sensitivity analysis
   D. PERT

55 Charlie is conducting a risk analysis where he, based upon a decision, must measure the probability and impact of various possible paths. Which analysis is he properly conducting?
   A. Sensitivity analysis
   B. Monte Carlo
   C. Decision tree
   D. Expected monetary value

56 When performing the quantitative risk analysis, it is important to analyze risk data and process performance information against what?
   A. Project objectives
   B. Established metrics
   C. Project constraints
   D. The risk management plan

57 Mary performs a quantitative risk analysis where she seeks to conduct a precise forecast analysis. What would be a good source?
   A. New information
   B. Historical information
   C. Both A and B
   D. Input from the trend analysis

58 Sandra has completed the quantitative risk analysis. Is it likely the risk weighting and risk priority have changed in the process?
   A. Yes, risk weighting and risk priority are likely to change in the process.
   B. Yes, risk weighting is likely to change in the process.
   C. Yes, risk priority is likely to change in the process.
   D. No change should be expected.

59 Ursula, the newly appointed project manager, has just completed the assessment of the probability and impact of all the identified risks. What should she do next?
   A. Identify the opportunities
   B. Assign risk responses to the identified risks
   C. Perform qualitative analysis
   D. Perform quantitative analysis

60 Monty is performing a quantitative analysis where his team is focusing on the critical path, as the deadline is set in stone and consequences are severe. What risk analysis tool or technique could support this emphasis during the quantitative analysis?
   A. Examine the sensitivity of the activities on the critical path
   B. Examine EVM, so an SPI higher than 1 should put more effort into risk mitigation
   C. Identify more risks with a focus on planning
   D. Check if milestones are still valid

61 Oliver is working with his team on the risk analysis in which they try to assess project risk complexity. Which tool or technique could best support this endeavor?
   A. Cause and effect diagram
   B. Decision tree analysis
   C. Interviews
   D. Brainstorming

62 An agile team is assessing project risk complexity. Which of the following tools and techniques should not be applied?
   A. SWOT analysis
   B. Ishikawa diagram
   C. Tree diagram
   D. Benefit-cost analysis

63 Ursula is performing impact analysis and assessing project objectives. Which of the following should she include?
   A. Stakeholders
   B. Assumptions
   C. Constraints
   D. Issues

64 Jim is performing impact analysis and assessing project objectives with his team. Which of the following should not be included?
   A. Project scopes
   B. Schedule
   C. Resources
   D. Legal

65 When assessing project compliance objectives against organizational strategic objectives, which of the following would be the best resource for this work?
   A. Impediment log
   B. Issue log
   C. Gantt chart
   D. Budget

66 When assessing project compliance objectives against organizational strategic objectives, which of the following should not be included?
   A. Procedures
   B. Procurement governance
   C. Corporate governance
   D. Project governance

67 Walid wants to engage his stakeholders to work more independently but to perform which task?
   A. Identify threats
   B. Assess project risk complexity
   C. Perform impact analysis on project objectives
   D. Identify threats and opportunities

68 Walid has empowered the stakeholders to independently identify threats and opportunities. Which of the following is the best example of this work?
   A. Requirements are unclear.
   B. It will never snow during project execution.
   C. It will rain for sure during project execution.
   D. It might be windy during project execution.

69 Which of the following is an appropriate risk response strategy for managing threats?
  A. Enhance
  B. Accept
  C. Share
  D. Exploit

70 Which of the following is not an appropriate risk response strategy for managing opportunities?
  A. Escalate
  B. Accept
  C. Mitigate
  D. Share

71 John, the project manager, has activated the risk response, which resulted in an additional resource being forced to work on an activity in order to keep the work on track. What risk response strategy has been applied?
  A. Accept
  B. Share
  C. Mitigate
  D. Escalate

72 When determining the appropriate risk response strategy it is also important to identify a person to act when the trigger happens. What is this role called?
  A. Risk owner
  B. Action owner
  C. Product owner
  D. Risk manager

73 Which of the following tools is a good way to illustrate and communicate the effectiveness of the risk response strategies?
  A. Product backlog
  B. Dot plots
  C. Information radiator
  D. Vision statement

74 Which of the following tasks is the least important when performing risk response strategies?
  A. Determine the workaround
  B. Allocate responsibilities
  C. Outline an appropriate responsibility matrix for a metricized project environment
  D. Reevaluate all risks

75 When planning risk response strategies, which should be applied first if the impact of the risk is high?
   A. Exploit
   B. Avoid
   C. Mitigate
   D. Escalate

76 When should the action owner implement the risk response?
   A. As per risk trigger
   B. If the risk is close to occurring
   C. If the risk impact is high and proximity is near
   D. All of the above

77 Paul is discussing with his team whether all risks should have a risk response plan. What is the right solution to this debate?
   A. All risks identified should have a risk response plan.
   B. All risks except risks on the watchlist should have a risk response plan.
   C. All risks with high probability and impact should have a risk response plan.
   D. It is a team decision to decide which risks should have a risk response plan.

78 Georg wants to encourage the project stakeholders to be more engaged in risk management. What would be a suitable task when implementing risk responses?
   A. Encourage stakeholders to discuss risk prioritization
   B. Encourage stakeholders to identify risks
   C. Encourage stakeholders to assess risks
   D. Encourage stakeholders to provide feedback on the risk response

79 The team evaluates and reacts to secondary risks from the response implementation. What is a good example of this?
   A. The risk response reduces probability and impact of the risk, but it is still active.
   B. The risk response causes a new risk to materialize.
   C. The risk response is aligned with the fallback plan.
   D. The risk response is aligned with the contingency plan.

80 The team evaluates and reacts to residual risks from the response implementation. What is a good example of this?
   A. The risk response reduces the probability of the risk.
   B. The risk response causes two new risks to materialize.
   C. The risk response can be measured in monetary value.
   D. The risk response can be measured in time.

81 Which of the following tasks would not be relevant when implementing risk responses?
   A. Execute the risk response plan(s)
   B. Execute fallback plans
   C. Execute the contingency plan(s)
   D. Evaluate and react to secondary and residual risks from the response implementation

82 When gathering and analyzing performance data on planning, which planning components may be relevant to reconcile performance data and reports from?
   A. Activities
   B. Work packages
   C. Milestones
   D. Epics

83 Which of the following is not a tool, technique, or meeting for gathering and analyzing performance in an agile environment?
   A. User stories
   B. Information radiator
   C. Iteration review
   D. Daily standup

84 When analyzing data to determine the completion status against the baseline, which of the following is not a common applied baseline?
   A. Scope
   B. Time
   C. Risk
   D. Cost

85 When trying to determine how the project is doing compared to where the project is supposed to be, which tool or technique could provide this?
   – Variance analysis
   – Benchmarking
   – Trend analysis
   – Information radiator

86 When gathering and analyzing performance data, which of the following task is most relevant?
   A. Reconcile performance data and reports from risk-relevant activities
   B. Analyze data to determine the completion status against the work packages
   C. Perform a variance analysis
   D. Monitor impact against overall project risk appetite to enterprise

87 Tony is updating the risk register after monitoring a residual risk. Which of the following entries fits this task?
   A. New risk identified after risk response implemented
   B. Change in budget after risk response implemented
   C. Risk no longer valid
   D. Reduced probability after risk response implemented

88 When would Tommy most likely encounter a new secondary risk?
   A. When identifying new risks
   B. When mitigating residual risks
   C. As the result of a risk response
   D. When measuring expected monetary value

89 When monitoring risk responses for secondary risk, which risk response is least relevant?
   A. Mitigate
   B. Accept
   C. Transfer
   D. Exploit

90 When assessing the possible impact of residual and secondary risks, which of the following illustrates this?
   A. Increase in the risk contingency budget
   B. Schedule delayed by 2 months
   C. Lack of stakeholder engagement
   D. No legal complaints during procurement

91 Which of the following tasks is the most relevant when monitoring residual and secondary risks?
   A. Monitor risk response and document positive risk
   B. Monitor risk response for negative risks
   C. Assess the impact of negative and positive risks on project objectives
   D. Update and communicate the impact of residual and secondary risks

92 Which of the following documents should not be updated during the monitoring and controlling?
   A. Risk register
   B. Lessons learned repository
   C. Project management plan
   D. Change logs

93 In the risk register which risk data are most likely to be updated?
   A. Description
   B. Category
   C. Probability and impact before risk response
   D. Probability and impact after risk response

94 When should risks be monitored?
   A. Monitored continuously and updated before end of phase
   B. Monitored and documented iteratively
   C. When risks are likely to occur
   D. In agile after each iteration

95 What would be a good reason to close a risk?
   A. Probability and impact are low.
   B. The risk is not included in the risk contingency budget.
   C. It is impossible for the risk to happen.
   D. The risk has occurred.

96 Which of the following documents would be the best resource when updating the risk register?
   A. Budget
   B. Schedule
   C. Work breakdown structure
   D. Lessons learned

97 In an agile Scrum-based environment who is responsible for the overall monitoring of the project risk levels?
   A. Scrum team
   B. Scrum master
   C. Chapter lead
   D. Product owner

98 In an agile Scrum-based environment how can one most effectively assess project risk levels during an iteration?
   A. Attend daily standup
   B. Ask the Scrum master
   C. Refine the iteration backlog
   D. Look at the information radiator for answers

99 Roger is a project manager of a construction project. His team is constantly monitoring project risk levels. Now he wants to prepare a risk report for the key stakeholders. What consideration is important to keep in mind when preparing the report?
   A. Stakeholders are different and may require different reports or reporting.
   B. Key stakeholders have similar needs that need to be included.
   C. Stakeholders are just like you and me, so if Roger makes a report for himself, it will also work for them.
   D. The team's reporting should be based upon the situation: short if things are going well, detailed if there are risks being discussed.

100 Which of the following tasks is the least important when monitoring project risk levels?

A. Assess threats

B. Assess the project risk level

C. Prepare reports for different stakeholders

D. Communicate risk levels to key stakeholders

9.2 Full Practice Exam 1 Answers

1 Murray, the project manager of a big healthcare project, is working on the preliminary document analysis. Which of the following documents should he review prior to the risk identification?

A. Risk management plan

B. **Industry benchmarks**

C. The lessons learned from his healthcare project

D. All of the above

Explanation: Option A is wrong as it is not yet completed. Option B is the best option. Alternatives are previous lessons learned, historical data, and such. Option C is wrong. Lessons learned from previous projects would be a good example; however, the healthcare project has limited lessons learned now. Option D is wrong as A and C are wrong.

2 Mary, the product owner of an agile software development team, is considering performing a preliminary document analysis. What does she need to do?

A. **She needs to determine and assign who is responsible for the preliminary document analysis.**

B. She needs to refine the product backlog and have the team working on the tasks.

C. She needs to do it herself as the PO.

D. She should discuss it with the Scrum master, who can facilitate the process

Explanation: Option A is correct. Various core roles, stakeholders, and subject matter experts should be involved. Option B is wrong as tasks may not be solved by the team, and the analysis might be done before the team is up and running. Option C could work, however, it could be a lot of work, and she may not have all the needed knowledge and expertise to do the full work. Option D is wrong as it will delay the work, and for many Scrum masters this task is outside of Scrum, so their expertise of the process might be limited.

3 Jimmy is working on a hybrid project where his task is to establish documents relevant to the risk process as part of the preliminary document analysis. Which of the following documents should he discard as the least relevant for his work?
A. The company's risk procedures
B. The project charter
C. **The benefit realization plan**
D. The team charter
Explanation: Option A is highly relevant as it states the risk process. Option B is relevant as the project charter may include high-level risk information. Option C is the least relevant as benefits in most cases may have little impact on the risk process. Option D is relevant as it states how the team works, which may include risk process components.

4 Pete has assessed the project environment for threats and opportunities. Several top opportunities were found that may have major impact on the realization of the business case benefits if delivered early. However, the project scope is not settled. Which project methodology is needed?
A. **Agile**
B. Waterfall
C. Hybrid
D. Waterfall with incremental deliverables
Explanation: Option A is the best choice for its early value delivery and unclear scope. Option B requires clear scope, and value delivery is in the end of the project. Option C might work as early value delivery and unclear scope may be included from agile; however, the question holds no evidence for the plan-based components. Option D is wrong. It requires clear scope, but value delivery can happen after each deliverable.

5 Pete has assessed the project environment for threats and opportunities. However, he failed to take the stakeholders into account. What should he do next?
A. Talk with the steering committee
B. **Conduct a stakeholder analysis**
C. Get an interview with the sponsor
D. Read lessons learned from previous projects
Explanation: Option A could work, but it is not the best option. The steering committee may provide input; however, it may not have the time for this engagement or the full view of the stakeholders. Option B is correct. Pete needs to conduct a stakeholder analysis. Option C is like option A, just with the sponsor. Option D is not the best option as it is just an extra/wasted step before doing the analysis.

6 Pete has assessed the project environment and analyzed constraints to risk management. Which of the following is he least likely to include in his assessment?
A. Market rules
B. Market laws
C. Technical risks
D. **Secondary risks**
Explanation: Constraints to risk management are fx. Government, market laws/rules, organizational, environmental, and technical risks. Options A, B, and C are correct. Option D is not a constraint and relevant now.

7 Otto, the project manager, is eager to ensure the risk threshold of the project is on the right level. What should it be aligned with to manage this?
A. Risk tolerance
B. **Risk appetites**
C. Risk capacity
D. Risk adverse
Explanation: The risk threshold of the project should be based upon the risk appetites. Option B is correct. Options A and C are wrong, out of the threshold and hold the same understanding. Option D is one of the various risk appetites the project stakeholders may have, just like neutral or seeker.

8 Otto, the project manager, aims at calculating the risk the organization can absorb. Which of the following is he least likely to consider?
A. Financial
B. Scope
C. Legal
D. **Procurement**
Explanation: The common factors are financial, scope, environmental, technical, legal, schedule, quality, contract, etc. Options A, B, and C seem likely. Contract is part of procurement, however, procurement is broader and the least likely candidate in this context.

9 Otto, the project manager, wants to confirm the risk thresholds based on risk appetites. What would be a good topic for the next steering committee meeting?

A. Calculate the risk appetite

B. **Discuss risk thresholds**

C. Discuss the calculations of the risk threshold based upon the risk budget

D. Discuss the risk contingency

Explanation: Option A is wrong. It may not be fully calculated, and it is part of the risk threshold, which should be discussed. Option B is the best option. Options C and D are wrong. Any budgets and contingencies should be settled after the risk threshold is set based on the risk appetite.

10 Otto, the project manager, is working on confirming the risk thresholds based on risk appetites. What should he expect?

A. He should have it signed as soon as possible to avoid too many conflicts.

B. He should invite the stakeholders for a review session so they are familiar with the content.

C. **He must lead conflict resolutions between stakeholders in agreeing on risk appetite.**

D. He should mentor and coach about risk appetite.
Explanation: Option A is wrong. The document is not signed, and conflicts are not necessarily a bad thing as they may help create even better material. Option B is wrong as the key stakeholders should be familiar with the content and a review session is not enough if disagreements are expected. Option C is the best option. Option D is not a bad option; however option C is just better.

11 Jane is an agile product owner in a hybrid environment. She is considering whether or not her project/team should establish a risk management strategy. Which of the following would highlight the need for a risk management strategy?

A. It is a mandatory section of the risk management plan

B. **To establish risk processes and tools**

C. An assumption for coaching the team on risk management best practices

D. Support servant leadership

Explanation: Option A is wrong. The risk management plan does contain the risk management strategy, but it is not mandatory nor should be the main reason for developing it. Option B is correct. Part of establishing a risk management strategy is to establish risk processes and tools. Option C is wrong. It is important to coach the team on risk management best practices;, however, the risk management strategy is not an assumption. Option D is wrong. Servant leadership may support the implementation of the risk management strategy not vice versa nor a main reason for its use.

12 Jane, an agile product owner in a hybrid environment, has decided to establish a risk management strategy. The PMO informs her that the risk management strategy should determine risk metrics. Which of the following would be a good example of a risk metric for her team to use?
    A. Escaped defects
    B. Schedule performance index
    C. Cost variance
    D. **Risk exposure based upon expected monetary value**
    Explanation: Option A is wrong. Escaped defects is a metric where the team measures the number of defects found by the business. Options B and C are wrong. SPI and CV are both earned value management measurements, which focus on time and cost, not risks. Option D is correct. Expected Monetary Value (EMV) is calculated by multiplying probability with impact using real monetary values like 10 % x $10.000 equals EMV of $1000.

13 Jane, an agile product owner in a hybrid environment, has decided to establish a risk management strategy. Her team wants to create an RBS. Which of the following would be a good approach to identify risk categories?
    A. Ask one of the project managers to share their RBS
    B. **See if they can find some historical data to be used as a basis for the development of an RBS**
    C. Forget it; risk categories are of little value in agile environments
    D. Have the Scrum master facilitate the development of the RBS by the team
    Explanation: Option A is wrong. A project manager of a predictive project with an RBS may have little value for a hybrid team. Option B is the best option. An RBS can be built upon historical data. Option C is wrong. An RBS does provide value in a value environment. Option D is wrong. The RBS could be developed by a team; however, it requires resources and has little value.

14 Jane, an agile product owner in a hybrid environment, has decided to establish a risk management strategy. What approach could support the coaching/mentoring of the team on risk management best practices?
    A. Resources for a training effort
    B. Adaptive leadership
    C. **Servant leadership**
    D. Sessions by the Scrum master
    Explanation: Option A is wrong. Resources for training may support the coaching/mentoring, but it is not the best option. Option B is wrong. Adaptive leadership is commonly used by the product owner but not for coaching or mentoring. Option C is correct. Coaching and mentoring is strengthened and supported using servant leadership. Option D is wrong. It may provide some value, but the Scrum master also relies on servant leadership to make the sessions work.

15 When documenting the risk management plan, which tool and technique could help in defining organizational risk roles and responsibilities?
A. RACI
B. Responsibility assignment matrix
C. RASI
D. **All of the above**
Explanation: Option D is correct as options A, B, and C all are tools for defining roles and responsibilities. Options A and C are both examples of a RAM, option B.

16 When documenting the risk management plan, which question could outline the key risk management activities?
A. Who?
B. What?
C. When?
D. **All of the above**
Explanation: Option D is correct as options A, B, and C all are questions that could outline key risk management activities. Other questions to ask are where and how.

17 How can the risk breakdown structure (RBS) support the risk management plan?
A. Highlights the key activities
B. **Categories for risk identification**
C. Mandatory for performing the qualitative risk assessment
D. Important input for most of the quantitative tools and techniques
Explanation: Option A is wrong. The RBS does not include activities. Option B is correct. The RBS can give the categories and risks for further use. Option C is wrong. Qualitative risk assessment can be performed without an RBS. It is not mandatory. Option D is wrong. The RBS is not an input or used to a high degree in quantitative risk analysis.

18 When documenting the risk management plan, other plans are needed. Which plan would provide the most value when documenting the risk management plan?
A. **The risk communication plan**
B. Project management plan
C. Project communication plan
D. Risk management approaches
Explanation: Option A is correct as the risk communication plan is needed. Option B is wrong. The project management plan contains all the plans, which is too much and broad. Option C is wrong. The risk communication plan is contained in the project communication plan, so Option B is more precise to the point. Option D is wrong. Risk management approaches are a made-up term.

19 The project team plans to engage the stakeholders in upcoming risk management activities. What would be an activity in which to engage the stakeholders?

   A. Engage stakeholders in developing the RBS

   B. Engage stakeholders in defining roles and responsibilities

   C. **Engage stakeholders in the risk prioritization process**

   D. Engage stakeholders in defining risk strategies

   Explanation: Option A is wrong. The stakeholders may provide input to the RBS; however, it is mainly based upon lessons learned, historical data, and such. Option B is wrong as roles and responsibilities are defined by the leadership part of the planning. Option C is correct and a good example of how to engage the stakeholders in risk management activities. Option D is wrong as risk strategies are defined in the risk management plan. The challenge is not the strategies but how to apply them to the actual risks.

20 When planning risk management activities with the key stakeholders, how can the project tailor the risk communication for the stakeholders?

   A. Ensure all stakeholders receive the full and comprehensive project communication all the time

   B. **Try to understand the need of the stakeholders and then adapt the communication to fit these needs**

   C. Follow company procedures on project risk communication

   D. Limit risk communication to avoid information overload

   Explanation: Option A is wrong. Communication is not tailored. Option B is correct. This is a good example of adapting the communication to the need of the stakeholders. Option C is wrong. A standard company approach may require some tailoring. Option D is wrong. Risk communication is limited, but needs might be more.

21 When planning risk management activities with the key stakeholders, how can the project educate the stakeholders on risk management to foster engagement?

   A. Provide project management training

   B. **Share understanding of risk principles**

   C. Invite the stakeholders to the team's daily standup meetings

   D. Teach the stakeholders about risk management facilitation

   Explanation: Option A is wrong. Standard project management training is too generic. It provides too little value. Option B is correct as it is important for stakeholder engagement to understand the risk principles. Option C is wrong. Stakeholders should not take part in the dailies, and they would include little on risk management or foster engagement. Option D is wrong. The stakeholders should not facilitate risk management activities. The training has little value to foster engagement.

22 When planning risk management activities with the key stakeholders, what is the goal of training, coaching, and educating the stakeholders on risk principles and processes?
A. General risk management awareness
B. To reduce conflicts with the team
C. To engage the stakeholders in performing activities
D. **To foster engagement in risk management**
Explanation: Option A is wrong. It is not the goal to provide general training. Option B is wrong. Training may not reduce conflicts, and conflicts if managed properly can have a positive impact. Option C is wrong. Stakeholders should not be engaged in performing activities. Option D is correct. Stakeholders are educated in the shared understanding to foster engagement in risk management.

23 Murray and Kim are both parts of an agile Scrum team. When would it be the most suitable time to identify risks?
A. Arrange a kickoff meeting before sprint 0
B. Only during sprint planning and sprint review
C. **During the process**
D. Include it in the sprint retrospective
Explanation: Option A is wrong. It could work, but the most suitable time is iterative. A one-time meeting is not enough. Option B is wrong. It is important to identify risks during sprint planning and the sprint review; however, it is not only during these events. Option C is correct. Identification of risks is an ongoing and iterative process during the sprint, at any time or meeting. Option D is wrong. It is fine to identify risks during the sprint retrospective, but it also must happen much sooner and iteratively.

24 John, the project manager of a plan-based construction project, is in the process of planning various activities for risk identification. John has identified several good activities, but one activity is probably not the most effective one. Which activity should John not include?
A. Meetings with various subject matter experts
B. Interviews with key stakeholders
C. Focus groups with industry representatives
D. **Obtain lessons learned from the agile development teams**
Explanation: Options A, B, and C are wrong because this is a "not" question. Meetings, interviews, and focus groups are all good activities for identification of risks. Option D is the right one since it should not be included. Lessons learned are often a good idea; however, the value from agile development teams is likely to be limited for a plan-based construction project.

25 Pete is working in a hybrid environment and needs to come up with a good activity or process for risk identification that benefits the predictive and agile approach his project is combining. Which of the following would be the most valued activity or change of process?

A. **Make sure risks are identified iteratively (all the time) like in Scrum**

B. Make sure risks are identified when starting each phase

C. Make sure lessons learned are collected from all types of projects to cover the hybrid approach

D. Make sure risks are identified before reaching a milestone

Explanation: Option A is correct. In hybrid, iterative identification of risks is needed. Option B is wrong. Identification of risks when starting a new phase is fine, but more is needed. Option C is wrong. It is always good to collect lessons learned from similar kinds of projects, however, more is needed. Option D is wrong. It is OK to identify risks before reaching a milestone, perhaps a bit late, but unless you have many milestones more is needed. Identification of risks and milestones are typically not aligned.

26 The IT healthcare project has identified a bunch of risks that have been described in the risk register. However, many of the columns in the Excel sheet lack data. What could be the next step to increase the quality of the identified risks?

A. Assign risk owners

B. Examine the risks for possible secondary or residual risks

C. **Perform detailed analyses of risk identification exercise results**

D. Conduct a qualitative risk assessment

Explanation: Option A is wrong. Risk owners should be assigned at some point; however, it would not increase the quality of the risks identified now. Option B is wrong. It is not possible to identify possible secondary or residual risks without considering the risk responses, which have not been done. Option C is correct; more analyses are needed. Option D is wrong. Qualitative risk analysis would be a good next step, but more quality data are needed.

27 When conducting various risk identification exercises, it is important to understand the business context of the information. Which of these examples is not the best representation of this concept?

A. Documents

B. Audio transcripts

C. Telemetry data

D. **Sprint retrospective**

Explanations: Options A, B, and C are all good examples of data applied to understand the business context of the information. Option D is right since it is not the best representation of the concept. The sprint retrospective is a team meeting and may contain some business context, but focus is on the continuous improvement of the team's performance. In this case, options A, B, and C are better presentations of these concepts.

28 The project has spent a lot of time and resources on examining assumptions and constraints. How could the project proactively leverage the results of the assumption and constraint analysis?

A. **Convert some assumptions and constraints into risks**

B. Update the risk register with the new insights

C. Allocate risk contingency to fit with the findings

D. Update lessons learned based upon the results

Explanation: Option A is correct. The assumption and constraint analysis can be used to convert them into risks. Option B is wrong. Assumptions and constraints are typically not included in the risk register unless converted into risks. Option C is wrong. The risk contingency budget depends on the identified risks, not assumptions and constraints. Funds may be allocated, but now it is not the most proactive approach either. Option D is wrong. Updating lessons learned is ongoing and could contain assumptions and constraints; however, it is not proactive in helping us going forward this point in time.

29 The project has spent a lot of time and resources on examining assumptions and constraints. Now the project has a list of these. What could the team do next?

A. Convert all of them into risks

B. **Categorize the assumptions and constraints**

C. Conduct a qualitative analysis on the assumptions

D. Conduct a quantitative analysis on the constraints

Explanation: Option A is wrong. It may not be possible nor the best solution to convert all assumptions and constraints into risks. Option B is correct. A categorization is often needed. Option C is wrong. The qualitative risk analysis is not conducted on assumptions. Option D is wrong. The quantitative analysis is not conducted on constraints.

30 The project has spent a lot of time and resources on examining assumptions and constraints. Some are converted, the rest have been categorized. What would be a good next step?

A. Update the risk contingency budget

B. Provide input to the planning of the risk activities

C. **Assess the risks associated with each assumption and/or constraint**

D. Perform an assessment of the probability and impact on monetary values of the risks associated with each assumption and/or constraint

Explanation: Option A is wrong. It is too early to update the budget, and it provides little value now. Option B is wrong. This work does not provide input to the planning of the risk activities. Option C is correct. Option D is wrong. The EMV analysis described is a quantitative analysis, which is conducted on risks not assumptions and/or constraints.

31 When examining the assumption and constraint analysis, which is the best example to recognize the relationship between assumptions and/or constraints and project objectives?

A. **The holiday season may have a cascade effect on the project timeline.**

B. Investments in risk responses may influence the risk budget.

C. Lack of risk management may result in more issues.

D. Poor project management may influence the project deliveries.

Explanation: Option A is correct. The holiday season is a constraint that may impact the project objective. Options B, C, and D are all wrong. There is a clear relationship between risk management and possible issues, however, they are not assumptions and/or constraints.

32 Which of the following assumptions and/or constraints may not have an impact on a project objective?

A. Key stakeholders available during the Chinese New Year period

B. Lack of skilled labor

C. In July, no work is possible due to bad weather/windy conditions

D. **Funding not approved**

Explanation: Option A is wrong. The constraint would have an impact on the project objective. Option B is wrong. The constraint would have an impact on the project objective. Option C is wrong. The assumption would have an impact on the project objective. Option D is correct. This is an issue.

33 Assumption and constraint analyses work best with the involvement of the stakeholders. Which of the following tasks would be a good use of the stakeholders' active engagement?

A. Encourage stakeholders to convert assumptions and constraints to risks

B. Encourage stakeholders to categorize assumptions and constraints

C. **Encourage stakeholders to challenge assumptions and constraints**

D. All of the above

Explanations: Option A is wrong. Conversations are done by the project team. Option B is wrong. The categorizations are done by the project team. Option C is correct. This is a great way of involving the stakeholders. Option D is wrong. Options A and B are wrong, so option D must also be wrong.

34 Paul is updating the risk registers and finds various risk triggers. Which one of these should he ask the team to reassess and document?

A. Structural failure of crane

B. Incorrect loading

C. Operator overextends load

D. **Dropped object**

Explanation: Options A, B, and C are all valid triggers. Option D is correct as this is a risk not a risk trigger.

35 Paul is updating the risk registers and now has updated the various risk triggers. However, risk triggers are related to causes. He examines one trigger where a crane drops a heavy object. Which one of these causes should he ask the team to reassess and document?
A. **Strong winds**
B. Overload protection
C. Use lifting plan
D. Check safety manifest
Explanation: Option A is the correct answer. It is a risk trigger not a cause and should be reassessed. Options B, C, and D are all valid causes and should not be reassessed.

36 Paul is updating the risk registers and now has updated the various risk triggers and causes. He examines one risk where a crane drops a heavy object. Which one of these risk consequences is valid?
A. Load too heavy
B. Pre-lift crane check
C. **Use lifting plan**
D. Object dropped in sea
Explanation: Option A is wrong. It is a risk trigger. Option B is wrong. It is a risk cause. Option C is correct. It is a risk sequence. Option D is wrong. It is a risk impact.

37 Which of the following is not a good example of the risk impact where the risk is a crane drops a heavy object?
A. Personnel hit by object
B. **Object may not be dropped**
C. Object dropped in sea
D. Object impacts ground
Explanation: Option A is wrong as it is a risk impact. Option B is correct. This is not a risk impact, but deals with the probability of the crane dropping the object. Option C is wrong. This is a risk impact. Option D is wrong. This is a risk impact.

38 Which quantitative analysis assesses and documents risk triggers, causes, consequences, and/or impact?
A. Decision tree
B. **Bowtie analysis**
C. Monte Carlo simulation
D. Analytical hierarchy process
Explanation: Option A is wrong. It includes decision, probabilities, and impacts. Option B is correct. Option C is wrong. The Monte Carlo can simulate various parameters but not all the listed items. Option D is wrong. It is a method to calibrate preferences for achieving the different objectives of a project.

39 When documenting risk triggers and thresholds based on the context/ environment, which of the following tasks is the least important?
   A. Assess, confirm, and document risk compliance thresholds and categories against updated risk data
   B. Assess and document risk triggers, causes, and timing
   C. **Assess and document risk probabilities and/or impact**
   D. Empower stakeholders to challenge existing thresholds
   Explanation: Options A, B, and D are all wrong as these are important tasks. Option C is correct as it is the least important. This assessment should not include risk probability, which is included in the qualitative risk analysis.

40 When developing a risk register, it is important to analyze the validity of certain elements. What are these elements?
   A. **Identified risks and triggers**
   B. Probabilities and impacts
   C. Risk attributes
   D. Risk ownership
   Explanation: Option A is correct. It is important to analyze the validity of the identified risks and triggers. Option B is wrong. Probabilities and impacts should be examined but not necessarily the validity. Option C is wrong. Risk attributes like probability, impact, and urgency should be examined but not necessarily the validity. Option D is wrong. It is important to establish risk origin and ownership, but it has nothing to do with the validity.

41 When developing a risk register, it is important to examine the relevant risk attributes. Which of the following do not fall into that category?
   A. Probability
   B. Impact
   C. Urgency
   D. **Opportunity**
   Explanation: Options A, B, and C are all relevant risk attributes. Option D is correct as it is not a relevant risk attribute. Opportunity is a positive risk, not a risk attribute.

42 Which of these risks should be classified as a threat in the risk register?
   A. Probability of increased sales due to close ties with the customer
   B. **Increased costs due to bad weather**
   C. Increased savings due to effective production
   D. Fewer team members leaving the team due to close cooperation
   Explanation: Option A is wrong. This is an opportunity. Option B is correct. This is a negative risk, also called a threat. Option C is wrong. This is an opportunity. Option D is wrong. This is an opportunity.

43 Which of these risks should not be classified as an opportunity in the risk register?

A. Reduced material use due to use of new technology

B. Happy stakeholders due to increased engagement

C. Increased stock rates due to good reputation

D. **Increased resource use due to planning**

Explanation: Option A is wrong. This is an opportunity. Option B is wrong. This is an opportunity. Option C is wrong. This is an opportunity. Option D is correct. This is not an opportunity but a negative risk or threat.

44 When developing the risk register, it is important to establish risk origin and ownership. Which of the following does not fit this statement?

A. Internal stakeholders

B. External subject matter expert

C. **Increased probability and impact**

D. Derived from the risk breakdown structure

Explanation: Option A is wrong. Ownership can be at internal stakeholders. Option B is wrong. Ownership can be at external subject matter experts. Option C is correct as probability and impact do not establish origin or ownership. Option D is wrong. A risk origin may be in the RBS.

45 John, the project manager of an IT project, is in the process of developing the risk register. Which of the following tasks is hardly relevant for this work?

A. Examine the risk attributes like probability, impact, urgency

B. **Classify risks only as threats**

C. Establish risk origin and ownership, e.g., internal/external

D. Analyze the validity of identified risks and triggers

Explanation: Option A is wrong. This is a valid task. Option B is correct. It is important to classify risks as threats or opportunities, not only as threats. Option C is wrong. This is a valid task. Option D is wrong. This is a valid task.

46 Murray, the project manager of a large healthcare project, is in the process of performing the qualitative analysis where some of the risks are identified using the RBS. Which document provides the classification used in the RBS?

A. Risk management strategy

B. Project management plan

C. **Risk management plan**

D. Project charter

Explanation: Option A is wrong. The risk management strategy does not provide detailed information for the RBS. Option B is wrong. The project management plan does contain the component of the risk management plan, however, it would be a better choice or more precise to choose a different option. Option C is correct. The RBS classifications are described in the risk management plan. Option D is wrong. The project charter does contain risks but not the categories.

47 Which of the following is not an example of a commonly applied classification of risks in an RBS?

A. Environment

B. Organizational

C. Project management

D. **Leadership**

Explanation: Options A, B, and C are all common classifications found in the RBS, but are wrong answers because this is a "not" question. Option D is correct. Leadership is not an example of a commonly applied classification of risks in an RBS.

48 When performing the qualitative analysis, the estimate of the impact of risks may affect various project objectives. Which of the following is not one of them?

A. **Quality**

B. Project schedule

C. Budget

D. Scope

Explanation: Option A is correct. Quality is commonly one of the project objectives assessed; however, if done so it is often related to budget, scope, or schedule. Options B, C, and D are wrong. They are project objective where impacts are estimated.

49 Pete is performing the qualitative analysis with his team. Which two parameters need to be assessed?

A. Probability and likelihood

B. **Probability and impact**

C. Consequence and impact

D. Time and materials

Explanation: Option A is wrong. Probability and likelihood are the same. Option B is correct. Option C is wrong. Consequence and impact are the same. Option D is wrong. Time and materials are a way for charging for services; see project procurement management for details.

50 Ann, the product owner, wants to apply the risk matrices part of the core team qualitative analysis. She found several good resources; however, one of them is not the best resource. Which one?

A. Agreed-upon assessment approach

B. Historical information

C. Preestablished criteria

D. **Definition of done from previous iterations**

Explanation: Options A, B, and C are all wrong as these are good resources. Option D is correct as it is not the best resource. The definition of done is not relevant here and if it is an old agreement, then a newer version might also exist.

51 Jimmy, the project manager, has key stakeholders in his project with limited knowledge of the risk categorization strategies his project could apply. What would be the best approach to more engagement of the stakeholders?

A. **Coach the stakeholders on risk categorization strategies**

B. Provide formal training to all the stakeholders

C. Find a mentor for the key stakeholders

D. Allow the key stakeholders to participate in various risk management activities

Explanation: Option A is correct. This is the best and more effective approach. Option B is wrong. Training might work, a bit broad but to all stakeholders it is not the best approach. Option C is wrong. A mentor is not a bad solution; however, it is a bit general. Option D is wrong. It is not a bad option, however, more knowledge is needed before they get value out of joining the activities and it is not as effective as the other options.

52 When performing the qualitative analysis, which task should be included?

   A. Estimate the impact of risk on only project schedule, budget, and resources

   B. Prioritize the risk based on impact and detectability

   C. Apply only the risk matrices based upon historical information and preestablished criteria

   D. **Perform an ordinal classification**

   Explanation: Option A is wrong. Scope is missing for this task to work. Option B is wrong. Detectability is not part of the prioritization. Option C is wrong. It is not only based upon these two sources. Option D is correct.

53 Allan, the project manager, has completed the qualitative analysis and now wants to perform the quantitative analysis. Several techniques have been selected, however, one is not applied for quantitative analysis. Which one is it?

   A. Sensitivity analysis

   B. Decision tree

   C. **Earned value management**

   D. Expected monetary value

   Explanation: Options A, B, and D are all wrong. These are techniques for quantitative analysis. Option C is relevant for monitoring and forecasting cost and time.

54 Paula, the business analyst, wants to see which risks and activities on the critical path have the highest standard deviation. Which technique can support this work?

   A. Monte Carlo simulation

   B. Benchmarking

   C. **Sensitivity analysis**

   D. PERT

   Explanation: Option A is wrong. This quantitative technique may simulate various outcomes but not standard deviation. Option B is wrong. Benchmarking is not relevant here. Option C is correct. The sensitivity analysis can describe which risks or activities have high or low sensitivity or standard deviation. Option D is wrong. This technique works fine for estimation and can support calculation of standard deviation.

55 Charlie is conducting a risk analysis where he, based upon a decision, must measure the probability and impact of various possible paths. Which analysis is he properly conducting?
A. Sensitivity analysis
B. Monte Carlo
C. **Decision tree**
D. Expected monetary value
Explanation: Options A, B, and D are all wrong. These techniques do not fit the description. Option C is correct.

56 When performing the quantitative risk analysis, it is important to analyze risk data and process performance information against what?
A. Project objectives
B. **Established metrics**
C. Project constraints
D. The risk management plan
Explanation: Options A, B, and D are all wrong. These are not relevant here. Option B is correct.

57 Mary performs quantitative risk analysis where she seeks to conduct a precise forecast analysis. What would be a good source?
A. New information
B. Historical information
C. **Both A and B**
D. Input from the trend analysis
Explanation: Options A and B are both good sources but the wrong option. Option C is correct as options A and B are good sources. Option D is wrong. The trend analysis is like the forecast analysis. The input used is similar, so it is unlikely they both have the same data.

58 Sandra has completed the quantitative risk analysis. Is it likely the risk weighting and risk priority have changed in the process?
A. **Yes, risk weighting and risk priority are likely to change in the process.**
B. Yes, risk weighting is likely to change in the process.
C. Yes, risk priority is likely to change in the process.
D. No changed should be expected.
Explanation: Option A is correct. Risk weighting and priority are likely to change during the process. Options B, C, and D are all wrong.

59 Ursula, the newly appointed project manager, has just completed assessment of the probability and impact of all the identified risks. What should she do next?

A. Identify the opportunities

B. Assign risk responses to the identified risks

C. Perform qualitative analysis

D. **Perform quantitative analysis**

Explanation: Option A is wrong. Risks and opportunities have been identified. Option B is wrong. Risk responses are assigned after the quantitative analysis. Option C is wrong. This assessment has just been completed. Option D is correct. Following the qualitative assessment, the quantitative assessment can be conducted.

60 Monty is performing a quantitative analysis where his team is focusing on the critical path, as the deadline is set in stone and consequences are severe. What risk analysis tool or technique could support this emphasis during the quantitative analysis?

A. **Examine sensitivity of the activities on the critical path**

B. Examine EVM, so an SPI higher than 1 should put more effort into risk mitigation

C. Identify more risks with a focus on planning

D. Check if milestones are still valid

Explanation: Option A is correct. Sensitivity analysis works well with a focus on the critical path. Option B is wrong. If SPI is higher than 1, the team is ahead of time and should not mitigate but perhaps take more chances. Option C is wrong. Most risks should have been identified. Option D is wrong. Milestones should be checked and valid; however, it is not necessary during the quantitative analysis.

61 Oliver is working with his team on the risk analysis in which they try to assess project risk complexity. Which tool or technique could best support this endeavor?

A. **Cause and effect diagram**

B. Decision tree analysis

C. Interviews

D. Brainstorming

Explanation: Option A is correct. The cause-effect, Ishikawa, fishbone diagram – the diagram has multiple names – would be effective in supporting this work. Option B is wrong. Tree diagrams may work but this refers to the quantitative technique. Options C and D are both wrong. These techniques are mostly for data gathering.

62 An agile team is assessing project risk complexity. Which of the following tools and techniques should not be applied?
A. SWOT analysis
B. Ishikawa diagram
C. Tree diagram
D. **Benefit-cost analysis**
Explanation: Options A, B, and C are all wrong. These are tools and techniques for assessing project risk complexity. Option D is correct. This method is for assessing projects and often used in the business case. This is not a technique for assessing project risk complexity.

63 Ursula is performing an impact analysis and assessing project objectives. Which of the following should she include?
A. **Stakeholders**
B. Assumptions
C. Constraints
D. Issues
Explanation: Option A is correct. This is a valid project objective to assess because stakeholders have a major influence on project objectives. Options B, C, and D are all wrong. These may influence project objectives, but they are not project objectives.

64 Jim is performing an impact analysis and assessing project objectives with his team. Which of the following should not be included?
A. Project scopes
B. Schedule
C. Resources
D. **Legal**
Explanation: Options A, B, and C are all valid project objectives. Option D is correct as this is not a project objective.

65 When assessing project compliance objectives against organizational strategic objectives, which of the following would be the best resource for this work?
A. Impediment log
B. Issue log
C. **Gantt chart**
D. Budget
Explanation: Options A, B, and D are all wrong. These resources do not contain organizational strategic objectives. Option D has some merit. However, option C is correct and a better resource.

66 When assessing project compliance objectives against organizational strategic objectives, which of the following should not be included?

A. Procedures

B. **Procurement governance**

C. Corporate governance

D. Project governance

Explanation: Options A, C, and D are all valid resources. These options are all wrong as this is a "not" question. Option B is correct as this is not a resource to be included.

67 Walid wants to engage his stakeholders to work more independently but to perform which task?

A. Identify threats

B. Assess project risk complexity

C. Perform an impact analysis on project objectives

D. **Identify threats and opportunities**

Explanation: Option A is wrong. It lacks opportunities. Option B and C are both valid options;, however, they should be conducted by the team. Option D is correct. This is a task for the stakeholders.

68 Walid has empowered the stakeholders to independently identify threats and opportunities. Which of the following is the best example of this work?

A. Requirements are unclear.

B. It will never snow during project execution.

C. It will rain for sure during project execution.

D. **It might be windy during project execution.**

Explanation: Option A is wrong. This is an issue. Option B is wrong as it is not a risk as the probability is never. Option C is wrong as it is not a risk as the probability is certain. Option D is correct and a good example of this work.

69 Which of the following is an appropriate risk response strategy for managing threats?

A. Enhance

B. **Accept**

C. Share

D. Exploit

Explanation: Options A, C, and D are all valid risk response strategies for managing opportunities, not threats. Option B is a valid risk response for managing threats.

70 Which of the following is not an appropriate risk response strategy for managing opportunities?
A. Escalate
B. Accept
C. **Mitigate**
D. Share
Explanation: Options A, B, and D are all wrong as these are all valid risk response strategies for managing opportunities. Option C is correct as this is not a valid risk response strategy for managing opportunities but for threats.

71 John, the project manager, has activated the risk response, which resulted in an additional resource being forced to work on an activity in order to keep the work on track. What risk response strategy has been applied?
A. Accept
B. Share
C. **Mitigate**
D. Escalate
Explanation: Option A is wrong. Actions were taken so it can't be accepted. Option B is wrong. This is not an opportunity. Option C is correct. This is an example of mitigating a risk. Option D is wrong. This risk is mitigated not escalated.

72 When determining the appropriate risk response strategy it is also important to identify a person to act when the trigger happens. What is this role called?
A. Risk owner
B. **Action owner**
C. Product owner
D. Risk manager
Explanation: Option A is wrong. A risk owner may own the risk, but someone else can act upon it. Option B is correct. Option C is wrong. The agile product owner may only have a few risks to act upon and this question is generic. Option D is wrong. This is a general role that often facilitates the process not action owners.

73 Which of the following tools is a good way to illustrate and communicate the effectiveness of the risk response strategies?
A. Product backlog
B. **Dot plots**
C. Information radiator
D. Vision statement
Explanation: Option A is wrong. The effectiveness of the response strategy is not captured in the product backlog. Option B is correct. This is a good tool like a burndown chart and such. Option C is wrong. This is a bit too generic and option B is a more precise option. Option D is wrong. It is not included in the vision statement.

74 Which of the following tasks is the least important when performing risk response strategies?

A. Determine the workaround

B. Allocate responsibilities

C. Outline an appropriate responsibility matrix for a metricized project environment

D. **Reevaluate all risks**

Explanation: Options A, B, and C are all valid tasks to be performed. Option D is correct because it is the least important task; the reevaluating should only involve organizational risks, not all risks.

75 When planning risk response strategies, which should be applied first if the impact of the risk is high?

A. Exploit

B. **Avoid**

C. Mitigate

D. Escalate

Explanation: Option A is wrong. This strategy is for managing opportunities, not threats. Option B is correct. When the impact is high, the project should try to avoid it. Option C is wrong. It may not be enough to mitigate a high impact risk. Option D is wrong. Escalate may not solve it and impact is high.

76 When should the action owner implement the risk response?

A. **As per risk trigger**

B. If the risk is close to occurring

C. If the risk impact is high and proximity is near

D. All of the above

Explanation: Option A is correct. The risk trigger is the time the risk response should be executed. Option B is wrong. A risk close to occurring might be too late. Option C is wrong. This might be too late and unclear. Option D is wrong since option B and option C are wrong.

77 Paul is discussing with his team whether all risks should have a risk response plan. What is the right solution to this debate?

A. All risks identified should have a risk response plan.

B. **All risks except risks on the watchlist should have a risk response plan.**

C. All risks with high probability and impact should have a risk response plan

D. It is a team decision to decide which risks should have a risk response plan.

Explanation: Option A is wrong. All risks should not have a risk response plan. Low probability and low impact risks may not have a risk response plan. Option B is correct. Option C is wrong. These risks might have a risk response plan, but others may also be relevant. Option D is wrong. This is not a team decision.

78 Georg wants to encourage the project stakeholders to be more engaged in risk management. What would be a suitable task when implementing risk responses?
   A. Encourage stakeholders to discuss risk prioritization
   B. Encourage stakeholders to identify risks
   C. Encourage stakeholders to assess risks
   D. **Encourage stakeholders to provide feedback on the risk response**
   Explanation: Options A, B, and C are all wrong. Risk prioritization, identification, and assessment of risks should have already been performed. Option D is correct.

79 The team evaluates and reacts to secondary risks from the response implementation. What is a good example of this?
   A. The risk response reduces probability and impact of the risk, but it is still active.
   B. **The risk response causes a new risk to materialize.**
   C. The risk response is aligned with the fallback plan.
   D. The risk response is aligned with the contingency plan.
   Explanation: Option A is wrong. This is a residual risk. Option B is correct. Option C is wrong. This alignment is hardly relevant. Option D is wrong. This alignment is hardly relevant.

80 The team evaluates and reacts to residual risks from the response implementation. What is a good example of this?
   A. **The risk response reduces the probability of the risk.**
   B. The risk response causes two new risks to materialize.
   C. The risk response can be measured in monetary value.
   D. The risk response can be measured in time.
   Explanation: Option A is correct. A residual risk is still active after the risk response. It may cause the probability and/or impact to be reduced. Option B is wrong. This is a secondary risk. Option C is wrong. This is hardly relevant. Option D is wrong. This is hardly relevant.

81 Which of the following tasks would not be relevant when implementing risk responses?
   A. Execute the risk response plan(s)
   B. **Execute fallback plans**
   C. Execute the contingency plan(s)
   D. Evaluate and react to secondary and residual risks from the response implementation
   Explanation: Options A, C, and D are all valid tasks, but this is a "not" question so these options are all wrong. Option B is correct. Fallback plans could be relevant, however, it is not a defined task.

82 When gathering and analyzing performance data on planning, which planning components may be relevant to reconciling performance data and reports?

A. Activities

B. **Work packages**

C. Milestones

D. Epics

Explanation: Option A is wrong. Activities might be too detailed. Option B is correct. Option C is wrong. Milestones are not relevant for performance data. Option D is wrong. Epics are agile requirements on a high level.

83 Which of the following is not a tool, technique, or meeting for gathering and analyzing performance in an agile environment?

A. **User stories**

B. Information radiator

C. Iteration review

D. Daily standup

Explanation: Option A is correct. User stories are not used for analyzing performance. Option B is wrong. Boards hold information for performance measurements. Option C is wrong. The iteration review is a meeting where performance is known. Option D is wrong. The daily standup is a meeting where performance is known.

84 When analyzing data to determine the completion status against the baseline, which of the following is not a commonly applied baseline?

A. Scope

B. Time

C. **Risk**

D. Cost

Explanation: Option A is wrong. Scope is one of the performance measurement baselines. Option B is wrong. Time is also one of the performance measurement baselines. Option C is correct. Risk is not a baseline. Option D is wrong. Cost is also one of the performance measurement baselines.

85 When trying to determine how the project is doing compared to where the project is supposed to be, which tool or technique could provide this?

A. **Variance analysis**

B. Benchmarking

C. Trend analysis

D. Information radiator

Explanation: Option A is correct. A variance analysis could provide the comparison. Option B is wrong. This tool does not provide this. Option C is wrong. This tool does not provide this. Option D is wrong. The board provides information on status, not the context described.

86 When gathering and analyzing performance data, which of the following tasks is most relevant?

A. Reconcile performance data and reports from risk-relevant activities

B. Analyze data to determine the completion status against the work packages

C. **Perform a variance analysis**

D. Monitor impact against overall project risk appetite to enterprise

Explanation: Option A is wrong. Activities are wrong in this statement. Option B is wrong. Work packages are wrong in this statement. Option C is correct. Option D is wrong. Risk appetite is wrong in this statement.

87 Tony is updating the risk register after monitoring a residual risk. Which of the following entries fits this task?

A. New risk identified after risk response implemented

B. Change in budget after risk response implemented

C. Risk no longer valid

D. **Reduced probability after risk response implemented**

Explanation: Option A is wrong. This sounds like a secondary risk. Option B is wrong. Change in the budget is not the best choice and most likely outcome. Option C is wrong. A residual risk is still active. Option D is correct.

88 When would Tommy most likely encounter a new secondary risk?

A. When identifying new risks

B. When mitigating residual risks

C. **As the result of a risk response**

D. When measuring expected monetary value

Explanation: Option A is wrong. Identification of new risks may not result in new secondary risks. Option B is wrong. Residual and secondary risks are not related. Option C is correct. Secondary risks are the result of the risk response. Option D is wrong. This is a made-up consequence.

89 When monitoring risk responses for secondary risk, which risk response is least relevant?

A. Mitigate

B. Accept

C. Transfer

D. **Exploit**

Explanation: Options A, B, and C are all valid risk responses for secondary risk. These are not correct as this is a "least relevant" question. Option D is correct. This risk response is wrong. This positive risk response is the least relevant option as secondary risks are negative risks.

90 When assessing the possible impact of residual and secondary risks, which of the following illustrates this?
A. Increase in the risk contingency budget
B. **Schedule delayed by 2 months**
C. Lack of stakeholder engagement
D. No legal complaints during procurement
Explanation: Option A is wrong. This is not a project objective. Option B is correct. This is a project objective. Options C and D are both wrong. These are not project objectives.

91 Which of the following tasks is the most relevant when monitoring residual and secondary risks?
A. Monitor risk response and document positive risk
B. Monitor risk response for negative risks
C. Assess the impact of negative and positive risks on project objectives
D. **Update and communicate the impact of residual and secondary risks**
Explanation: Options A, B, and C are all wrong. These tasks should not involve positive and negative risks. Option D is correct. This is the most relevant task.

92 Which of the following documents should not be updated during the monitoring and controlling?
A. Risk register
B. **Lessons learned repository**
C. Project management plan
D. Change logs
Explanation: Options A, C, and D are all valid documents that should be updated. These are wrong as this is a "not" question. Option B is correct as it is wrong to update a repository. Lessons learned should be updated but not the repository.

93 In the risk register, which risk data are most likely to be updated?
A. Description
B. Category
C. Probability and impact before risk response
D. **Probability and impact after risk response**
Explanation: Option A is wrong. The description will hardly change much, if defined properly. Option B is wrong. Early on the category is settled and hardly changed. Option C is wrong. Before the risk response, probability and impact should not change much unless new information comes up, minor updates, and such. Option D is correct. It is likely that probability and impact will change if the risk is residual after the risk response.

94 When should risks be monitored?
   A. Monitored continuously and updated before end of phase
   B. **Monitored and documented iteratively**
   C. When risks are likely to occur
   D. In agile after each iteration
   Explanation: Option A is wrong. Risks should be monitored continuously but updated before the end of phase is not enough. Option B is correct. Monitoring and documentation should happen all the time. Option C is wrong. This is too late and not enough. Option D is wrong. In agile, risks are monitored iteratively.

95 What would be a good reason to close a risk?
   A. Probability and impact are low.
   B. The risk is not included in the risk contingency budget.
   C. It is impossible for the risk to happen.
   D. **The risk has occurred.**
   Explanation: Option A is wrong. The risk should still be active on the watchlist. Option B is wrong. The risk can still be active without budget allocated. Option C is wrong. This is an issue and should not be in the risk register. Option D is correct. It is a good time to close a risk when it has occurred.

96 Which of the following documents would be the best resource when updating the risk register?
   A. Budget
   B. **Schedule**
   C. Work breakdown structure
   D. Lessons learned
   Explanation: Option A is wrong. The budget may contain some useful information, but it is not the best resource. Option B is correct. This is properly the best resource as several risks may be related to the project objective time. Option C is wrong. The WBS should not change much, and the work packages are decomposed into activities which are found in the schedule. Option D is wrong. Lessons learned documented during the project have little knowledge for the ongoing management of risks.

97 In an agile Scrum-based environment, who is responsible for the overall monitoring of the project risk levels?
   A. Scrum team
   B. Scrum master
   C. Chapter lead
   D. **Product owner**
   Explanation: Option A is wrong. The Scrum team may be responsible for several risks but not have overall responsibility. Option B is wrong. The Scrum master may be responsible for several risks but not have overall responsibility. Option C is wrong. This is not a common Scrum role and if applied should only manage individual risks. Option D is correct. The overall responsibility is the product owner's.

98 In an agile Scrum-based environment, how can one most effectively assess project risk levels during an iteration?
    A. Attend daily standup
    B. Ask the Scrum master
    C. Refine the iteration backlog
    D. **Look at the information radiator for answers**
    Explanation: Option A is wrong. The daily standup has three questions that do not include an assessment of the project risk levels. Option B is wrong. The Scrum master may have the answer, however, it is not the most effective option. Option C is not correct. Refinement might hold some assessment; however, the iteration backlog is not refined. Option D is correct. The board or information radiator should hold this answer.

99 Roger is a project manager of a construction project. His team is constantly monitoring project risk levels. Now he wants to prepare a risk report for the key stakeholders. What consideration is important to keep in mind when preparing the report?
    A. **Stakeholders are different and may require different reports or reporting.**
    B. Key stakeholders have similar needs that need to be included.
    C. Stakeholders are just like you and me, so if Roger makes a report for himself, it will also work for them.
    D. The team's reporting should be based upon the situation: short if things are going well, detailed if there are risks being discussed.
    Explanation: Option A is correct. Options B, C, and D are all wrong. Stakeholders are most likely not similar, may have different needs than yourself, and the reporting should not be based upon the status.

100 Which of the following tasks is the least important when monitoring project risk levels?
    A. **Assess threats**
    B. Assess project risk level
    C. Prepare reports for different stakeholders
    D. Communicate risk levels to key stakeholders
    Explanation: Option A is correct. This is the least important, as threats are included on the project risk level. Also, opportunities are missing here. Options B, C, and D are all valid tasks, but are wrong here since this is a "least important" question.

Chapter 10

Full Practice Exam 2

The PMI-RMP full practice exam 2 consists of 100 questions that should be completed in no more than 2.5 hours in total. The PMI exam does contain 115 questions; however, 15 questions are not scored. Table 10.1 gives the overview of the PMI-RMP exam breakdown, which you should use if you need to go back and revisit the chapter and as a confirmation of all content has been covered, understood, and mastered. All the test questions are split equally between the predictive, hybrid, and agile approaches as you will encounter at the actual exam.

Section 10.1 contains the questions and space for answering the questions. Each question includes four possible answers; however, only one is correct. Section 10.2 includes all the answers and explanations. At this stage you should have at least 70 correct questions before moving on to the actual certification exam.

Do not attempt to take the full practice exams before you are ready. You will not get the full benefit, and retaking the exam may result in flawed results. These are the last practice exams you should take before getting above average on the actual PMI exam.

DOI: 10.4324/9781003304012-10

Table 10.1 PMI-RMP Practice Exam 2 Breakdown

Domain	Split	Questions	Test questions
Risk Strategy and Planning	22%	22	
Task 1 Perform a preliminary document analysis		3	1–3
Task 2 Assess project environment for threats and opportunities		3	4–6
Task 3 Confirm risk thresholds based on risk appetites		4	7–10
Task 4 Establish risk management strategy		4	11–14
Task 5 Document the risk management plan		4	15–18
Task 6 Plan and lead risk management activities with stakeholders		4	19–22
Risk Identification	23%	23	
Task 1 Conduct risk identification exercises		5	23–27
Task 2 Examine assumption and constraint analyses		6	28–33
Task 3 Document risk triggers and thresholds based on context/environment		6	34–39
Task 4 Develop risk register		6	40–45
Risk Analysis	23 %	23	
Task 1 Perform qualitative analysis		7	46–52
Task 2 Perform quantitative analysis		8	53–60
Task 3 Identify threats and opportunities		8	61–68
Risk Response	13%	13	
Task 1 Plan risk response		7	69–75
Task 2 Implement risk response		6	76–81
Monitor and Close Risks	19%	19	
Task 1 Gather and analyze performance data		5	82–86
Task 2 Monitor residual and secondary risks		5	87–91
Task 3 Provide information required to update relevant project documents		5	92–96
Task 4 Monitor project risk levels		4	97–100
Summary	100%	100	1–100

10.1 Full Practice Exam 2 Questions

1 Werner, the project manager of a large ERP project, is in the process of performing a preliminary document analysis and has gathered and reviewed industry benchmarks and previous lessons learned. What additional information would be most useful?
A. Historical data
B. Previous risk management plans
C. Interviews with sponsors of similar projects
D. Knowledge of continuous improvement approaches in the firm

2 Julie is the product owner for an agile Scrum team. She understands the importance of performing a preliminary document analysis; however, she is not sure who should be assigned as responsible for the preliminary document analysis. Who should she assign?
A. The Scrum master
B. The Scrum team
C. The core roles
D. Just do it herself

3 Pete is just finalizing his preliminary document analysis for his hybrid construction project. The only task missing is establishing documents relevant to the risk process. He found a lot of relevant documents. However, which of the following is the least relevant and not to be applied?
A. Lessons learned
B. Burnup chart
C. Project charter
D. Risk breakdown structure

4 Tony is working with his team on assessing the project environment for threats and opportunities. Now the team is considering which project methodology is needed. The project has a fixed deadline. Multiple deliverables are needed. The scope is not defined yet, and it is changing all the time. The budget has not been approved. Quality is a big concern. The team knows about agile approaches, but experience is limited. Many team members are mature people with loads of experience from working predictive. Which project methodology should the team apply?
A. Agile
B. Waterfall
C. Hybrid
D. Incremental

5 Ben and his team are brainstorming on the internal stakeholders of the IT infrastructure project. Which of the following statements is not relevant for the stakeholder analysis?
   A. The IT enterprise architect is an important stakeholder.
   B. Stakeholders could be analyzed based on influence and interest in the project.
   C. We need to remember to place the IT manager on the steering committee.
   D. Has DevOps high or low power?

6 Evan and his team are assessing the project environment with emphasis on determining the business drivers of the project. Which of the following is the most relevant business driver for his project?
   A. Many stakeholders like the idea of this project.
   B. The project, when implemented, is expected to save the company $200,000 monthly in operating costs.
   C. The project must be completed by the end of 2023.
   D. The cost of the project is expected to be high.

7 What are project risk thresholds based on?
   A. Risk tolerances
   B. Risk appetites
   C. How much risk the organization can absorb
   D. The result of the conflict resolutions between stakeholders in agreeing on risk levels

8 Noah, the project risk manager, is considering how to calculate how much risk the organization can absorb. Which of these calculations would be the least recommended?
   A. The financial impacts
   B. Change of scope and/or increase in scope
   C. Increases in errors, defects, and bugs
   D. Changes in stakeholders' attitudes

9 Julie is the product owner for an agile Scrum team. Her stakeholders are arguing about the risk appetite for the team. Who should lead conflict resolutions between the stakeholders in agreeing on risk appetite?
   A. She must do it herself (she is the PO).
   B. This is a clear case for the Scrum master.
   C. The Scrum team should be able to handle this.
   D. The Scrum master should facilitate a meeting for all core team members to be engaged with the stakeholders.

10 The project has agreed with its key stakeholders that the risk thresholds should be based on risk appetites. But whose risk appetite?
    A. The stakeholders'
    B. The project's
    C. The organization's
    D. None of the above

11 John is working with his team on identifying possible risk categories to validate the current RBS. Which of the identified categories is the least useful?
A. Commercial risks
B. Requirements risks
C. Technical risks
D. Stakeholders' risks

12 John and his team have identified the following risks: unclear customer structure, user not committed to project, and management and users disagree. In which risk category should these risks be listed?
A. Relationship risks
B. Subcontractor risks
C. Planning and resource risks
D. Commercial risks

13 John and his team have just presented the risk breakdown structure to the key stakeholders. The stakeholders had a hard time understanding it, so John and his team plan to remake the RBS into a different format but with the same content. They have found several good concepts. Which one is the least preferred?
A. Ishikawa diagram
B. Force field diagram
C. Cause-and-effect diagram
D. Herringbone diagram

14 John and his team have just changed the RBS into a fishbone diagram and presented it to the key stakeholders. One of them asked, "What is illustrated as the sides and head of the fish?"
A. The sides are all the risks, while the head of the fish is the risk category such as financial.
B. The sides are all the risks with low probability and impact, while the risks near the head have a higher probability and impact.
C. The sides are risk categories, while the head of the fish illustrates the project risks.
D. The sides illustrate risks on the watchlist, while the risks near the head are the ones to be managed.

15 John and his team are in the process of documenting the risk management plan. Part of this work is assigning organizational risk roles and responsibilities. To support this they have agreed upon using a RACI chart. John and his team have identified most parts, but one is off. Which one?
A. Consulted
B. Informed
C. Accountable
D. Reliable

16 Pete and his agile team are discussing the possible use of a RAM or RACI diagram. Which of the following statements is correct in that regard?

A. The RACI chart is the only type of RAM.

B. The RACI chart is just a type of RAM.

C. The RACI must include various people in each of the four roles.

D. The RAM is just a type of RACI chart.

17 Mary is trying to explain to the project's key stakeholders how the risk breakdown structure (RBS) can be used to support the project and the risk management plan. Which statement best supports her case?

A. The risk breakdown structure (RBS) guides the risk management activities.

B. The risk breakdown structure (RBS) supports the qualitative assessment of the risks.

C. The risk breakdown structure (RBS) provides a framework in which risks have been identified, often based upon historical data.

D. The risk breakdown structure (RBS) is the basis for creating the work breakdown structure.

18 Erik and his team are in the process of documenting the risk management plan. They have defined risk roles and responsibilities, prepared a list of the key artifacts/resources that will be used to compile a risk management plan, and listed the key risk management activities. Which of the following tasks is the least important to finish this work?

A. Define a risk communication plan

B. Define risk prioritization criteria

C. Define stakeholder empowerment and education strategy

D. Assign roles and responsibilities with a project RAM chart

19 Joan and her team want to leverage the stakeholder analysis to plan and lead the risk management activities with stakeholders. How can this work be best applied?

A. It illustrates the skills and knowledge of the key stakeholders.

B. It serves as the basis for stakeholder engagement in risk management activities.

C. It shows who is against the project and therefore should be avoided.

D. It illustrates who are the most important stakeholders, who should be engaged first.

20 Joan and her team are planning the risk management activities with the stakeholders. Now they have leveraged the stakeholder analysis done by the project manager. However, more work is needed. Which of the following tasks is the least important?
A. Manage stakeholders' risk appetites and attitudes
B. Engage stakeholders in the risk prioritization process
C. Set appropriate expectations with stakeholders
D. Tailor the risk management process to fit the stakeholders

21 Brian, the product owner, wants to train, coach, or educate the stakeholders on risk principles and processes to create a shared understanding of principles and processes and foster engagement in risk management. What should Brian do next?
A. Plan comprehensive training on risk principles and processes
B. Arrange a meeting with the key stakeholders where Brian explains what Scrum and the agile principles are all about
C. Figure out a way to measure what understanding the stakeholders have, so he can tailor the activities to their needs
D. Book the Scrum master, Jill, to do one-on-one training with the stakeholders

22 Brian, the product owner, meets with the key stakeholders to discuss the rules of engagement. Which of the following statements or rules should be applied by project?
A. Everyone should be able to express their views openly during the daily standup meetings.
B. Risks can be identified and assessed during any ceremony by the participants.
C. The key stakeholders should be engaged in the assessment of all the risks with high probability and impact.
D. Key stakeholders should participate in the iteration retrospective to cover risk management.

23 Ian and his agile Scrum team are in the process of identifying risks. Which of the following tools and techniques can help identify risks and is aligned with the agile way of working?
A. Brainwriting session where participants draw a risk and then discuss the drawings.
B. The Scrum master should conduct a structured interview of the key stakeholders.
C. The product owner should interview the team members one-on-one.
D. The stakeholders should meet up, discuss the risk, and provide the product owner with joint input.

24 Donald and his team have gathered all kinds of risk identification data to be analyzed. Which of these resources should he and his team not consider?
   A. All kinds of documents
   B. A bunch of audio transcripts
   C. Loads of telemetry data
   D. Most data from the Project Management Information System (PMIS)

25 Donald, the project manager, learned a mnemonic technique during a PMP training course. The term was BIRDS and was used to identify risk. His notes stated that S = SWOT analysis, D = Delphi, R = Root-cause analysis, but what were B and I?
   A. B was brainstorming and I was interview.
   B. B meant bullets (the importance of) and I meant interpretation.
   C. The tool was called BI, so it was the name of the technique.
   D. B was brainwriting and I was a semi-structured interview.

26 Irving has just completed a detailed risk identification exercise with his team and key stakeholders. What should they do next?
   A. Update lessons learned
   B. Perform detailed analyses of risk identification exercise results
   C. Identify responses for each of the identified risks
   D. Perform a detailed quantitative analysis of each of the risks identified

27 Kim, the newly appointed project manager for the healthcare project, is starting to conduct various risk identification exercises. Which of the following is the least important of these tasks?
   A. Conduct meetings, interviews, focus groups, and other SME support activities
   B. Perform detailed analyses of risk identification exercise results
   C. Analyze documents, audio transcripts, telemetry data, etc., and understand the business context of information
   D. Assemble the final risk report

28 Kim, the newly appointed project manager for the healthcare project, and her dedicated team are working on the assumption and constraint analysis. Which of these statements is an assumption?
   A. Product ZXY is expected to be ready for deployment in July 2023.
   B. Product ZXY needs comprehensive testing before deployment.
   C. Product ZXY is not documented.
   D. Product ZXY has not received final medical trial 4 approval.

29 Kim, the newly appointed project manager for the healthcare project, and her dedicated team are working on the assumption and constraint analysis. Which of these statements is a constraint?
   A. Product ZXY may not work properly and may cause unexpected actions.
   B. Product ZXY has not received funding.
   C. Product ZXY requires US resources to deploy it.
   D. Product ZXY is expected to be used with Product ZXYXZ.

30 Kim, the newly appointed project manager for the healthcare project, and her dedicated team are working on the assumption and constraint analysis where they have identified a constraint on resources to be used with the product. Which of the following describes the least possible risk associated with the constraint?

A. Documentation of the product might be delayed due to a lack of resources.

B. The activities related to the implementation of the product might be delayed.

C. The cost of the resources might increase as they are scarce.

D. The scope has changed.

31 Paul and his team have identified various assumptions and constraints that can be false. They also figured out that if the assumptions and constraints are false, then they would affect the project objective. What is a possible next step?

A. Convert them into monetary values

B. Do nothing

C. Convert them into risks

D. Convert them into issues

32 Paul and his team have examined the assumption and constraint analysis. They are in doubt whether this analysis takes both positive and negative effects on project objectives into account. What is correct?

A. It takes only negative effects on project objectives into account.

B. It takes only positive effects on project objectives into account.

C. It takes positive and negative effects on project objectives into account.

D. It takes positive and negative effects on project objectives into account, if the probability or impact is high.

33 Paul and his team have examined the assumption and constraint analysis. They have categorized and leveraged the results of the assumption and constraint analysis. Several tasks need to be completed. Which one is the least likely?

A. Assess the risks associated with each assumption and/or constraint

B. Recognize the relationship between assumptions and/or constraints, and project objectives

C. Encourage stakeholders to challenge assumptions and constraints

D. Categorize assumptions and constraints into risks and issues

34 Paul and his team are having a hard time explaining the term "risk trigger" to the key stakeholders. What would be a suitable alternative?

A. Information radiator

B. Warning signs

C. Risk impacts

D. When it is too late to activate the risk response

35 Paul and his team are in the process of documenting risk triggers. The risk is the probability of activity (activity X) on the critical path being delayed. Which of the following would be the best risk trigger here?
   A. Activity X is starting earlier than expected.
   B. The schedule performance index is still above 1.
   C. About 80% of the resources for activity X have been used, but progress is 20%.
   D. Activity X is not completed on July 10 as expected.

36 Pete and his team need to document risk compliance thresholds. How do they perform the update?
   A. Against updated risk data
   B. Against the risk triggers
   C. Against the risk consequences and/or impact
   D. All of the above

37 Freddy, the agile coach of a Scrum team, is working with the product owner to empower the key stakeholders to challenge existing thresholds. How should that be done?
   A. The key stakeholders should participate in the iteration planning and question the team's estimates.
   B. The key stakeholders should work with the PO on finding the right thresholds.
   C. The key stakeholders should work with the team so thresholds with the iterations are stable.
   D. The key stakeholders should be coached by the agile coach, so they can learn to say no.

38 Freddy, the agile coach, is working with Pete, the project manager of a hybrid project, on documenting risk triggers and thresholds based on context/environment. They have assessed, confirmed, and documented risk compliance thresholds and categories against updated risk data. Which of the following tasks is the least likely to be missing?
   A. Assess and document risk triggers, causes, and timing
   B. Assess and document probabilities
   C. Assess and document risk consequences and/or impact
   D. Empower stakeholders to challenge existing thresholds

39 Freddy, the agile coach, is discussing with his agile Scrum team what is a good example of a risk impact. Which of the following statements should he put forward as a good example?
   A. John, the tester, is expected to be sick for another 4 days.
   B. Ulla, the lead developer, does not have access to GitHub.
   C. Task B might take 2 days longer than estimated.
   D. William, the new programmer, has left the team after just 2 days.

40 Roger is developing a risk register for his first risk workshop. During the workshop he and some SMEs are going to examine various risk attributes. Which of the following is not a risk attribute?
A. Probability
B. Impact
C. Urgency
D. Ability to define a valid trigger

41 Roger is developing a risk register for his first risk workshop. During the workshop he and some SMEs are going to classify some risks. Which of the following would be the best classification?
A. Positive and negative threats
B. Threats or opportunities
C. Risks and issues
D. Probability and impact

42 Freddy, the agile coach, is discussing with his agile Scrum team who should have risk ownership of the DevOps environment. Who would be the best owner?
A. The product owner and he/she owns the product.
B. The Scrum master, as this may become an impediment soon.
C. The DevOps team, as this is a shared service.
D. It should be owned by the external vendor of most of the software.

43 The team is faced with the risk of not being able to solve a technical issue due to some missing hardware configuration. What is the risk origin here?
A. The team
B. Missing hardware configuration
C. Technical issue
D. Poor planning

44 Eddy and Peter are in the process of developing a risk register for the ERP project. Which of the following content should not be included?
A. Risk ID
B. Categorization
C. Source
D. Author

45 Eddy and Peter have developed a risk register and now need to update it. Which of the following information is least likely to be updated when a risk response is triggered?
A. Description
B. Probability
C. Impact
D. Risk contingency

46 The team is in the process of performing the qualitative analysis of the identified risk. What factors are assessed?
  A. Time and money
  B. Probability and likelihood
  C. Probability and impact
  D. Impact and consequence

47 Which of the following is the least beneficial for Paul and his team in using a risk breakdown structure?
  A. Provide a classification, e.g., environment
  B. Categories for the identified risks
  C. Framework for the application of historical risk data, e.g., identified risks
  D. Support the assessment of the risks

48 Tony and his agile team are using an RBS and now discover that one category, project management, has been empty. What are the consequences for Tony and his team?
  A. They should identify some project management risks and populate the RBS shortly.
  B. They should escalate the issue to the PMO as this is clearly a mistake.
  C. It is not a problem as agile teams do not have project managers.
  D. Historical data on project management seems to be lacking. Tony and his agile team need to identify the risks, and in due time they might be part of the RBS.

49 Risks in the RBS use classifications from the risk management plan. However, which of the following is the least likely categorization?
  A. Organizational
  B. Project management
  C. Issues
  D. Technical

50 When estimating the impact of an identified risk, "Missing configuration hardware," which of the following would be best applied?
  A. Time
  B. Cost
  C. Scope
  D. Uncertainty

51 Pete and his team have prioritized risks based upon the impact but the assessment is not complete - what else does Peter and his needs to include when prioritizing risks?
  A. Urgency
  B. Uncertainty
  C. Risk origin
  D. Risk ownership

52 John, the product owner, has just engaged a new Scrum master to coach the key stakeholders on performing the qualitative analysis. What would be a good topic for the sessions?
  A. Expected monetary analysis
  B. Risk categorization strategies
  C. How to make the Monte Carlo simulation run smoothly
  D. Affinity estimating

53 John and his team are about to embark on performing a quantitative analysis. Which of the following tools and techniques does not fit that description?
  A. Monte Carlo
  B. Probability and impact analysis
  C. Influence diagrams
  D. Sensitivity analysis

54 John and his team are still working on performing the quantitative analysis. They would like a tool or technique that can tell them the probability that the schedule is completed in 11 or 23 days. Which tool and technique could solve that problem?
  A. Monte Carlo
  B. Decision trees
  C. Expected monetary value
  D. None of the above

55 John and his team are still working on performing quantitative analysis. They found a technique they can use to calculate the project's risk contingency. What technique did they most likely discover?
  A. Monte Carlo
  B. Decision trees
  C. Expected monetary value
  D. Sensitivity analysis

56 A team wants to perform a forecast and trend analysis. What information would be required?
  A. New information
  B. Historical information
  C. New and historical information
  D. None of the above

57 A team has just performed a qualitative analysis and now plans on performing the quantitative analysis. What is the big difference between qualitative analysis and quantitative analysis?
   A. The qualitative assessment examines the individual risks, while the quantitative assessment analyzes all the risks.
   B. The assessments are the same, but the quantitative assessment is more detailed for high-risk projects.
   C. The assessments are the same, but the quantitative assessment requires tooling such as Monte Carlo simulation software.
   D. The qualitative assessment gives a prioritization, while the quantitative assessment analyzes only the impact on the monetary values.

58 Tony has examined his schedule and found the standard deviation of the tasks in his plan. Which tool or technique, when performing the quantitative analysis, may provide a similar type of outcome for risks?
   A. Monte Carlo
   B. Decision trees
   C. Expected monetary value
   D. Sensitivity analysis

59 Which of the following tasks should not be conducted when performing the quantitative analysis?
   A. Analyze risk data and process performance information against established metrics
   B. Analyze a project's general risks
   C. Document lessons learned on risk management activities
   D. Perform risk weighting and calculate risk priority

60 Tony is an expert planner. Which tool or technique used in scheduling may support Tony when forecasting?
   A. Critical path analysis
   B. Critical chain analysis
   C. Expected monetary value
   D. Earned value management

61 Tony, the expert planner, and his team are in the middle of assessing project risk complexity. Which of the following tools and techniques should be applied?
   A. SWOT analysis
   B. Earned value management
   C. Expected monetary value
   D. Benchmarking

62 Tony, the expert planner, and his team are in the middle of assessing project risk complexity. Which of the following tools and techniques should not be applied?
   A. SWOT analysis
   B. Ishikawa diagram
   C. Tree diagram
   D. Iteration retrospective

63 Emma and her agile Scrum team want to perform an impact analysis. Which of the following is the least of her concerns?
   A. Project scope
   B. Schedule cost
   C. Resources
   D. Environment

64 Tom has conducted a detailed study of business activities, dependencies, and infrastructure. Which kind of analysis has he just conducted?
   A. SWOT analysis
   B. Benchmarking
   C. Impact analysis
   D. Trend analysis

65 When assessing project compliance objectives against organizational strategic objectives, which of the following project artifacts would be most helpful?
   A. Risk register
   B. Issue log
   C. Budget
   D. Project plans

66 Roger and his team are assessing project compliance objectives against organizational strategic objectives. They have identified the importance of the various governance requirements. Which of the following is the least important?
   A. Corporate governance
   B. Project governance
   C. Team governance
   D. Regulatory governance

67 Tommy, the agile Scrum product owner, has empowered the key stakeholders to independently identify threats and opportunities. The stakeholders report the following to Tommy. Which one should he take into consideration?
   A. The written user stories are unclear.
   B. The team did not complete all tasks during the sprint.
   C. The definition of done may not cover all quality concerns.
   D. The daily standups have been skipped.

68 Tommy, the agile Scrum product owner, has empowered the key stake-holders to independently identify threats and opportunities. This has been working; however, most stakeholders only identify threats, not opportunities. Tommy arranged a workshop where the following were identified. Which of the following should he include as an opportunity?
    A. Pair programming would increase quality greatly
    B. Applying DevOps might also increase velocity
    C. Refactoring should solve the technical debt of the past
    D. Team ownership increases the quality of the team's work

69 Tommy, the agile Scrum product owner, has selected a risk response strategy where he works with a partner who provides more resources, which should increase the probability of the risk. What strategy is this?
    A. Transfer
    B. Share
    C. Escalate
    D. Exploit

70 Tommy and his team are struggling with key stakeholders who only work with negative risks. Which of the following risk response strategies would work for both positive and negative risks?
    A. Mitigate
    B. Avoid
    C. Accept
    D. Transfer

71 Pete, the project manager of a major project, has a risk with a high prob-ability and a huge negative impact. Which risk response strategy should he try out first?
    A. Exploit
    B. Mitigate
    C. Transfer
    D. Avoid

72 When would be a good time for Pete, the project manager of a major project, to be using a workaround?
    A. When his client asks him to do so
    B. When all options have been tried
    C. As he sees fit
    D. When risk contingency has been spent

73 Pete, the project manager, wants to assess the effectiveness of the risk response mitigation actions on a risk regarding lack of resources for the implementation of the solution. How can Pete, when examining the risk register, verify the effectiveness?
   A. The risk is gone as it is no longer relevant.
   B. The risk description and origin have been updated.
   C. Probability and/or impact might have increased.
   D. Probability and/or impact might have decreased.

74 Andy, the team lead, wants to allocate responsibilities for managing risk responses. What kind of responsibilities would most likely be allocated?
   A. Help the risk owner watch the risk
   B. Support the risk action owner
   C. Take on the role of risk action owner
   D. Manage the risk budget

75 When dealing with the planning of risk responses, which of the following tasks is the least important?
   A. Illustrate and communicate the effectiveness of the risk response strategies
   B. Allocate responsibilities within the team
   C. Outline an appropriate responsibility matrix for a metricized project environment
   D. Reevaluate organizational risks

76 Victor and his team are discussing the goals of executing the risk response plans. Which of the following states one or more of these goals?
   A. Determining ways to keep the risk contingency budget within the tolerance
   B. Determining ways to reduce or eliminate any threats to the project
   C. Determining ways to ensure all risks are mitigated
   D. Determining ways to maximize opportunities obtained

77 When should Victor and his team execute the contingency plan of a certain risk dealing with the risk of the organization not using the implemented solution?
   A. The plan is to lessen the damage of the risk when it occurs.
   B. The plan should be triggered so it can prevent the risk from occurring.
   C. The plan should be executed if the fallback plan fails.
   D. The plan should be activated by the direction of the sponsor and steering committee.

78 What might be the consequence for Georg and his team for not having a contingency plan for a high-impact risk?
   A. Without the plan in place, the project cannot avoid the risk.
   B. Without the plan in place, the project cannot aim for opportunities.
   C. Without the plan in place, the full impact of the risk could greatly affect the project.
   D. Without the plan in place, the project cannot fully measure the expected monetary value.

79 Roger hears this statement from the sponsor: "The contingency plan is the last line of defense against the risk." What is the most exact respond?
   A. Yes, you are right.
   B. Yes, you are right, but if it is not effective or fails, we have a fallback plan.
   C. No, you are wrong. The risk response strategy is the last line of defense.
   D. No, you are wrong. We still have the risk owner and risk action owner who will intervene.

80 Roger and his team are working with the key stakeholders to encourage them to provide feedback on the risk responses. What could Roger and his team do to further this?
   A. Tell the key stakeholders to provide written feedback at any time
   B. Encourage the stakeholders to review the risk register
   C. Encourage the stakeholders to sign up as risk owners
   D. Invite the key stakeholders to participate in a risk workshop

81 Which of the following tasks is the least important when implementing risk responses?
   A. Execute the risk response plan(s)
   B. Assess the watchlist
   C. Encourage stakeholders to provide feedback on the risk response
   D. Evaluate and react to secondary and residual risks from the response implementation

82 Pete and his team are in the process of gathering and analyzing performance data. Currently they are examining schedule risk. Should they reconcile data from both work and planning packages?
   A. Yes, all kinds of data are relevant.
   B. No, only work package data.
   C. No, only planning package data.
   D. No, work and planning package data are not relevant.

83 Pete and his team are in the process of gathering and analyzing performance data. There seems to be a schedule concern with the performance of several teams working predictive. What can Pete and his team do to clarify this concern?
   A. Examine the trend analysis
   B. Check if CPI is higher than 1
   C. Perform a variance analysis
   D. Reexamine the burndown chart

84 Pete and his team are in the process of gathering and analyzing performance data. They want to monitor impacts against overall project risk exposure, but whom would be affected?
   A. The enterprise
   B. The project
   C. The program
   D. The value streams

85 When gathering and analyzing performance data, what is the most important aspect of the baseline?
   A. It helps the team to stay within the schedule.
   B. It supports formal change control.
   C. It is fundamental for configuration management.
   D. The team can determine the completion status against the baseline.

86 When gathering and analyzing performance data, which of the following tasks is the least important?
   A. Reconcile performance data and reports from risk-relevant work packages
   B. Analyze data to determine the completion status against the baseline
   C. Perform a trend analysis
   D. Monitor impact against overall project risk exposure to the enterprise

87 Ian has identified some risks and documented them in the risk register. Which of them should be considered a residual risk?
   A. A risk that arises due to another risk response.
   B. It is just another word for a secondary risk.
   C. A risk that is still present even after the risk response.
   D. A risk that has been fully mitigated and no longer relevant.

88 Ian has identified some risks and documented them in the risk register. They found a risk where the impact has been greatly reduced due to the risk response. However, probability is still high, and the impact was not completely removed. What type of risk is this?
   A. Residual risk
   B. Secondary risk
   C. Known risk
   D. Unknown risk

89 Some years ago, an oil platform burned in the Mexican gulf and there was a risk that oil would pollute the sea. Various chemicals were used to avoid this. However, it turned out that these chemicals might also damage the sea. What kind of risk is this?
   A. Residual risk
   B. Secondary risk
   C. High-impact risk
   D. Unknown risk

90 Ian has identified some risks and documented them in the risk register. When assessing the impact of residual and secondary risks, which is most important?
   A. The project manager can do it.
   B. It can be done in a few hours as it must be repeated throughout the project's lifetime.
   C. It is done on project objectives.
   D. It works in Scrum.

91 Ian and his team are monitoring residual and secondary risks. Which of the following tasks is the least important?
   A. Monitor risk response and document residual risk
   B. Monitor risk response for threats and opportunities
   C. Assess the impact of residual and secondary risks on project objectives
   D. Update and communicate the impact of residual and secondary risks

92 Ian and his team are in the process of updating relevant project documents. Which of the following is the least relevant to update with aggregated and summarized risk data?
   A. Risk register
   B. Lessons learned
   C. Project management plan
   D. Issue log

93 Ian and his team are in the process of updating relevant project documents. Currently, they are updating the risk register. What data is likely to be updated?
   A. Change status for expired risks
   B. Risk origin
   C. Risk description
   D. Risk response

94 Ian and his team are in the process of updating relevant project documents. Which of the following risks should be closed out as expired?
   A. A risk that has been mitigated so probability and impact are greatly reduced, but the risk is still present
   B. A risk that arises due to the risk response to another risk
   C. A risk where the risk response exploit has been successfully applied
   D. A risk where the risk response is avoid; however, the risk trigger has not yet occurred

95 When Ian and his team are updating relevant project documents with aggregated and summarized risk data, who or what is the least likely source of data?
   A. Project team
   B. Sponsor
   C. Work performance data
   D. Work performance information

96 Ian and his team are updating relevant project documents with aggregated and summarized risk data. What needs to be done?
   A. Achieve lessons learned
   B. Update the project management plan
   C. Update the change logs
   D. Monitor and close out expired risks

97 Trevor and his team are monitoring project risk levels. Which of the following tasks is the least important?
   A. Assess secondary and residual risks
   B. Assess the project risk level
   C. Prepare reports for different stakeholders
   D. Communicate risk levels to key stakeholders

98 Trevor and his team are monitoring project risk levels for a major IT project with many high-ranking key stakeholders of a certain age and from across the world. In that process they prepare reports for different stakeholders. Which report best represents the needs of the stakeholders?
   A. Comprehensive and detailed for all key stakeholders
   B. Tailored for each key stakeholder
   C. Standardized and available on a collaborative platform
   D. Short and overview format for all key stakeholders as they are busy people

99 How should Andrew and his team on the construction project working with local on-site officials communicate the risk levels to these people?
   A. Give them access to a collaborative platform, so they can pull the information when needed
   B. Push it out as a monthly newsletter to all key stakeholders
   C. Arrange a monthly interactive meeting to discuss it
   D. Have a talk with each of them to figure out their needs

100 Which of the following tasks should not be conducted when assessing project risk level?
   A. Identify new risks
   B. Assess probabilities
   C. Assess impacts
   D. Confirm risks are expired

10.2 Full Practice Exam 2 Answers

1 Werner, the project manager of a large ERP project, is in the process of performing a preliminary document analysis and has gathered and reviewed industry benchmarks and previous lessons learned. What additional information would be most useful?
   A. **Historical data**
   B. Previous risk management plans
   C. Interviews with sponsors of similar projects
   D. Knowledge of continuous improvement approaches in the firm
   Explanation: Option A is correct. Historical data should be gathered and reviewed. Option B is wrong. This is not relevant for the preliminary document analysis. Option C is wrong. This is hardly relevant or even documented. Option D is wrong. This is not relevant for this analysis.

2 Julie is the product owner for an agile Scrum team. She understands the importance of performing a preliminary document analysis. However, she is not sure who should be assigned as responsible for the preliminary document analysis. Who should she assign?
   A. The Scrum master
   B. The Scrum team
   C. The core roles
   D. **Just do it herself**
   Explanation: Options A, B, and C are all wrong. In Scrum it is the responsibility of the product owner. Option D is correct. Option C is wrong as it should not be shared when it is a clear PO task. For option B, the Scrum team could do some work; however, it should be assigned to them by the PO during the iteration planning.

3 Pete is just finalizing his preliminary document analysis for his hybrid construction project. The only task missing is establishing documents relevant to the risk process. He found a lot of relevant documents. However, which of the following is the least relevant and not to be applied?
A. Lessons learned
B. Burnup chart
C. Project charter
D. **Risk breakdown structure**
Explanation: Option A is wrong as it is relevant. The lesson learned may cast light on the risk process. Option B is wrong as the burnup chart can provide relevant information. Option C is wrong as the project charter may hold relevant information for the risk process. Option D is correct as the RBS is generic and based upon historical data, but it contains little information on the risk process. It is therefore the least relevant document of the options.

4 Tony is working with his team on assessing the project environment for threats and opportunities. Now the team is considering which project methodology is needed. The project has a fixed deadline. Multiple deliverables are needed. The scope is not defined yet, and it is changing all the time. The budget has not been approved. Quality is a big concern. The team knows about agile approaches, but experience is limited. Many team members are mature people with loads of experience from working predictive. Which project methodology should the team apply?
A. Agile
B. Waterfall
C. **Hybrid**
D. Incremental
Explanation: Option A is wrong. Deadline, quality, budget, and team experience are not clear indicators for agile. Option B is wrong. Scope is an issue. Option C is correct. This project needs to combine the best of agile and predictive. Option D is wrong. The project does contain agile elements, which are not part of the incremental approach.

5 Ben and his team are brainstorming on the internal stakeholders of the IT infrastructure project. Which one of the following statements is not relevant for the stakeholder analysis?
A. The IT enterprise architect is an important stakeholder.
B. Stakeholders could be analyzed based upon influence and interest in the project.
C. **We need to remember to place the IT manager on the steering committee.**
D. Has DevOps high or low power?
Explanation: Option A is wrong. This is a relevant identified stakeholder, but this is a "not" question. Option B is wrong. These factors are relevant when assessing stakeholders, but this is a "not" question. Option C is correct. The IT manager is a relevant stakeholder, but here the focus is on governance, which is not included in the stakeholder analysis. Option D is wrong. It is relevant for the stakeholder analysis to discuss the low power of a certain stakeholder, but this is a "not" question.

6 Evan and his team are assessing the project environment with emphasis on determining the business drivers of the project. Which of the following is the most relevant business driver for his project?
A. Many stakeholders like the idea of this project.
B. **The project when implemented is expected to save the company $200,000 monthly in operating costs.**
C. The project must be completed by the end of 2023.
D. The cost of the project is expected to be high.
Explanation: Option A is wrong. Stakeholder attitude is not a formal business driver. Option B is correct. These are the benefits. Option C is wrong. This is a constraint. Option D is wrong. These are the costs; however, high costs would not likely drive a project forward unless benefits are stated and higher.

7 What are project risk thresholds based on?
A. Risk tolerances
B. **Risk appetites**
C. How much risk the organization can absorb
D. The result of the conflict resolutions between stakeholders in agreeing on risk levels
Explanation: Options A, C, and D are all wrong. Option B is correct. The risk thresholds are based on risk appetites, which may be the result of conflict resolution between stakeholders.

8 Noah, the project risk manager, is considering how to calculate how much risk the organization can absorb. Which of these calculations would be the least recommended?

A. The financial impacts

B. Change of scope and/or increase in scope

C. Increases in errors, defects, and bugs

D. **Changes in stakeholders' attitudes**

Explanation: Options A, B, and C are all wrong. Financial, scope, and quality are all methods to calculate how much risk the organization can absorb. Option D is correct as this is a "least" question. Measuring stakeholders' attitude is not a common method to calculate how much risk the organization can absorb.

9 Julie is the product owner for an agile Scrum team. Her stakeholders are arguing about the risk appetite for the team. Who should lead conflict resolutions between stakeholders in agreeing on risk appetite?

A. **She must do it herself (she is the PO).**

B. This is a clear case for the Scrum master.

C. The Scrum team should be able to handle this.

D. The Scrum master should facilitate a meeting for all core team members to be engaged with the stakeholders.

Explanation: Option A is correct. Dealing with stakeholders is a task for the PO. Option B is wrong. The Scrum master may facilitate discussions if required by the PO; however, this is not a Scrum master task when dealing with stakeholders. Option C is wrong. The team should not spend time on this. Option D is wrong. All core members should not waste time on this. The PO can ask the Scrum master to facilitate the meeting if needed; however, team participation should be reduced.

10 The project has agreed with its key stakeholders that the risk thresholds should be based on risk appetites. But whose risk appetite?

A. The stakeholders'

B. The project's

C. **The organization's**

D. None of the above

Explanation: Option A is wrong. The stakeholder appetite is factored in; however, it's not the main cause. Option B is wrong. The project's appetite is not the main cause. Option C is correct. Option B should be derived from option C with input from option A, so option C is the best option. Option D is wrong as option C is correct.

11 John is working with his team on identifying possible risk categories to validate the current RBS. Which of the identified categories is the least useful?

A. Commercial risks

B. Requirements risks

C. Technical risks

D. **Stakeholders' risks**

Explanation: Options A, B, and C are all common risk categories and wrong options as this is a "least useful" question. Stakeholders' risk is rarely a category and, in this question, the right option. Option D is correct.

12 John and his team have identified the following risks: unclear customer structure, user not committed to project, and management and users disagree. In which risk category should these risks be listed?

A. **Relationship risks**

B. Subcontractor risks

C. Planning and resource risks

D. Commercial risks

Explanation: Option A is correct. These risks are often found in this category. Options B, C, and D are all wrong. These risks do not belong here.

13 John and his team have just presented the risk breakdown structure to the key stakeholders. The stakeholders had a hard time understanding it, so John and his team plan to remake the RBS into a different format but with the same content. They have found several good concepts. Which one is the least preferred?

A. Ishikawa diagram

B. **Force field diagram**

C. Cause-and-effect diagram

D. Herringbone diagram

Explanation: Options A, C, and D are all the same. They are common RBS structures, just various names for the same concept. Option B is correct as the least preferred one, as the force field analysis is not relevant here and a force field diagram is a made-up term.

14 John and his team have just changed the RBS into a fishbone diagram and presented it to the key stakeholders. One of them asked, "What is illustrated as the sides and head of the fish?"
   A. The sides are all the risks, while the head of the fish is the risk category such as financial.
   B. The sides are all the risks with low probability and impact, while the risks near the head have a higher probability and impact.
   C. **The sides are risk categories, while the head of the fish illustrates the project risks.**
   D. The sides illustrate risks on the watchlist, while the risks near the head are the ones to be managed.
   Explanation: Option C is correct. Options A, B, and D are all made-up variations that are wrong.

15 John and his team are in the process of documenting the risk management plan. Part of this work is assigning organizational risk roles and responsibilities. To support this they have agreed to use a RACI chart. John and his team have identified most parts, but one is off. Which one?
   A. Consulted
   B. Informed
   C. Accountable
   D. **Reliable**
   Explanation: Options A, B, and C are all wrong as these are parts of the RACI chart. Option D is correct. This should have been responsible.

16 Pete and his agile team are discussing the possible use of a RAM or RACI diagram. Which of the following statements is correct in that regard?
   A. The RACI chart is the only type of RAM.
   B. **The RACI chart is just a type of RAM.**
   C. The RACI must include various people in each of the four roles.
   D. The RAM is just a type of RACI chart.
   Explanation: Option A is wrong. The RACI chart is just one type of RAM. Many do exist. Option B is correct. Option C is wrong. You just need one for the key roles, and not all roles are required, just accountable. Option D is wrong. The info is reversed.

17 Mary is trying to explain to the project's key stakeholders how the risk breakdown structure (RBS) can be used to support the project and the risk management plan. Which statement best supports her case?

A. The risk breakdown structure (RBS) guides the risk management activities.

B. The risk breakdown structure (RBS) supports the qualitative assessment of the risks.

C. **The risk breakdown structure (RBS) provides a framework in which risks have been identified, often based upon historical data.**

D. The risk breakdown structure (RBS) is the basis for creating the work breakdown structure.

Explanation: Option A is wrong. The RBS and the activities are not related. Option B is wrong. The RBS and the qualitative assessment are not related; the RBS can provide input in terms of risks for the assessment. Option C is correct. An RBS lists risks based upon best practices and historical data. Option D is wrong. The RBS and WBS are related; however, the RBS does not serve as a basis for the WBS.

18 Erik and his team are in the process of documenting the risk management plan. They have defined risk roles and responsibilities, prepared a list of the key artifacts/resources that will be used to compile a risk management plan, and listed the key risk management activities. Which of the following tasks is the least important to finish this work?

A. Define a risk communication plan

B. Define risk prioritization criteria

C. Define stakeholder empowerment and education strategy

D. **Assign roles and responsibilities with a project RAM chart**

Explanation: Options A, B and C are all wrong, and these are important tasks during this process. Option D is correct, as this is a "least important" question. This work has already been done when roles and responsibilities were defined.

19 Joan and her team want to leverage the stakeholder analysis to plan and lead the risk management activities with stakeholders. How can this work be best applied?

A. It illustrates the skills and knowledge of the key stakeholders.

B. **It serves as the basis for stakeholder engagement in risk management activities.**

C. It shows who is against the project and therefore should be avoided.

D. It illustrates who are the most important stakeholders who should be engaged first.

Explanation: Option A is wrong. Skills and knowledge are not included in the common stakeholder's analysis. Option B is correct. Option C is wrong. Stakeholders who are against it should not necessarily be avoided. Option D is wrong. Stakeholder engagement is not solely based upon power.

20 Joan and her team are planning the risk management activities with the stakeholders. Now they have leveraged the stakeholder analysis done by the project manager. However, more work is needed. Which of the following tasks is the least important?
   – Manage stakeholders' risk appetites and attitudes
   – Engage stakeholders in the risk prioritization process
   – Set appropriate expectations with stakeholders
   – **Tailor the risk management process to fit the stakeholders**
Explanation: Options A, B, and C are all valid tasks to be completed. These are wrong options in this case as the question focus is on "least important" task. Option D is correct as it is the least important. The project should tailor the risk management process and activities to fit the projects needed. However, not the stakeholders. Stakeholders' needs should be taken into considerations; however, project needs come first.

21 Brian, the product owner, wants to train, coach, or educate the stakeholders on risk principles and processes to create a shared understanding of principles and processes and foster engagement in risk management. What should Brian do next?
   A. Plan comprehensive training on risk principles and processes
   B. Arrange a meeting with the key stakeholders where Brian explains what Scrum and the agile principles are all about
   C. **Figure out a way to measure what understanding the stakeholders have, so he can tailor the activities to their needs**
   D. Book the Scrum master, Jill, to do one-on-one training with the stakeholders
Explanation: Options A and B are both wrong. Brian does not know whether these activities are relevant or not. Option C is correct. He needs to understand the stakeholders' needs and knowledge to plan the activities properly. Option D is wrong. It could work or it could not work, but Brian does not know.

22 Brian, the product owner, meets with the key stakeholders to discuss the rules of engagement. Which of the following statements or rules should be applied by the project?

A. Everyone should be able to express their views openly during the daily standup meetings.

B. **Risks can be identified and assessed during any ceremony by the participants.**

C. The key stakeholders should be engaged in the assessment of all the risks with high probability and impact.

D. Key stakeholders should participate in the iteration retrospective to cover risk management.

Explanation: Option A is wrong. During the daily standup meeting it is only the team who should speak and answer the three questions. Option B is correct. Option C is wrong. Key stakeholders can be engaged in the assessment but not in all risks, no matter the severity. Option D is wrong. Key stakeholders should not take part in the iteration retrospective, which is a team meeting.

23 Ian and his agile Scrum team are in the process of identifying risks. Which of the following tools and techniques can help identify risks and is aligned with the agile way of working?

A. **Brainwriting session where participants draw a risk and then discuss the drawings.**

B. The Scrum master should conduct a structured interview of the key stakeholders.

C. The product owner should interview the team members one-on-one.

D. The stakeholders should meet up, discuss the risks, and provide the product owner with joint input.

Explanations: Option A is correct. This is a tool that is built upon individuals and interactions from the agile manifesto. Option B is wrong. This is not a task for the Scrum master, and interactions with the stakeholders should be performed by the product owner. Option C is wrong. The product owner can discuss risks with the team; however, one-on-one is not preferred. Option D is wrong. Input from the stakeholders should be discussed with the product owner on a regular basis.

24 Donald and his team have gathered all kinds of risk identification data to be analyzed. Which of these resources should he and his team not consider?

A. All kinds of documents

B. A bunch of audio transcripts

C. Loads of telemetry data

D. **Most data from the Project Management Information System (PMIS)**

Explanation: Option A, B, and C are all valid data to be gathered and analyzed. These are wrong options as this question focuses on what not to consider. Option D is correct, as the team may find useful data on the PMIS; however, most data is not likely.

25 Donald, the project manager, learned a mnemonic technique during a PMP training course. The term was BIRDS and used to identify risk. His notes stated that S = SWOT analysis, D = Delphi, R = Root-cause analysis, but what were B and I?

A. **B was brainstorming and I was interview.**

B. B meant bullets (the importance of) and I meant interpretation.

C. The tool was called BI, so it was the name of the technique.

D. B was brainwriting and I was a semi-structured interview.

Explanation: Option A is correct. Options B, C, and D are all wrong and made-up alternatives.

26 Irving has just completed a detailed risk identification exercise with his team and key stakeholders. What should they do next?

A. Update lessons learned

B. **Perform detailed analyses of risk identification exercise results**

C. Identify responses for each of the identified risks

D. Perform a detailed quantitative analysis of each of the risks identified

Explanation: Option A is wrong. This should be done, but now may not be the best of times. Option B is correct. Option C is wrong. Risk responses are assigned after the assessment, not at this time. Option D is wrong. Quantitative assessment is done for all the risks and commonly after the qualitative assessment, which has not yet been conducted in this scenario.

27 Kim, the newly appointed project manager for the healthcare project, is starting to conduct various risk identification exercises. Which of the following is the least important of these tasks?

A. Conduct meetings, interviews, focus groups, and other SME support activities

B. Perform detailed analyses of risk identification exercise results

C. Analyze documents, audio transcripts, telemetry data, etc., and understand the business context of information

D. **Assemble the final risk report**

Explanation: Options A, B, and C are all valid tasks but wrong options as this is a "least important" question. Option D is correct as writing the risk report is not done at this point in time.

28 Kim, the newly appointed project manager for the healthcare project, and her dedicated team is working on the assumption and constraint analysis. Which of these statements is an assumption?

A. **Product ZXY is expected to be ready for deployment in July 2023.**

B. Product ZXY needs comprehensive testing before deployment.

C. Product ZXY is not documented.

D. Product ZXY has not received final medical trial 4 approval.

Explanation: Option A is correct. This is an assumption. Option B is wrong. This is a constraint. Option C is wrong. This is an issue. Option D is wrong. This is an issue.

29 Kim, the newly appointed project manager for the healthcare project, and her dedicated team are working on the assumption and constraint analysis. Which of these statements is a constraint?

A. Product ZXY may not work properly and may cause unexpected actions.

B. Product ZXY has not received funding.

C. **Product ZXY requires US resources to deploy it.**

D. Product ZXY is expected to be used with Product ZXYXZ.

Explanation: Option A is wrong. This is a risk. Option B is wrong. This is an issue. Option C is correct. Use of US resources is a constraint. Option D is wrong. This is an assumption.

30 Kim, the newly appointed project manager for the healthcare project, and her dedicated team are working on the assumption and constraint analysis where they have identified a constraint on resources to be used with the product. Which of the following describes the least possible risk associated with the constraint?
   A. Documentation of the product might be delayed due to a lack of resources.
   B. The activities related to the implementation of the product might be delayed.
   C. The cost of the resources might increase as they are scarce.
   D. **The scope has changed.**
   Explanation: Options A, B, and C are all likely risks, and these options are wrong as this question is a "least" question. Option D is correct as this is not a risk but an issue.

31 Paul and his team have identified various assumptions and constraints that can be false. They also figured out that if the assumptions and constraints are false, then they would affect the project objectives. What is a possible next step?
   A. Convert them into monetary values
   B. Do nothing
   C. **Convert them into risks**
   D. Convert them into issues
   Explanation: Option A is wrong. This is a made-up option. Option B is wrong. This would not help. Option C is correct. This is the assumption and constraint analysis. Option D is wrong. Converting them into issues would not help.

32 Paul and his team have examined the assumption and constraint analysis. They are in doubt whether this analysis takes both positive and negative effects on project objectives into account. What is correct?
   A. It takes only negative effects on project objectives into account.
   B. It takes only positive effects on project objectives into account.
   C. **It takes positive and negative effects on project objectives into account.**
   D. It takes positive and negative effects on project objectives into account, if probability or impact is high.
   Explanation: Options A and B are both wrong. Option C is correct. This is the correct application of the assumption and constraint analysis. Option D is wrong. This is a made-up application.

33 Paul and his team have examined the assumption and constraint analysis. They have categorized and leveraged the results of the assumption and constraint analysis. Several tasks need to be completed. Which one is the least likely?

A. Assess the risks associated with each assumption and/or constraint

B. Recognize the relationship between assumptions and/or constraints, and project objectives

C. Encourage stakeholders to challenge assumptions and constraints

D. **Categorize assumptions and constraints into risks and issues**

Explanation: Options A, B, and C are all wrong as these are likely tasks to be completed. Option D is correct as it is a made-up task and makes little sense. Assumptions and constraints may be converted into risks; however, categorization is not possible and converting them into issues is of little value or even possible.

34 Paul and his team are having a hard time explaining the term "risk trigger" to the key stakeholders. What would be a suitable alternative?

A. Information radiator

B. **Warning signs**

C. Risk impacts

D. When it is too late to activate the risk response

Explanation: Option A is wrong. The information radiator is an agile board. Option B is correct. Warning signs or risk symptoms are suitable alternatives. Option C is wrong. Risk impacts are something else. Option D is wrong. The trigger is not too late.

35 Paul and his team are in the process of documenting risk triggers. The risk is the probability of an activity (activity X) on the critical path being delayed. Which of the following would be the best risk trigger here?

A. Activity X is starting earlier than expected.

B. The schedule performance index is still above 1.

C. About 80% of the resources for activity X have been used, but progress is 20%.

D. **Activity X is not completed July 10 as expected.**

Explanation: Option A is wrong. Starting early might be positive. Option B is wrong. SPI above 1 means the schedule is ahead of time, but activity X might still be delayed. Option C is wrong. It is a concern, but high resource usage and low progress may not be a problem depending on the work. Option D is correct. We have a delay, and it should trigger the risk response.

36 Pete and his team need to document risk compliance thresholds. How do they perform the update?

A. **Against updated risk data**

B. Against the risk triggers

C. Against the risk consequences and/or impact

D. All of the above

Explanation: Option A is correct. Risk compliance thresholds should be documented and categorized against updated risk data. Option B is wrong. This does not make sense as triggers vary. Option C is wrong. These impacts could be included in the risk data but cannot stand alone. Option D is wrong since options B and C are also wrong.

37 Freddy, the agile coach of a Scrum team, is working with the product owner to empower the key stakeholders to challenge existing thresholds. How should that be done?

A. The key stakeholders should participate in the iteration planning and question the team's estimates.

B. **The key stakeholders should work with the PO on finding the right thresholds.**

C. The key stakeholders should work with the team so thresholds with the iterations are stable.

D. The key stakeholders should be coach by the agile coach, so they can learn to say no.

Explanation: Option A is wrong. The stakeholders should not take part in the planning. Option B is correct. The PO sets the risk threshold in dialogue with the stakeholders. Option C is wrong. This is not a team task. Option D is wrong. Coaching may be fine, but it is not an issue about saying no.

38 Freddy, the agile coach, is working with Pete, the project manager of a hybrid project, on documenting risk triggers and thresholds based on context/environment. They have assessed, confirmed, and documented risk compliance thresholds and categories against updated risk data. Which of the following tasks is the least likely to be missing?

A. Assess and document risk triggers, causes, and timing

B. **Assess and document probabilities**

C. Assess and document risk consequences and/or impact

D. Empower stakeholders to challenge existing thresholds

Explanation: Options A, C, and D are all valid tasks to be completed, but these are wrong as this is a "least likely" question. Option B is correct. This is not relevant here. Probability is assessed as part of the qualitative assessment.

39 Freddy, the agile coach, is discussing with his agile Scrum team what is a good example of a risk impact. Which of the following statements should he put forward as the good example?

A. John, the tester, is expected to be sick for another 4 days.

B. Ulla, the lead developer, does not have access to GitHub.

C. **Task B might take 2 days longer than estimated.**

D. William, the new programmer, has left the team after just 2 days.

Explanation: Option A is wrong. He is sick for another 4 days, which is a decent example but the impact is uncertain. Option B is wrong. This is an impediment. Option C is correct. The risk impact is 2 days. Option D is wrong. This is an issue.

40 Roger is developing a risk register for his first risk workshop. During the workshop he and some SMEs are going to examine various risk attributes. Which of the following is not a risk attribute?

A. Probability

B. Impact

C. Urgency

D. **Ability to define a valid trigger**

Explanation: Options A, B, and C are all valid risk attributes. These options are wrong as this is a "not" question. Option D is correct. This is not a risk attribute.

41 Roger is developing a risk register for his first risk workshop. During the workshop he and some SMEs are going to classify some risks. Which of the following would be the best classification?

A. Positive and negative threats

B. **Threats or opportunities**

C. Risks and issues

D. Probability and impact

Explanation: Option A is wrong. Positive and negative risks, not threats. Option B is correct because we label as positive or negative or as threats or opportunities. The alternative is positive and negative risks. Options C is wrong. Issues are not relevant here. Option D is wrong. Probability and impact belong to the qualitative risk assessment.

42 Freddy, the agile coach, is discussing with his agile Scrum team who should have risk ownership of the DevOps environment. Who would be the best owner?

A. The product owner and he/she owns the product.

B. The Scrum master, as this may become an impediment soon.

C. **The DevOps team, as this is a shared service.**

D. It should be owned by the external vendor of most of the software.

Explanation: Option A is wrong. The product owner of one team should not own this as several teams may use it. Option B is wrong. The Scrum master should not own risks, and it is not sure it will become an impediment. Even if, then solving an impediment is not a reason for owning a risk. Option C is correct. This is a shared service; however, it is outside the team, which some may not prefer. Option D is wrong. This would not work out, and they would not be able to take full ownership anyway.

43 The team is faced with the risk of not being able to solve a technical issue due to some missing hardware configuration. What is the risk origin here?

A. The team

B. **Missing hardware configuration**

C. Technical issue

D. Poor planning

Explanation: Option A is wrong. The risk did not come from the team. Option B is correct. The origin is missing hardware configuration, which is the root-cause. Option C is wrong. This is not generic. Option D is wrong. This might worsen it, but we don't have the risk due to poor planning based on the scenario.

44 Eddy and Peter are in the process of developing a risk register for the ERP project. Which of the following content should not be included?

A. Risk ID

B. Categorization

C. Source

D. **Author**

Explanation: Options A, B, and C are all wrong. This content should be included in the risk register. Option D is correct as this question is a "not" question but a bit tricky. Some might argue source and author are similar. Source is more versatile than author and therefore the better choice.

45 Eddy and Peter have developed a risk register and now need to update it. Which of the following information is least likely to be updated when a risk response is triggered?
   A. **Description**
   B. Probability
   C. Impact
   D. Risk contingency
   Explanation: Option A is correct. The description is not likely to change due to risk response. IT can be updated along the way but not due to risk response. Options B, C, and D are all information that may be updated. These options are all wrong as this is a "not" question.

46 The team is in the process of performing the qualitative analysis of the identified risk. What factors are assessed?
   A. Time and money
   B. Probability and likelihood
   C. **Probability and impact**
   D. Impact and consequence
   Explanation: Option A is wrong. It is made up. Option B is wrong. Probability and likelihood are very similar. Option C is correct. Option D is wrong. Impact and consequence are very similar.

47 Which of the following is the least beneficial for Paul and his team in using a risk breakdown structure?
   A. Provide a classification, e.g., environment
   B. Categories for the identified risks
   C. Framework for the application of historical risk data, e.g., identified risks
   D. **Support the assessment of the risks**
   Explanation: Options A, B, and C are all valid benefits for Paul and his team in using an RBS. These options are all wrong as this is a "least" question. Option D is correct as this is not a benefit. The RBS does not provide guidance on the actual assessment of the risks.

48 Tony and his agile team are using an RBS and discover that one category, project management, has been empty. What are the consequences for Tony and his team?
   A. They should identify some project management risks and populate the RBS shortly.
   B. They should escalate the issue to the PMO as this is clearly a mistake.
   C. It is not a problem as agile teams do not have project managers.
   D. **Historical data on project management seems to be lacking. Tony and his agile team need to identify the risks and in due time they might be part of the RBS.**
   Explanation: Option A is wrong. Risks identified should not necessarily be included in the RBS shortly. Option B is wrong. This is not a mistake. Option C is wrong. This is not relevant. Option D is correct.

49 Risks in the RBS use classifications from the risk management plan.
    However, which of the following is the least likely categorization?
    A. Organizational
    B. Project management
    C. **Issues**
    D. Technical
    Explanation: Options A, B, and D are all common categorizations, and
    these options are all wrong as this is a "least likely" question. Option C
    is correct. "Issues" is hardly a category of use.

50 When estimating the impact of an identified risk, "Missing configuration
    hardware," which of the following would be best applied?
    A. Time
    B. Cost
    C. **Scope**
    D. Uncertainty
    Explanation: Option A is wrong. Schedule would be more relevant than
    time. Option B is wrong. Budget would be more precise than cost.
    Option C is correct. Scope, resource, schedule, and budget would be
    relevant. Option D is wrong. This is not relevant.

51 Pete and his team have prioritized risks based upon the impact but
    the assessment is not complete - what else does Peter and his needs to
    include when prioritizing risks?
    A. **Urgency**
    B. Uncertainty
    C. Risk origin
    D. Risk ownership
    Explanation: Option A is correct. Options B, C, and D are all wrong and
    not valid options here.

52 John, the product owner, has just engaged a new Scrum master to coach
    the key stakeholders on performing the qualitative analysis. What would
    be a good topic for the sessions?
    A. Expected monetary analysis
    B. **Risk categorization strategies**
    C. How to make the Monte Carlo simulation run smoothly
    D. Affinity estimating
    Explanation: Options A and C are both wrong. Quantitative assessment is
    not relevant here. Option B is correct. Option D is wrong. Estimation is
    not relevant here.

53 John and his team are about to embark on performing a quantitative analysis. Which of the following tools and techniques does not fit that description?

A. Monte Carlo

B. **Probability and impact analysis**

C. Influence diagrams

D. Sensitivity analysis

Explanation: Options A, C, and D are all wrong as this is a "not" question. These techniques are all fit for quantitative analysis. Option B is correct as it is a qualitative analysis not quantitative.

54 John and his team are still working on performing the quantitative analysis. They would like a tool or technique that can tell them the probability that the schedule is completed in 11 or 23 days. Which tool and technique could solve that problem?

A. **Monte Carlo**

B. Decision trees

C. Expected monetary value

D. None of the above

Explanation: Option A is correct. This is an example of the Monte Carlo simulation. Options B, C, and D are all wrong. Options B and C are quantitative tools but do not fit the description.

55 John and his team are still working on performing the quantitative analysis. They found a technique they can use to calculate the project's risk contingency. What technique did they most likely discover?

A. Monte Carlo

B. Decision trees

C. **Expected monetary value**

D. Sensitivity analysis

Explanation: Options A, B, and D are all wrong. These are quantitative techniques but do not fit the description. Option C is correct. The EMV analysis can provide monetary values of all risks to be used in the contingency budget.

56 A team wants to perform a forecast and trend analysis. What information would be required?

A. New information

B. Historical information

C. **New and historical information**

D. None of the above

Explanation: Options A and B are both wrong as both are needed. Option C is correct. Option D is wrong as the right option is listed.

57 A team has just performed a qualitative analysis and now plans on performing the quantitative analysis. What is the big difference between qualitative analysis and quantitative analysis?

A. **The qualitative assessment examines the individual risks, while the quantitative assessment analyzes all the risks.**

B. The assessments are the same, but the quantitative assessment is more detailed for high-risk projects.

C. The assessments are the same, but the quantitative assessment requires tooling such as Monte Carlo simulation software.

D. The qualitative assessment gives a prioritization, while the quantitative assessment analyzes only the impact on the monetary values.

Explanation: Option A is correct. This explains it nicely. Options B and C are wrong. The assessments are not the same. Some use the quantitative assessment for high-risk projects and it may require tooling, but it is not the same as the qualitative assessment. Option D is wrong. The qualitative assessment can provide prioritization, but the quantitative assessment does not only provide monetary values.

58 Tony has examined his schedule and found the standard deviation of the tasks in his plan. Which tool or technique when performing the quantitative analysis may provide a similar type of outcome for risks?

A. Monte Carlo

B. Decision trees

C. Expected monetary value

D. **Sensitivity analysis**

Explanation: Options A, B, and C are all wrong. These are quantitative techniques but do not fit the description. Option D is correct. Sensitivity analysis and standard deviation both represent uncertainty in various matters.

59 Which of the following tasks should not be conducted when performing the quantitative analysis?

A. Analyze risk data and process performance information against established metrics

B. Analyze a project's general risks

C. **Document lessons learned on risk management activities**

D. Perform risk weighting and calculate risk priority

Explanation: Options A, B, and D are all wrong and these are relevant tasks, but this is a "not" question. Option C is correct as this task is not done during the quantitative analysis.

60 Tony is an expert planner. Which tool or technique used in scheduling may support Tony when forecasting?

A. Critical path analysis

B. Critical chain analysis

C. Expected monetary value

D. **Earned value management**

Explanation: Options A, B, and C are all wrong. These techniques may not support forecasting. Option D is correct. Earned value management analysis can provide status, time, and costs.

61 Tony, the expert planner, and his team are in the middle of assessing project risk complexity. Which of the following tools and techniques should be applied?

A. **SWOT analysis**

B. Earned value management

C. Expected monetary value

D. Benchmarking

Explanation: Option A is correct. Options B, C, and D are all wrong. These tools and techniques do not assess project risk complexity.

62 Tony, the expert planner, and his team are in the middle of assessing project risk complexity. Which of the following tools and techniques should not be applied?

A. SWOT analysis

B. Ishikawa diagram

C. Tree diagram

D. **Iteration retrospective**

Explanation: Options A, B, and C are valid tools and techniques for assessing project risk complexity, but this is a "not" question. Option D is correct. This technique is agile and does not necessarily assess risk complexity.

63 Emma and her agile Scrum team want to perform an impact analysis. Which of the following is the least of her concerns?

A. Project scope

B. Schedule cost

C. Resources

D. **Environment**

Explanation: Options A, B, and C are all valid project objectives, but these options are wrong as this is a "least" question. Not all options are highly relevant for an agile team, but they are still better than option D. Option D is correct. The impact analysis is done on project objectives. Environment is not a project objective.

64 Tom has conducted a detailed study of business activities, dependencies, and infrastructure. Which kind of analysis has he just conducted?
A. SWOT analysis
B. Benchmarking
C. **Impact analysis**
D. Trend analysis

Explanation: Options A, B, and D are all wrong. These analyses are not mentioned here. Option C is correct. The context fits the real-life application of the impact analysis.

65 When assessing project compliance objectives against organizational strategic objectives, which of the following project artifacts would be most helpful?
– Risk register
– Issue log
– Budget
– **Project plans**

Explanation: Options A, B, and C are all wrong. These options are not relevant here. Option D is correct as the project plan is highly relevant. The only artifact coming close is the budget, but it is not the most helpful artifact.

66 Roger and his team are assessing project compliance objectives against organizational strategic objectives. They have identified the importance of the various governance requirements. Which of the following is the least important?
A. Corporate governance
B. Project governance
C. **Team governance**
D. Regulatory governance

Explanation: Options A, B and D are all valid, but this is a "least important" question. Option C is correct as this is not important. The term "team governance" is made up. Team charter, ground rules, and other artifacts may cover this aspect.

67 Tommy, the agile Scrum product owner, has empowered the key stakeholders to independently identify threats and opportunities. The stakeholders report the following to Tommy. Which one should he take into consideration?
A. The written user stories are unclear.
B. The team did not complete all tasks during the sprint.
C. **The definition of done may not cover all quality concerns.**
D. The daily standups have been skipped.

Explanation: Options A, B, and D are all wrong. These are all issues. Option C is correct. This is a threat dealing with the probability of a quality impact.

68 Tommy, the agile Scrum product owner, has empowered the key stakeholders to independently identify threats and opportunities. This has been working; however, most stakeholders only identify threats, not opportunities. Tommy arranged a workshop where the following were identified. Which of the following should he include as an opportunity?

A. Pair programming would increase quality greatly

B. **Applying DevOps might also increase velocity**

C. Refactoring should solve the technical debt of the past

D. Team ownership increases the quality of the team's work

Explanation: Options A, C, and D are all wrong as these are not risks. No uncertainty. Option B is correct. This is an opportunity for increased velocity.

69 Tommy, the agile Scrum product owner, has selected a risk response strategy where he works with a partner who provides more resources, which should increase the probability of the risk. What strategy is this?

A. Transfer

B. **Share**

C. Escalate

D. Exploit

Explanation: Option A is wrong. This is a negative strategy, and the risk is positive. Option B is correct. Option C is wrong. The risk is not being escalated but shared with a partner. Option D is wrong. The risk is not certain to happen.

70 Tommy and his team are struggling with key stakeholders who only work with negative risks. Which of the following risk response strategy would work for both positive and negative risks?

A. Mitigate

B. Avoid

C. **Accept**

D. Transfer

Explanation: Option A is wrong. This is a negative risk strategy only. Option B is wrong. This is a negative risk strategy only. Option C is correct. Accept and escalate work for positive and negative risks. Option D is wrong. This is a negative risk strategy only.

71 Pete, the project manager of a major project, has a risk with a high probability and huge negative impact. Which risk response strategy should he try out first?

A. Exploit

B. Mitigate

C. Transfer

D. **Avoid**

Explanation: Options A, B, and C are all wrong. These options deal with negative risks; however, with a huge negative impact these strategies should not be applied first. Option D is correct. Avoid first, if possible, with high-impact risks. Then mitigate, transfer, and accept.

72 When would be a good time for Pete, the project manager of a major project, to be using a workaround?

A. When his client asks him to do so

B. **When all options have been tried**

C. As he sees fit

D. When risk contingency has been spent

Explanation: Option A is wrong. This is not a decision made by the client. Option B is correct. The workaround is commonly applied when all risk responses have failed. Option C is wrong. It is partly correct as he can use it when he sees fit, but it may not always be a good time. Option D is wrong. Lack of funds may result in a workaround, but it should not be the preferred solution.

73 Pete, the project manager, wants to assess the effectiveness of the risk response mitigation actions on a risk regarding lack of resources for the implementation of the solution. How can Pete, when examining the risk register, verify the effectiveness?

A. The risk is gone as it is no longer relevant.

B. The risk description and origin have been updated.

C. Probability and/or impact might have increased.

D. **Probability and/or impact might have decreased.**

Explanation: Option A is wrong. Mitigation might not eliminate the risk. Option B is wrong. This information should not be updated due to risk response. Option C is wrong. A negative risk response should not increase the probability or impact of a negative risk. Option D is correct. The mitigate strategy should decrease the probability and/or impact, which should be visible in the risk register.

74 Andy, the team lead, wants to allocate responsibilities for managing risk responses. What kind of responsibilities would most likely be allocated?
A. Help the risk owner watch the risk
B. Support the risk action owner
C. **Take on the role as risk action owner**
D. Manage the risk budget
Explanation: Option A and B are both wrong. These scenarios are not likely. Option C is correct. The risk action owner's responsibility is important and needs to be assigned. Option D is wrong. The risk budget should not be assigned by the team lead.

75 When dealing with the planning of risk responses, which of the following tasks is the least important?
A. Illustrate and communicate the effectiveness of the risk response strategies
B. **Allocate responsibilities within the team**
C. Outline an appropriate responsibility matrix for a metricized project environment
D. Reevaluate organizational risks
Explanation: Options A, C, and D are all valid tasks but this is a "least important" question. Option B is correct as allocating responsibilities is important but not only within the team.

76 Victor and his team are discussing the goals of executing the risk response plans. Which of the following states one or more of these goals?
A. Determining ways to keep the risk contingency budget within the tolerance
B. **Determining ways to reduce or eliminate any threats to the project**
C. Determining ways to ensure all risks are mitigated
D. Determining ways to maximize opportunities obtained
Explanation: Option A is wrong. The main purpose is not keeping track of the budget. Option B is correct. The purpose is determining ways to reduce or eliminate any threats to the project and the opportunities to increase their impact. Option C is wrong. The plan does not ensure all risks are mitigated. Option D is wrong. Opportunities is part of it, but the plan does not necessarily maximize opportunities obtained.

77 When should Victor and his team execute the contingency plan of a certain risk dealing with the risk of the organization not using the implemented solution?

A. **The plan is to lessen the damage of the risk when it occurs.**

B. The plan should be triggered so it can prevent the risk occurring.

C. The plan should be executed if the fallback plan fails.

D. The plan should be activated by the direction of the sponsor and steering committee.

Explanation: Option A is correct. Option B is wrong. This is not related to the risk trigger. Option C is wrong. The contingency plan is executed before the fallback plan, not after. Option D is wrong. The execution is not governed by the sponsor or steering committee but when the risk occurs.

78 What might be the consequence for Georg and his team for not having a contingency plan for a high-impact risk?

A. Without the plan in place, the project cannot avoid the risk.

B. Without the plan in place, the project cannot aim for opportunities.

C. **Without the plan in place, the full impact of the risk could greatly affect the project.**

D. Without the plan in place, the project cannot fully measure the expected monetary value.

Explanation: Option A is wrong. The plan does not help to avoid risks. Option B is wrong. The plan has nothing to do with positive risk responses. Option C is correct. Option D is wrong. The plan is not related to measuring EMV.

79 Roger hears this statement from the sponsor: "The contingency plan is the last line of defense against the risk." What is the most exact response?

A. Yes, you are right.

B. **Yes, you are right, but if it is not effective or fails, we have a fallback plan.**

C. No, you are wrong. The risk response strategy is the last line of defense.

D. No, you are wrong. We still have the risk owner and risk action owner who will intervene.

Explanation: Option A is wrong. The statement is correct, however, it is not the most exact response. Option B is correct. Option C is wrong. The risk responses are activated before not after the contingency plan. Option D is wrong. These people should act with a risk response when the risk trigger occurs not after.

80 Roger and his team are working with the key stakeholders to encourage them to provide feedback on the risk responses. What could Roger and his team do to further this?

A. Tell the key stakeholders to provide written feedback at any time

B. Encourage the stakeholders to review the risk register

C. Encourage the stakeholders to sign up as risk owners

D. **Invite the key stakeholders to participate in a risk workshop**

Explanation: Options A and B are both wrong. Written feedback or review may work, but they are not the best solutions to foster engagement. Option C is wrong. Signing up would not encourage feedback. Option D is correct. This is a good way to engage the stakeholders.

81 Which of the following tasks is the least important when implementing risk responses?

A. Execute the risk response plan(s)

B. **Assess the watchlist**

C. Encourage stakeholders to provide feedback on the risk response

D. Evaluate and react to secondary and residual risks from the response implementation

Explanation: Options A, C, and D are all wrong as these are valid options and important when implementing risk responses. Option B is correct as this is a "least" question. Assessing the watchlist is hardly relevant. The watchlist contains the list with low probability and impact. It should be assessed for changes but not now.

82 Pete and his team are in the process of gathering and analyzing performance data. Currently they are examining schedule risk. Should they reconcile data from both work and planning packages?

A. Yes, all kinds of data are relevant.

B. **No, only work package data.**

C. No, only planning package data.

D. No, work and planning package data are not relevant.

Explanation: Option A is wrong. All data are not equally relevant. Option B is correct. Work package data includes scheduling data. Option C is wrong as the planning package does not contain schedule data. Option D is wrong as work package data are relevant.

83 Pete and his team are in the process of gathering and analyzing performance data. There seems to be a schedule concern with the performance of several teams working predictive. What can Pete and his team do to clarify this concern?

A. Examine the trend analysis

B. Check if CPI is higher than 1

C. **Perform a variance analysis**

D. Reexamine the burndown chart

Explanation: Option A is wrong. This may not clarify the concern. Option B is wrong. CPI is the cost performance index, and the concern is schedule related. Option C is correct. Option D is wrong. The teams are working predictive and may not use an agile burndown chart.

84 Pete and his team are in the process of gathering and analyzing performance data. They want to monitor impacts against overall project risk exposure, but whom would be affected?

A. **The enterprise**

B. The project

C. The program

D. The value streams

Explanation: Option A is correct. The overall project risk exposure would affect the enterprise. Options B, C, and D are all wrong options. The project, program, or value streams are not affected.

85 When gathering and analyzing performance data, what is the most important aspect of the baseline?

A. It helps the team to stay within the schedule.

B. It supports formal change control.

C. It is fundamental for configuration management.

D. **The team can determine the completion status against the baseline.**

Explanation: Option A is wrong. The schedule baseline is the target, and it is not necessary to help the team to keep it and it is not relevant for gathering and analyzing performance data. Option B is wrong. Baselines are governed by change control; however, it is not relevant here. Option C is wrong. Change and configuration controls are relevant, but are out of context here. Option D is correct.

86 When gathering and analyzing performance data, which of the following tasks is the least important?

A. Reconcile performance data and reports from risk-relevant work packages

B. Analyze data to determine the completion status against the baseline

C. **Perform a trend analysis**

D. Monitor impact against overall project risk exposure to the enterprise

Explanation: Options A, B, and D are valid tasks, but option C is correct as this is the least important task. It is relevant to perform variance analysis, but a trend analysis is not recommended now.

87 Ian has identified some risks and documented them in the risk register. Which of them should be considered a residual risk?

A. A risk that arises due to another risk response.

B. It is just another word for a secondary risk.

C. **A risk that is still present even after the risk response.**

D. A risk that has been fully mitigated and is no longer relevant.

Explanation: Options A and B are both wrong. These are secondary risks. Option C is correct. Option D is wrong as it is no longer a risk.

88 Ian has identified some risks and documented them in the risk register. They found a risk where impact has been greatly reduced due to the risk response. However, probability is still high, and impact was not completely removed. What type of risk is this?

A. **Residual risk**

B. Secondary risk

C. Known risk

D. Unknown risk

Explanation: Option A is correct. It is still residual with probability and impact left. Option B is wrong. It is not another risk due to the risk response. Options C and D are both wrong. This classification is not relevant now.

89 Some years ago, an oil platform burned in the Mexican gulf and there was a risk that oil would pollute the sea. Various chemicals were used to avoid this. However, it turned out that these chemicals might also damage the sea. What kind of risk is this?

A. Residual risk

B. **Secondary risk**

C. High-impact risk

D. Unknown risk

Explanation: Option A is wrong. The risk is the result of another risk response. Option B is correct. Option C is wrong and just made up. Option D is wrong. This classification is not relevant now.

90 Ian has identified some risks and documented them in the risk register. When assessing the impact of residual and secondary risks, which is most important?

A. The project manager can do it.

B. It can be done in a few hours as it must be repeated throughout the project's lifetime.

C. **It is done on project objectives.**

D. It works in Scrum.

Explanation: Option A is wrong. The project manager should not do it alone. Option B is wrong. Time is not a concern. Option C is correct. It must be impacts those matters, that is project objectives like time and cost. Option D is wrong. It does work in Scrum; however, it is not the most important option.

91 Ian and his team are monitoring residual and secondary risks. Which of the following tasks is the least important?

A. Monitor risk response and document residual risk

B. **Monitor risk response for threats and opportunities**

C. Assess the impact of residual and secondary risks on project objectives

D. Update and communicate the impact of residual and secondary risks

Explanation: Options A, C, and D are all wrong as these are valid tasks, but this is a "least important" question. Option B is correct as this is not important. It should have been the focus on secondary risks, not threats and opportunities.

92 Ian and his team are in the process of updating relevant project documents. Which of the following is the least relevant to update with aggregated and summarized risk data?

A. Risk register

B. Lessons learned

C. Project management plan

D. **Issue log**

Explanation: Options A, B, and C are all relevant project documents to be updated. These options are all wrong as this is a "least" question. Option D is correct as it is the least relevant document because it is not commonly updated with aggregated and summarized risk data.

93 Ian and his team are in the process of updating relevant project documents. Currently they are updating the risk register. What data is likely to be updated?

A. **Change status for expired risks**

B. Risk origin

C. Risk description

D. Risk response

Explanation: Option A is correct. Options B, C, and D are all wrong options as these risk data are not likely to change or to be updated now.

94 Ian and his team are in the process of updating relevant project documents. Which of the following risks should be closed out as expired?

A. A risk that has been mitigated so probability and impact are greatly reduced, but the risk is still present

B. A risk arises due to the risk response to another risk

C. **A risk where the risk response exploit has been successfully applied**

D. A risk where the risk response is avoid; however, the risk trigger has not yet occurred

Explanation. Option A is wrong. This is a residual risk. Option B is wrong. This is a secondary risk. Option C is correct. The opportunity has been obtained with the exploit strategy. Option D is wrong. This risk is still active as the trigger has not been activated.

95 When Ian and his team are updating relevant project documents with aggregated and summarized risk data, who or what is the least likely source of data?

A. Project team

B. **Sponsor**

C. Work performance data

D. Work performance information

Explanation: Option A is wrong as the project team is a relevant source as they do much of the work. Option B is correct. The sponsor is least likely to provide data. Options C and D are both wrong as these are relevant data sources on work.

96 Ian and his team are updating relevant project documents with aggregated and summarized risk data. What needs to be done?

A. Achieve lessons learned

B. Update the project management plan

C. Update the change logs

D. **Monitor and close out expired risks**

Explanation: Option A is wrong. Lessons learned is updated but not necessarily achieved now. Option B and C are both wrong. These tasks were completed when updating relevant project documents. Option D is correct. This task has not yet been done.

97 Trevor and his team are monitoring project risk levels. Which of the following tasks is the least important?

A. **Assess secondary and residual risks**

B. Assess project risk level

C. Prepare reports for different stakeholders

D. Communicate risk levels to key stakeholders

Explanation: Option A is correct as it is the least important. This assessment should not be conducted when monitoring project risk levels. Options B, C, and D are all wrong as these are valid tasks now.

98 Trevor and his team are monitoring project risk levels for a major IT project with many high-ranking key stakeholders of a certain age and from across the world. In that process they prepare reports for different stakeholders. Which report best represents the needs of the stakeholders?

A. Comprehensive and detailed for all key stakeholders

B. **Tailored for each key stakeholder**

C. Standardized and available on a collaborative platform

D. Short and overview format for all key stakeholders as they are busy people

Explanation: Option A is wrong. It is uncertain if comprehensive and detailed is the need of the stakeholders. Option B is correct. Each stakeholder may or may not have different needs and expectations. Option C is wrong. One size does not necessarily fit all. More might be expected with high-level stakeholders. Option D is wrong. It is uncertain if short and overview fits the need of the stakeholders.

99 How should Andrew and his team on the construction project working with local on-site officials communicate the risk levels to these people?

A. Give them access to a collaborative platform, so they can pull the information when needed

B. Push it out as a monthly newsletter to all key stakeholders

C. Arrange a monthly interactive meeting to discuss it

D. **Have a talk with each of them to figure out their needs**

Explanation: Options A, B, and C are all wrong. Push, pull, and interactive communication may all work out nicely; however, the project should know the needs and requirements of the stakeholders. Option D is correct. The project should match the communication with the needs of the stakeholders.

100 Which of the following tasks should not be conducted when assessing project risk level?

A. Identify new risks

B. Assess probabilities

C. Assess impacts

D. **Confirm risks are expired**

Explanation: Options A, B, and C are all wrong as these are valid tasks. Option D is correct as the task should not focus on expired risks.

Appendix A: Agile Mindset and Principles

The agile approach is very different from the predictive approach. It is not just a matter of the spiral system development model being different than the waterfall system development model. Some may argue agile is just a new notion for reinvented predictive project management. This might hold some truth, but most agile methodologies, tools, and techniques include mindset, values, morals, and principles that are the key essence of being agile. Agile is a mindset, a diverse culture and that is what this chapter is all about. After reading this chapter it should be much easier to understand how Scrum works, Appendix B, and appreciate the underlying ideas and concepts, as Scrum and other frameworks are built upon the agile manifesto and principles.

Exercise A.1 Starting from zero or a lot – What do you know about the agile mindset and principles? Write it down or share it with the people in the room.

_____

_____

_____

_____

_____

Answer: No right or wrong answers.

Before going into detail about the agile manifesto, the 12 principles of agile software, and the declaration of interdependence for modern management, it is important to highlight that agile project management is not going to be agile if it violates the values and principles in the agile manifesto, the 12 principles of agile software, and the declaration of interdependence for modern management. This is fundamental for agile, agile history, and still very much relevant today.

Exercise A.2 Is the hybrid approach a violation of the essence of being agile?

_____

_____

_____

_____

_____

_____

Answer: Practitioners may have different views on this matter, however, I would argue that if you do hybrid properly, then it works fine with agile and predictive project management without any type of violations.

The second point to highlight is concepts like "doing agile versus being agile" by Highsmith (2002), which stresses the importance of being agile rather than just doing agile, meaning really understanding the benefits of agile and applying agile values and principles are so much more beneficial than just doing agile by applying the ceremonies and artifacts. This point is often downplayed on the team level.

A.1 Agile Is a Mindset, a Culture

When trying to fully understand that agile is a mindset I used the framework illustrated in Figure A.1. It starts with the agile mindset, which is included in this section. On top of the mindset all agile approaches are based upon Lean (Section A.2), which is the next part of the circle. The next part is agile values, which is the Agile Manifesto discussed in Section A.3. Following the Agile Manifesto are the 12 principles (Section A.4) and Declaration of Independence for Modern Management (Section A.5), which are the agile principles in the figure. Last is the agile practices (Section A.6), which are all the tools, techniques, ceremonies, and artifacts being applied. Understanding each of the elements of Figure A.1 will provide you with a detailed and comprehensive view of what the agile mindset and culture imply.

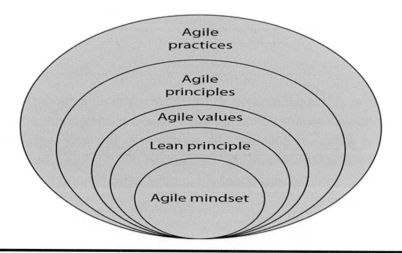

Figure A.1   Agile mindset.

The work on the "agile" mindset is built upon the book *Mindset*, written by Carol S. Dweck in 2006. It explains how we can learn to fulfill our potential. Her research has emphasis on two mindsets: fixed and growth. The growth mindset is sometimes referred to as agile. To briefly sum up the findings: Individuals who believe their talents can be developed (through hard work, good strategies, and input from others) have a growth mindset. People with a growth mindset tend to achieve more than those with a more fixed mindset (those who believe their talents are innate gifts). This is because they worry less about looking smart and they put more energy into learning. When entire companies embrace a growth mindset, their employees report feeling far more empowered and committed; they also receive far greater organizational support for collaboration and innovation. Both mindsets are illustrated Table A.1.

Table A.1 Mindsets

Fixed	*Growth (Agile)*
Ability – static, like height Goal – look good Challenge – avoid Failure – defines your identity Effort – for those with no talent Reaction to challenge – helplessness	Ability – can grow, like muscle Goal – to learn Challenge – embrace Failure – provides information Effort – path to mastery

One of the major challenges with the work by Dweck (2006) is the many misconceptions of the mindset. Later, Dweck explained in the *Harvard Business Review* article "What Having a 'Growth Mindset' Actually Means" (2016) the three most common misconceptions, which are shown in Table A.2.

Table A.2 Misconceptions of the Mindset

Misconception	Explanation
I already have it, and I always have.	People often confuse a growth mindset with being flexible or open-minded or with having a positive outlook — qualities they believe they've simply always had. My colleagues and I call this a false growth mindset. Everyone is actually a mixture of fixed and growth mindsets, and that mixture continually evolves with experience. A "pure" growth mindset doesn't exist, which we have to acknowledge in order to attain the benefits we seek.
A growth mindset is just about praising and rewarding effort.	This isn't true for students in schools, and it's not true for employees in organizations. In both settings, outcomes matter. Unproductive effort is never a good thing. It's critical to reward not just effort but learning and progress, and to emphasize the processes that yield these things, such as seeking help from others, trying new strategies, and capitalizing on setbacks to move forward effectively. In all of our research, the outcome — the bottom line — follows from deeply engaging in these processes.
Just espouse a growth mindset, and good things will happen.	Mission statements are wonderful things. You can't argue with lofty values like growth, empowerment, or innovation. But what do they mean to employees if the company doesn't implement policies that make them real and attainable? They just amount to lip service. Organizations that embody a growth mindset encourage appropriate risk-taking, knowing that some risks won't work out. They reward employees for important and useful lessons learned, even if a project does not meet its original goals. They support collaboration across organizational boundaries rather than competition among employees or units.

Exercise A.3 Even if we correct these misconceptions, it's still not easy to attain a growth mindset. What do you do or plan on doing?

_____

_____

_____

_____

_____

Answer: No right or wrong answers.

A.2 Lean Principles

The term "Lean software development" was first coined as the title for a conference organized by the ESPRIT initiative of the European Union, in Stuttgart, Germany, October 1992. Independently, the following year, Robert "Bob" Charette suggested the concept of Lean software development as part of his work exploring better ways of managing risk in software projects. The term "Lean" was coined to describe Toyota's management approach during the late 1980s by a research team headed by Jim Womack at MIT's International Motor Vehicle Program, which was described in the book *The Machine That Changed the World: The Story of Lean Production*. The idea that Lean might be applicable in software development was established early, only 1 to 2 years after the term was first used in association with trends in manufacturing processes and industrial engineering.

Today Lean thinking is behind the evolution of many agile processes and provides a context for discussions about customer value and process efficiency across the business. The major theories and key thinkers are the Toyota Way, Womack, Larman and Vodde, Reinertsen, and Poppendieicks, which are explained in the following sections. The core idea of Lean is to maximize customer value while minimizing waste. Simply, Lean means creating more value for customers with fewer resources.

Lean Philosophy of Management: The Toyota Way

The Toyota Way is a set of principles and behaviors that underlie the Toyota Motor Corporation's managerial approach and production system. Toyota first summed up its philosophy, values, and manufacturing ideals in 2001, calling it "The Toyota Way 2001." It consists of principles in four sections: long-term philosophy, the right process will produce the right results, add value to the organization by developing your people, and continuously solving root problems drives organizational learning.

- Long-term philosophy
  - Base your management decisions on a long-term philosophy, even at the expense of short-term financial goals.
- The right process will produce the right results
  - Create a continuous process flow to bring problems to the surface.
  - Use "pull" systems to avoid overproduction.
  - Level out the workload (heijunka). (Work like the tortoise, not the hare.)
  - Build a culture of stopping to fix problems, to get quality right the first time.
  - Standardized tasks and processes are the foundation for continuous improvement and employee empowerment.
  - Use visual control so no problems are hidden.
  - Use only reliable, thoroughly tested technology that serves your people and processes.
- Add value to the organization by developing your people
  - Grow leaders who thoroughly understand the work, live the philosophy, and teach it to others.

- Develop exceptional people and teams who follow your company's philosophy.
- Respect your extended network of partners and suppliers by challenging them and helping them improve.

■ Continuously solving root problems drives organizational learning
- Go and see for yourself to thoroughly understand the situation (Genchi Genbutsu).
- Make decisions slowly by consensus, thoroughly considering all options; implement decisions rapidly (nemawashi).
- Become a learning organization through relentless reflection (hansei) and continuous improvement (kaizen).

The Five Principles of Lean Thinking by Womack

The five principles of Lean thinking are value, value stream, flow, pull, and perfection. The five principles of Lean thinking are defined in Table A.3.

Table A.3 Five Principles of Lean Thinking by Womack

Principle	Definition
Value	Value is defined by the authors as a "capability provided to customers at the right time at an appropriate price, as defined in each case by the customer." Value is the critical starting point for Lean thinking and can only be defined by the ultimate end customer.
Value stream	The value stream is defined in Lean thinking as the set of all the "specific activities required to design, order, and provide a specific product, from concept to launch, order to delivery, and raw materials into the hands of the customer." There are three types of activities in the value stream: one kind adds value, and the other two are "Muda" (the Japanese word for waste). Value-added: Those activities that unambiguously create value. Type 1 Muda: Activities that create no value but seem to be unavoidable with current technologies or production assets. Type 2 Muda: Activities that create no value and are immediately avoidable.
Flow	The Lean principle of flow is defined as the "progressive achievement of tasks along the value stream so that a product proceeds from design to launch, order to delivery, and raw materials into the hands of the customer with no stoppages, scrap or backflows."
Pull	The fourth Lean principle of pull is defined by the authors as a "system of cascading production and delivery instructions from downstream to upstream in which nothing is produced by the upstream supplier until the downstream customer signals a need."
Perfection	The fifth and final Lean principle is perfection, defined again by the authors as the "complete."

Lean thinking applies the concepts of the three Lean principles – Muri, Mura, and Muda – which are illustrated in Table A.4.

Table A.4 The Three Lean Principles

Muri	Mura	Muda
Overburdening of people or equipment	Unevenness in workload	Waste or non-value adding activities

There is a relation between the three principles: Mura creates Muri leading to the inability to reduce Muda. Muda, or waste, can be reduced by solving problems of imbalanced loading and overstraining of people.

The 14 Principles of Lean Thinking by Larman

Larman and Vodde (2008) described in their book *Scaling Lean & Agile Development: Thinking and Organizational Tools for Large-Scale Scrum* the Lean thinking house and the Toyota Way with 14 principles, including grow leaders who thoroughly understand the work, live the philosophy, and teach it to others.

The Eight Principles of Flow by Reinertsen

The book *The Principles of Product Development Flow* by Donald G. Reinertsen (2009) includes the following principles:

- Economic
- Queueing
- Variability
- Batch size
- Constraint
- Flow control
- Fast feedback
- Decentralization

Several of these principles play a major role in agile. "Batch size" ensures an ongoing stream of small initiatives are completed. "Constraint" ensures flow with the theory of constrains and the managing of bottlenecks, which is supported by "flow control" with techniques such as work-in-progress (WIP) limits.

The Seven Principles of Lean Software Development by Poppendiecks

The work by Poppendiecks (2003) focuses on Lean software development, including Lean principles and tools that are highlighted in Table A.5.

Table A.5   Lean Principle by the Poppendiecks

Lean Principle	Lean Tools	Comments
Eliminate waste	Tool 1: Seeing Waste Tool 2: Value Stream Mapping	
Amplify learning	Tool 3: Feedback Tool 4: Iterations Tool 5: Synchronization Tool 6: Set-Based Development	The nature of software development
Decide as late as possible	Tool 7: Options Thinking Tool 8: The Last Responsible Moment Tool 9: Making Decisions	Concurrent development
Deliver as fast as possible	Tool 10: Pull Systems Tool 11: Queuing Theory Tool 12: Costs of Delays	
Empower the team	Tool 13: Self-Determination Tool 14: Motivation Tool 15: Leadership Tool 16: Expertise	Beyond scientific management
Build integrity in	Tool 17: Perceived Integrity Tool 18: Conceptual Integrity Tool 19: Refactoring Tool 20: Testing	Integrity
See the whole	Tool 21: Measurements Tool 22: Contracts	System thinking

The theory of constraints and Lean practices are very compatible. Lean is primarily oriented around principles. The theory of constraints emphasizes the strategic level and the ability to deliver resources even when faced with bottlenecks. Lean practices deal on the operational level with the various processes and activities, which may need to be reordered to remove waste.

The Lean Startup

The book *The Lean Startup* was written by Eric Ries in 2011 with emphasis on how constant innovation creates radically successful businesses. The content focuses on vision, steer, and accelerate, and several of these concepts are vital for agile. The vision section highlights the importance of validated learning and experiment for creating and measuring value, while steer had emphasis on the importance of testing and measuring. Finally, accelerate talks about adapting and reducing waste, which all are key elements in Lean and most agile settings.

Exercise A.4 Think about a board (information radiator) – Where do you experience the influence of Lean?

_____

_____

_____

_____

_____

Answers: WIP limit, transparency, batch sizes, pull, queuing, MVP, and such.

A.3 Agile Manifesto Values and Principles

On February 11-13, 2001, at The Lodge at Snowbird ski resort in the Wasatch Mountains of Utah (US), 17 advocates (14 took part in the meeting, just missing Ward Cunningham, Kent Back, and Dave Thomas) of lightweight development processes met to talk, ski, relax, and try to find common ground, and, of course, to eat. The intent of the conference was to write the Agile Manifesto to avoid codification of practice, but what emerged was the Agile Software Development Manifesto with an emphasis on technical practices, strong teams, and mindfulness. Representatives convened from extreme programming (Martin Fowler and Ron Jeffries), Scrum (Jeff Sutherland, Ken Schwaber, and Mike Beedle), DSDM, adaptive software development (Jim Highsmith), Crystal (Alistair Cockburn), feature-driven development, pragmatic programming (Andy Hunt), and others sympathetic (Bob Martin, James Grenning, Jon Kern, and such) to the need for an alternative to documentation driven, heavyweight software development processes. These people represent the agile movement and declared:

- We want to restore credibility to the word "methodology."
- We want to restore a balance.
- We embrace modeling but not to file some diagram in a dusty corporate repository.
- We embrace documentation but not hundreds of pages of never maintained and rarely used tomes.
- We plan but recognize the limits of planning in a turbulent environment.

The Agile Software Development Manifesto was developed with the purpose of uncovering better ways of developing software by doing it and helping others to do it. Later, Kern was quoted as saying, "Four measly bullets and all this s**t happened."

The Agile Software Development Manifesto contains four statements with the following syntax:

We value: <left> over <right>. That is, while there is value in the items on the right, we value the items on the left more. We are uncovering better ways of developing software by doing it and helping others to do it. Through this work, we have come to value:

- Individuals and interactions over processes and tools
- Working software over comprehensive documentation
- Customer collaboration over contract negotiation
- Responding to change over following a plan

Individuals and Interactions over Processes and Tools

The value and principle of "Individuals and interactions over processes and tools" has a strong emphasis on communication, management, and commitment. Project management and communication, for many years, has been intricately connected, as organizations have witnessed how projects have failed due to lack of communication, while other projects have performed far better than average with good communication practices. In agile, communication is a vital and integral part of various life cycles. These cycles can range from every few minutes with pair programming, every few hours with continuous integration, every day with daily standup meetings, to every iteration with a review and retrospective. For the team to achieve its full potential, agile management must provide a supportive environment where honesty, conflict resolution, and self-organization thrive. Agile methodologies facilitate commitment and self-organization by encouraging team members to pull items from a prioritized work list, manage their own work, and focus on improving their work practices.

"To create high-performing teams, Agile methodologies value individuals and interactions over processes and tools. Practically speaking, all of the Agile methodologies seek to increase communication and collaboration through frequent inspect-and-adapt cycles".

Working Software over Comprehensive Documentation

The principle of "Working software over comprehensive documentation" is perhaps the most important value that agile offers in the process of delivering small chunks of working software at set intervals. The phrase "working software" may have different meanings from team to team, so does the "definition of done" based on the working software. However, the use of working software is a great way for the team to demonstrate high value and high performance to stakeholders. It can foster increased communication and interactions, thereby supporting other values.

In terms of documentation, the manifesto does not value comprehensive documentation, but just enough documentation to get by. Kent Beck (2007) seems to suggest that well-written code is its own documentation. Hoda et al. (2010) suggests documentation pattern or framework that will ensure just enough documentation.

Customer Collaboration over Contract Negotiation

"Over the past two decades, project success rates have more than doubled worldwide. These improvements occurred because of smaller projects and more frequent deliveries, which allowed customers to provide feedback on working software at regular intervals".

Agile methodologies foster collaboration by having a customer advocate work together with the development team. Agile methods, such as Scrum and XP, turn to product owners and customers to create roles and foster an environment, where verbal customer collaboration adds value. This value stands in strong opposition to the written contract negotiation over software requirements or legal practicalities. In agile, we seek verbal customer collaboration as soon as possible to receive feedback. However, this does not mean that there were not contract negotiations.

Responding to Change over Following a Plan

For teams to create products that will please customers and provide business value, teams must respond to change. Industry data shows that over "60 percent of product or project requirements change during the development of software". One may argue that customers rarely know what they want (requirement churn) until they see the working software. If customers do not see the working software until the end of a project, it is too late to incorporate their feedback.

Exercise A.5 Manifesto that makes you go hmmm – You may recall the song "Things That Make You Go Hmmm..." from C&C Music Factory. However, read the following eight statements inspired by Cockburn and Highsmith (2002) and let us see if they make you go hmmm.

1. Can we have a successful agile team by delivering individuals and interactions with less emphasis on processes and tools?
2. Can we have a successful agile team by delivering processes and tools with less emphasis on individuals and interactions?
3. Can we have a successful agile team by delivering working software with less emphasis on comprehensive documentation?
4. Can we have a successful agile team by delivering comprehensive documentation with less emphasis on working software?
5. Can we have a successful agile team by delivering customer collaboration with less emphasis on contract negotiation?
6. Can we have a successful agile team by delivering contract negotiation with less emphasis on customer collaboration?
7. Can we have a successful agile team by delivering responding to change with less emphasis on following a plan?
8. Can we have a successful agile team by delivering following a plan with less emphasis on responding to change?

Answer: No right or wrong answers.

A.4 The 12 Principles of Agile Software

According to Kent Beck (2000), the Agile Software Development Manifesto is based on 12 principles of agile software. These values are not just something the creators of the Agile Software Development Manifesto intended to give lip service to and then forget. They are working values. Each individual agile methodology approaches these values in a slightly different manner, but all these methodologies have specific processes and practices that foster one or more of the following principles:

1. Our highest priority is to satisfy the customer through early and continuous delivery of valuable software.
2. Welcome changing requirements, even late in development. Agile processes harness change for the customer's competitive advantage.
3. We deliver working software frequently, from a couple of weeks to a couple of months, with a preference to the shorter timescale.

4. Businesspeople and developers must work together daily throughout the project.
5. We build projects around motivated individuals. We give them the environment and support they need and trust them to get the job done.
6. The most efficient and effective method of conveying information to and within a development team is face-to-face conversation.
7. Working software is the primary measure of progress.
8. Agile processes promote sustainable development. The sponsors, developers, and users should be able to maintain a constant pace indefinitely.
9. Continuous attention to technical excellence and good design enhances agility.
10. Simplicity – the art of maximizing the amount of work not done – is essential.
11. The best architectures, requirements, and designs emerge from self-organizing teams.
12. At regular intervals, the team reflects on how to become more effective and then tunes and adjusts its behavior accordingly.

To understand the underlying values and practical applications of the 12 principles of agile software, review the summary in Table A.6.

Table A.6 12 Principles of Agile Software

Name	Value	Principle	Practices
Our highest priority is to satisfy the customer through early and continuous delivery of valuable software.	Commitment Feedback	Satisfy the customer	Product backlog Whole team Incremental deployment Small releases Frequent delivery
Deliver working software frequently, from a couple of weeks to a couple of months, with a preference to the shorter timescale.	Focus Commitment	Frequent delivery	Incremental deployment Small releases Sprint review Definition of done Acceptance tests
Working software is the primary measure of progress.	Commitment Feedback	Working software	Incremental deployment Small releases Definition of done Acceptance tests
Welcome changing requirements, even late in development. Agile processes harness change for the customer's competitive advantage.	Openness Commitment Focus	Embrace change	Sprint planning Planning game Product backlog Customer involvement
Business people and developers must work together daily throughout the project.	Focus Commitment	Cross-functional collaboration	Real customer Involvement Whole team Osmotic communication Daily Scrum
Build projects around motivated individuals. Give them the environment and support they need, and trust them to get the job done.	Commitment Courage	Support and trust	Servant leadership Motivation

(Continued)

Table A.6 (Continued)   12 Principles of Agile Software

Name	Value	Principle	Practices
The most efficient and effective method of conveying information to and within a development team is face-to-face conversation.	Communication Openness	Face-to-face conversation	Osmotic communication Servant leadership
The best architectures, requirements, and designs emerge from self-organizing teams.	Simplicity Feedback Courage	Self-organization	Test-driven development Refactoring Osmotic communication Servant leadership
Continuous attention to technical excellence and good design enhances agility.	Courage Simplicity Focus	Technical excellence	Testing Sprint retrospective Pair programming Test-driven development Refactoring
Agile processes promote sustainable development. The sponsors, developers, and users should be able to maintain a constant pace indefinitely.	Commitment Communication	Sustainable pace	Real customer involvement Motivation
Simplicity – the art of maximizing the amount of work not done – is essential.	Focus Simplicity	Keep it simple	Product backlog Refactoring Seeing waste
At regular intervals, the team reflects on how to become more effective, then tunes and adjusts its behavior accordingly.	Commitment	Inspect and adapt	Sprint retrospective Root-cause Analysis Seeing waste Value stream mapping

It was difficult for the 17 people back in Utah to agree upon a detailed description of the values. This is because different backgrounds and philosophies come into play. But, when all was said and done, it was their hope that the Agile Software Development Manifesto and supporting values would give you enough information to build your own agile work habits on any level.

The Agile Software Development Manifesto and the 12 principles of agile software were written almost 20 years ago. Some years ago, Laurie Williams (2012) conducted two surveys at North Carolina State University to weigh the community's view of the principles and use of the associated practices. The findings were published in an ACM article (2012), "What Agile Teams Think of Agile Principles." It turned out that 11 of the 12 principles had a mean score of 4.1 out of 5 or higher, indicating a high level of support for principles that had been spelled out 10 years earlier.

The authors of the Agile Software Development Manifesto and the original 12 principles defined the essence of the Agile trend that has transformed the software industry over more than a decade. That is, "they nailed it" (Williams, 2012).

Exercise A.6 Align the practices of the twelve principles of agile software with the agile manifesto in Table A.7. Set a marker (X) if the practice has a central part of the principle and values. The four principles are listed next and found in Table A.7 with the matching letters.

A. Individuals and interactions over processes and tools
B. Working software over comprehensive documentation
C. Customer collaboration over contract negotiation
D. Responding to change over following a plan

Table A.7   12 Principles of Agile Software

The 12 Principles of Agile Software	Manifesto			
	A	B	C	D
1. Our highest priority is to satisfy the customer through early and continuous delivery of valuable software.				
2. Deliver working software frequently, from a couple of weeks to a couple of months, with a preference to the shorter timescale.				
3. Working software is the primary measure of progress.				
4. Welcome changing requirements, even late in development. Agile processes harness change for the customer's competitive advantage.				
5. Business people and developers must work together daily throughout the project.				
6. Build projects around motivated individuals. Give them the environment and support they need, and trust them to get the job done.				
7. The most efficient and effective method of conveying information to and within a development team is face-to-face conversation.				
8. The best architectures, requirements, and designs emerge from self-organizing teams.				
9. Continuous attention to technical excellence and good design enhances agility.				
10. Agile processes promote sustainable development. The sponsors, developers, and users should be able to maintain a constant pace indefinitely.				
11. Simplicity – the art of maximizing the amount of work not done – is essential.				
12. At regular intervals, the team reflects on how to become more effective and then tunes and adjusts its behavior accordingly.				

Answers: 1B, 2B, 3B, 4D, 5C, 6A, 7A, 8A, 9C, 10C, 11C, and 12A

A.5 Declaration of Interdependence for Modern Management

In 2005, a group headed by Alistair Cockburn and Jim Highsmith wrote an addendum for the principles – the Declaration of Interdependence for Modern Management – to guide software project management according to agile development methods. The group, not wanting to coin a new buzzword, instead worked out six rules of operation.

"The sentences were formed as two clauses: We accomplish X — by doing Y. That is, Y is what you can see us do, and the reason we all care about that is because we're trying to set up X".

The Declaration of Interdependence for Modern Management is as follows:

We …

- Increase Return on Investment by — making continuous flow of value our focus.
- Deliver reliable results by — engaging customers in frequent interactions and shared ownership.
- Expect uncertainty and manage it through — iterations, anticipation, and adaptation.
- Unleash creativity and innovation by — recognizing that individuals are the ultimate source of value and creating an environment where they can make a difference.
- Boost performance through — group accountability for results and shared responsibility for team effectiveness.
- Improve effectiveness and reliability through situational-specific strategies, processes and practices.

(Written in 2005 by David Anderson, Sanjiv Augustine, Christopher Avery, Alistair Cockburn, Mike Cohn, Doug DeCarlo, Donna Fitzgerald, Jim Highsmith, Ole Jepsen, Lowell Lindstrom, Todd Little, Kent McDonald, Pollyanna Pixton, Preston Smith, and Robert Wysocki)

Exercise A.7 Know the terminology – List the name of the term described: "a document created in 2001 that lays out the guiding principles of agile."

_____

_____

_____

_____

_____

Answer: Agile Software Development Manifesto

The Declaration of Interdependence for Modern Management is summarized in Table A.8 to demonstrate what is accomplished and how it is accomplished.

"One of the issues with the declaration of interdependence is that it may sound platitudes".

Table A.8 The Declaration of Interdependence for Modern Management

Accomplish This	By/Through This	And
Increased ROI	Focusing on "flow of value" (e.g., not "tracking effort")	Continuous (one-piece) flow, preferably
Reliable results	Engaging customers in frequent interactions	Shared ownership
Unleash creativity and innovation	Recognizing individual human beings as the ultimate source of value	Creation of an environment where individual people can make a difference
Manage uncertainty	Iterations, anticipation, and adaption	Anticipation and adaptation (i.e., think ahead, plan, iterate, deliver, reflect, adapt)
Improve effectiveness and reliability	Situational-specific strategies, processes and practices (i.e., no one answers, folks just get used to it)	
Boost performance	Group accountability for results (i.e., the whole group is singly accountable, no in-team blame)	Shared responsibility for team effectiveness

As it only identifies causes and effects, no bad guys, the application of the Declaration of Interdependence for Modern Management is to improve agile software development as a default mode of management and is appropriate for agile at any level.

Exercise A.8 Align the Declaration of Interdependence (DOI) with the 12 principles of agile software and with the Agile Manifesto in Table A.9. Set a marker (X) where the DOI aligns with the principles and manifesto.

Table A.9 DOI, 12 Principles, and Agile Manifesto

DOI	12 Principles (1–12)	Agile Manifesto (A–D)
Q. Increased ROI		
W. Reliable results		
E. Unleash creativity and innovation		
R. Manage uncertainty		
T. Improve effectiveness and reliability		
Y. Boost performance		

Answers: Q1B, W5C, E9C, R4D, T6A, and Y12A

Figure A.2 demonstrates the evolution of the Agile Manifesto to date. Please notice that currently the last two editions are not included in the PMI-RMP certification exam.

Figure A.2 Evolution of the Agile Manifesto.

A.6 Agile Practice

Agile practices are all the tools, techniques, and ceremonies agile teams apply to do and be agile. Figure A.3 was developed by Ahmed Sidkey and nicely explains how this chapter fits together and fits in with the concepts from Jim Highsmith on doing agile and being agile. The concepts are if you really want the benefits out of working agile you must be agile, not just do agile. Being agile means embracing the agile value, manifesto, and mindset; that is what this chapter is all about. Doing agile is how agile is applied, all the agile practices. Appendix B is a good example of how agile works in an agile framework – Scrum. To make this right it is important to understand this chapter before moving on to Scrum. Just using Scrum without really understanding agile values, principles, and mindset is just doing agile, which may be enough for some teams/organizations, however, it will never be high performing if participants don't really understand why they are using the various tools and techniques, having the ceremonies and such.

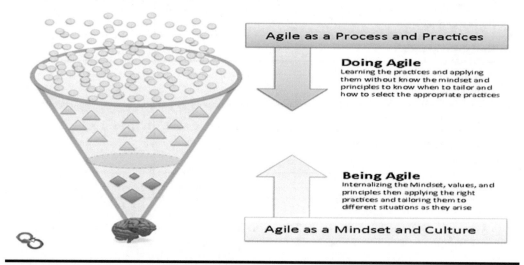

Figure A.3 Doing agile and being agile.

Exercise A.9 Turn to your neighbor – When this chapter has ended, discuss the two or three main points learned with other participants.

A.7 Sample PMI-RMP Exam Questions on Agile Mindset and Principles

This section contains five short exam questions in the PMI-RMP format for you to check your knowledge of the content presented in this chapter and check your readiness for the PMI-RMP exam. The answers will be provided in boldface following the questions section. If you make mistakes, you should go back and learn why mistakes were made. Do not learn the questions and answers; learn the content.

A.7.1 Questions

1 Identify the incorrect agile principle and its implications.
   A. Businesspeople and developers must work together daily throughout the project: it is mandatory for the stakeholders and the team to meet and converse daily.
   B. Continuous attention to technical excellence and good design enhances agility: it keeps the software maintainable.
   C. The best architectures, requirements, and designs emerge from self-organizing teams: self-organizing teams have a higher level of ownership in the designs they create.
   D. Deliver working software frequently: this ensures timely feedback that can be incorporated early in the product development process.

2 What agile concept is closely related to value stream mapping?
   A. Maximize business value
   B. Eliminate waste
   C. Incremental integration
   D. Minimize resource usage

3 The Agile Manifesto value "customer collaboration over contract negotia-tion" means that:
   A. Agile approaches encourage you not to focus too much on negotiating contracts, since most vendors are just out for themselves anyway.
   B. Agile approaches focus on what we are trying to build with our ven-dors rather than debating the details of contract terms.
   C. Agile approaches prefer not to use contracts, unless absolutely neces-sary, because they hamper our ability to respond to change requests.
   D. Agile approaches recommend that you only collaborate with vendors who are using agile processes themselves.

4 What is the relationship between the Agile Software Development Manifesto and the 12 principles of agile software?
   A. The 12 principles of agile software are the working values of the manifesto.
   B. They are written by the same people.
   C. The Agile Software Development Manifesto is voluntary to use, while the 12 principles of agile software are mandatory for agile teams.
   D. They are not related.

5 In which practice would you experience simplicity as described in the 12 principles of agile software?
   A. Test-driven development
   B. Refactoring
   C. Osmotic communication
   D. Seeing waste

A.7.2 Answers

1 Identify the incorrect agile principle and its implications.

A. **Businesspeople and developers must work together daily throughout the project: it is mandatory for the stakeholders and the team to meet and converse daily.**

B. Continuous attention to technical excellence and good design enhances agility: it keeps the software maintainable.

C. The best architectures, requirements, and designs emerge from self-organizing teams: self-organizing teams have a higher level of ownership in the designs they create.

D. Deliver working software frequently: this ensures timely feedback that can be incorporated early in the product development process.

Explanation: Option A is correct as this is an incorrect implication. It is not mandatory for stakeholders and team to meet. Also, the meeting between stakeholders and team are conducted by the product owner representing the team. Options B, C, and D are all wrong. These are correct understandings of the 12 principles.

2 What agile concept is closely related to value stream mapping?

A. Maximize business value

B. **Eliminate waste**

C. Incremental integration

D. Minimize resource usage

Explanation: Eliminate waste is closely related to value stream mapping, while the other options are irrelevant or made up in this case.

3 The Agile Manifesto value "customer collaboration over contract negotiation" means that:

A. Agile approaches encourage you not to focus too much on negotiating contracts, since most vendors are just out for themselves anyway.

B. **Agile approaches focus on what we are trying to build with our vendors, rather than debating the details of contract terms.**

C. Agile approaches prefer not to use contracts, unless absolutely necessary, because they hamper our ability to respond to change requests.

D. Agile approaches recommend that you only collaborate with vendors who are using agile processes themselves.

Explanation: The Agile Manifesto value "customer collaboration over contract negotiation" means that Agile approaches focus on what we are trying to build with our vendors, rather than debating the details of contract terms (B). Trying not to focus too much on negotiating contracts (A), not to use contracts (C), and only collaborate with vendors (D) are all wrong.

4 What is the relationship between the Agile Software Development Manifesto and the 12 principles of agile software?

A. **The 12 principles of agile software are the working values of the manifesto.**

B. They are written by the same people.

C. The Agile Software Development Manifesto is voluntary to use, while the 12 principles of agile software are mandatory for agile teams.

D. They are not related.

Explanations: Option A is correct. Option B is also correct, however, option A is more precise. Option C is wrong. It is not mandatory. Option D is wrong as they are related.

5 In which practice would you experience simplicity as described in the 12 principles of agile software?

A. Test-driven development

B. Refactoring

C. Osmotic communication

D. **Seeing waste**

Explanations: Options A, B, and C are all wrong. They are all agile practices but not necessarily related to simplicity. Option D is correct as seeing waste is a lean practice with emphasis on simplicity.

Appendix B: Scrum and Continuous Risk Management in Scrum

This chapter introduces agile frameworks before going into detail about Scrum. After Scrum has been described, the closing section of this chapter explains how risk management is conducted in Scrum. Make sure that you have read Appendix A before reading this chapter as it provides the background information you need to obtain maximum value out of this chapter.

Tip: Scrum uses the term "sprint"; the agnostic agile term is "iteration." They have the same meaning.

Exercise B.1 Think it, ink it – It is time to read about Scrum and risk management in Scrum. What do you already know? Think about it, then write it down.

_____

_____

_____

_____

_____

Answer: No right or wrong answers.

B.1 Agile Frameworks and Terminology

We can trace the history and influences of agile frameworks and terminology back to the early 1900s with Walter Shewhart's Plan–Do–Study–Act. By the mid-1900s, his work was modified by the likes of Edward Deming, SPC, TQM, Toyota Production System (continuous improvements, respect for people, long-term philosophy, develop the right process, develop your people and partners, and continuously solve root problems); and Peter Drucker, knowledge worker. The late 1900s saw the rise of Womack and Jones, *Lean Thinking*; Eli Goldratt, *Theory of Constraints*; Tom Gilb, Evo; and the Toyota Way.

The evolution of the agile methodologies started in the early 1990s with methods such as Crystal Methods, Lean Software Development, and Dynamic Software Development Method (DSDM). In the mid-1990s, agile methodologies of Feature Driven Development (FDD), Extreme Programming (XP), and Adaptive Software Development (ASD) saw the light of day. In early 2001, the Manifesto for Agile Software Development was developed, Scrum in 2002, and the Declaration of Interdependence in 2005. Frameworks, terminology, and processes that are based on the Agile Manifesto are called agile methodologies or agile methods. Agile methodology is an umbrella term, as illustrated in Figure B.1, in which the concept encompasses many different new lightweight software development methodologies.

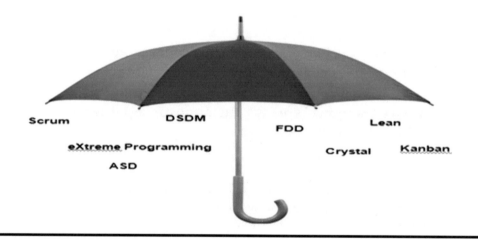

Figure B.1   Agile methodologies.

As opposed to heavyweight plan-driven processes, these new methodologies are lightweight, short cycled, less wasteful, and focus more on the human aspect in software development. Agile methods are characterized by iterative and incremental development, and promote frequent delivery of product features that are prioritized in consultation with the customers, aiming to deliver business value in each iteration. Agile methods address small, collocated, dedicated, and highly collaborative teams. In 2021 "The State of Agile" survey had Scrum as the most widely adopted agile method, which has been the case for years with adoption rates above 80%.

Some of the methods and methodologists that contributed to defining the agile frameworks are

- Extreme Programming (Beck, 1999, 2000)
- Crystal Methods (Cockburn, 2002)

- Adaptive Systems Development Method (J. A. Highsmith, 2000)
- Dynamic Systems Development Method (Stapleton, 1997)
- Pragmatic Programming (Hunt and Thomas, 2000)
- Scrum (Schwaber and Beedle, 2002)
- Open Unified Process
- Other practitioners and methodologists

The agile methodologists are illustrated in Figure B.2 as an agile timeline from the early waterfall approaches to the agile methods of today.

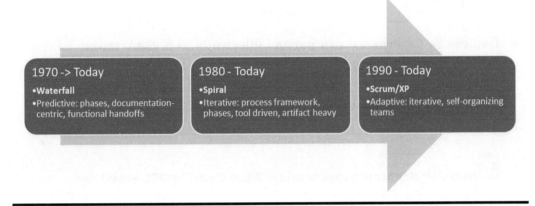

Figure B.2   Agile timeline.

B.2 Scrum

The origins of Scrum are found in writings by Takeuchi and Nonaka (Sutherland et al., 2006). In rugby, a scrum refers to the manner of restarting the game after a minor infraction; reflective of the way Ken Schwaber started his company. A later Scrum champion, Jeff Sutherland worked at the same time on a similar concept. In 2001, Ken Schwaber and Mike Beedle wrote the book *Agile Software Development with Scrum*, which may be considered as the official start of Scrum as we know it today.

Scrum is a simple approach or method. It contains five values and six principle that guide behavior and explain the why. The what is explained with three roles, four ceremonies, and some artifacts. The why and what can be traced back to the agile thinking of Appendix A.

> **Exercise B.2 Explain how Scrum works using the following terms: product owner, Scrum master, team, sprint planning, sprint review, daily standup, sprint retrospective, sprint backlog, product backlog, vision statement, transparency, and business value.**

_____

_____

_____

_____

_____

Answers: See Figure B.6 later in Appendix.

The five Scrum values (FORCC – not necessarily in any order) are

- Focus
- Openness
- Respect
- Commitment
- Courage

The five Scrum values address the human aspect of the method that are not directly addressed by the Scrum processes, ceremonies, and roles. Scrum values provide a

> framework for how we can interact effectively as a team, at the human level. If a team is aware and adhering to the Scrum values, then many of the interpersonal problems can be identified and solutions for various human issues can be addressed.

(Srinivasan, 2012)

Exercise B.3 Scrum mnemonic – What does C-FORC stand for?

_____

_____

_____

_____

_____

Answers: Commitment, Focus, Openness, Respect, and Courage

Table B.1 contains an overview of the Scrum values and possible behavior associated with the Scrum values.

Table B.1   Scrum Values

Scrum Value	Behavior
Focus	Have a clear role and clear goals within that role. Few things at a time.
Openness	Be open about the work, the progress, the learning, and the problems. To collaborate across disciplines and skills, also sharing feedback and learning from one another.
Courage	To trust the Scrum process to guide the work needed to satisfy the requirements of the product. Not to fear to raise impediments daily.
Commitment	Willing to create realistic goals and stick to them. Be present at the meetings.
Respect	Harmony is created by each role syncing and thereby creating a development rhythm as the project progresses. Individuals are shaped by their background and their experiences. It is important to accept the different people who comprise a team.

The six Scrum principles are the core guidelines for applying the Scrum framework and should be "mandatory" to be applied in all Scrum projects. Note that not all Scrum frameworks do include these six Scrum principles. The Scrum principles are illustrated Table B.2.

Table B.2   Scrum Principles

Principle	Description
Empirical process control	In Scrum, decisions are made based on observation and experimentation rather than on detailed upfront planning. Empirical process control relies on the three main ideas of transparency, inspection, and adaptation.
Self-organization	Scrum believes that employees are self-motivated and seek to accept greater responsibility.
Collaboration	Collaboration in Scrum refers to the team working together and interfacing with stakeholders to create and validate the deliverables of the project to meet the goals outlined in the project vision.
Value-based prioritization	The Scrum framework is driven by the goal of delivering maximum business value in a minimum time span.
Time-boxing	Time-boxing is maximum time for a ceremony.
Iterative development	Iterative (spiral model) development of deliverables.

Source: Adapted from the *SBOK Guide*, Third Edition.

The Scrum principle of empirical process control is based upon the three pillars of visibility, inspection, and adaptation, as illustrated in Table B.3.

The Scrum principle of empirical process control involves visibility/transparency, which is a concept relevant for meetings/ceremonies, artifacts, and

Table B.3   Empirical Process Control

Empirical Process Control	Explanation
Visibility/transparency	Visible outcome/artifacts/ceremonies
Inspection	Timely checks Deviations or differences
Adaptation	Adjusting the learning process/artifacts

for the information radiator, as illustrated in Figure B.3. Visibility or transparency is a major benefit of running Scrum. It makes visible how most roles are doing, the status of various elements ranging from a backlog to work being performed, and in addition information is quickly accessible just by looking at the board in the team space.

Meetings/Ceremonies		Artefacts		Information Radiators
•Sprint Planning •Sprint Review •Sprint Retrospective •Daily stand-up	→	•Product vision statement •Product backlog •Sprint backlog	→	•Burndown chart •Scrumboard

Figure B.3   Scrum transparency.

The second component of the Scrum principle empirical process control is inspection, which includes frequent feedback (that could include develop epic user stories, create prioritized product backlog, and release planning) and final inspection (that might include sprint review), as illustrated in Figure B.4.

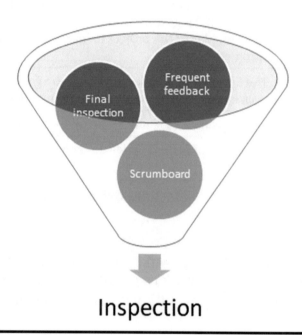

Inspection

Figure B.4   Inspections in Scrum.

The last component of the Scrum principle empirical process control is adaptation, which in Scrum happens along the way as ongoing changes, changes during the ceremonies, and improvements, as illustrated in detail in Figure B.5. Software must be written with future changes in mind, and within adaptation also includes the concept of not repeating yourself or DRY (Don't Repeat Yourself).

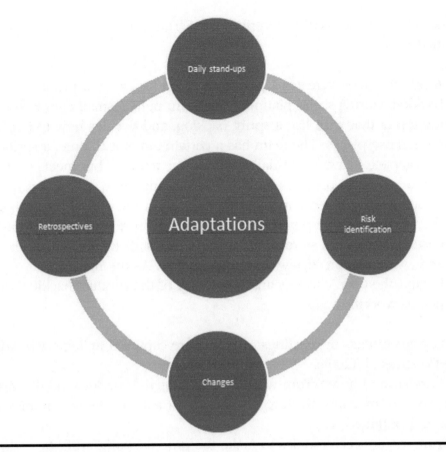

Figure B.5   Adaptations in Scrum.

The following sections will explain Scrum in terms of ceremonies/
meetings, artifacts and roles, the essential components of Scrum. Scrum hangs
all its practices on an iterative, incremental process skeleton, illustrated in
Figure B.6.

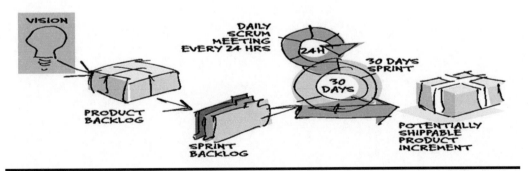

Figure B.6   Scrum flow.

The Agile Alliance (2012) describes the Scrum framework and process succinctly:

> A product owner creates a prioritized wish list called a product backlog. During sprint planning, the team pulls a small chunk from the top of that wish list, a sprint backlog, and decides how to implement those pieces. The team has a certain amount of time, a sprint, to complete its work – usually two to four weeks – but meets each day to assess its progress (daily scrum). Along the way, the Scrum Master keeps the team focused on its goal. At the end of the sprint, the work should be potentially shippable, as in ready to hand to a customer, put on a store shelf, or show to a stakeholder. The sprint ends with a sprint review and retrospective. As the next sprint begins, the team chooses another chunk of the product backlog and begins working again.

The key ceremonies or meetings of Scrum are captured in Table B.4, adapted from Cohen et al. (2003).

To understand how Scrum works, it is essential to understand the various ceremonies or meetings that are mandatory for a start. The ceremonies are explained in Table B.4.

Scrum requires ceremonies to make the process work, artifacts as documentation, and roles to ensure everyone knows what to do and when to do it. The Scrum ceremonies have just been covered, now it is time for the

Table B.4   Scrum Ceremonies/Meetings

Scrum Methodology	Description
Sprint planning	Sprint planning is first attended by the product owner and Scrum team, perhaps facilitated by the Scrum master. The sprint planning meeting is divided into two parts. The first part, the prioritized product backlog, is estimated by the Scrum team and based upon the product owner's prioritization of the Scrum team's commitment to a certain amount (based upon velocity) of work for the next sprint. After the Scrum team's commitment, the product owner leaves the sprint planning. The Scrum team then breaks the work into tasks then estimates them again. This meeting is time-boxed. The common duration is 2 or 4 hours depending on the length of the sprint.
Sprints	The sprint is the period where the Scrum teams works on the tasks in the Sprint backlog. The Sprint may have a duration of 1–6 weeks (time-boxed).
Daily standup	Every day during the sprint the Scrum team has a daily standup meeting. The daily standup is time-boxed for 15 minutes and during the meeting the Scrum team answers three questions. 1. What have I done since the last meeting? 2. What do I plan to do before the next meeting? 3. What impediments or obstacles (if any) am I currently facing?
Sprint review	The sprint review is the big exam for the Scrum team. This ceremony is facilitated by the product owner who may include stakeholders. The purpose of the meeting is to verify work has been completed and has the right quality. If work is approved, it is in theory ready for production, and if rejected, user stories are returned to the product backlog for renewed prioritization. This meeting is time-boxed. The common duration is 2 or 4 hours depending on the length of the sprint.
Sprint retrospective	The sprint retrospective is the last ceremony of the sprint. This is a Scrum team meeting that could be facilitated by the Scrum master. The purpose of the meeting is to reflect on the sprint and make improvements for the next sprint. This meeting is time-boxed. The common duration is 2 hours.
Backlog refinement	The backlog refinement or grooming activity is conducted by the product owner during the sprint. The purpose of this activity is to ensure the product backlog is ready for the next sprint planning. This is where the product owner elucidates new requirements, break epics into User stories, defines acceptance criteria, and such. Some use the term "definition of ready" meaning that the prioritized user stories for the next sprint are ready for sprint planning. This activity is ongoing and not time-boxed.

Scrum artifacts. Many Scrum artifacts do exist, but the most common artifacts are explained in Table B.5.

The Scrum ceremonies are covered in Table B.4, the Scrum artifacts are found in Table B.5, and Table B.6 contains the core Scrum roles. In Scrum, roles do play a major part. Three key roles are the product owner; development team, Scrum team, or team member; and the Scrum master. All roles are mandatory, in theory full time, and each person can only have one role.

Table B.5   Scrum Artifacts

Scrum Artifact	Description
Product backlog	This is the prioritized list of all work, features, and changes that have yet to be made to the system desired by multiple actors, such as customers, marketing and sales, and the project team. The product owner is responsible for maintaining and prioritizing the product backlog. This is the full list of all the considered work to be completed.
Sprint backlog	The sprint backlog is a subset of the product backlog. During the sprint planning the Scrum team and the product owners agree on which user stories should be completed in the next sprint by the Scrum team. This arrangement transfers the user stories from the product backlog to the sprint backlog, and then freeze it as no more changes can be made. The user stories are decomposed by the Scrum team into tasks, which also are placed on the Scrum board as a representation of the sprint backlog.
Burndown chart	A burndown or burnup chart is just a chart to illustrate progress. It could measure story points completed over time. The chart is often found on the Scrum board so it is visible for all.

Table B.6 Core Scrum Roles

Core Scrum Role	Description	Metaphor
Product owner	Ensures business justification Choose release date and content Financially responsible (owns the business case) Accepts or rejects deliverables Envisions the final product Represents the stakeholders "Voice of the customer" Communicates the vision Provides guidance and clarification to the team Tracks and forecasts progress Prioritizes the product backlog Responsible for ensuring epics and user stories are written Drives and measures benefits	The product owner is a CEO
Development team/Scrum team/team members	Delivers the product Self-organizing Cross-functional Demos work results Identifies risks, issues, and impediments Estimates user stories and tasks Decomposes user stories into tasks Selects the sprint goals and specifies work results Determines how it will accomplish the work	Workforce
Scrum master	Liaison between the product owner and the team Servant leader Manages impediments Coach and mentor to all participants Facilitates the Scrum ceremonies, if needed Helps update Scrum artifacts Guides agile principles and mindset Supports the team to become functional and productive Shields the team of external responsibilities Ensures Scrum processes are used properly	The Scrum master is a facilitator, coach, mentor, and bulldozer

Schwaber (2004) uses the expression "pigs" for people occupying one of the three Scrum roles (team, product owner, Scrum master) who have made a commitment and have the authority to fulfill it. The non-core roles were described as "chickens." These terms are found throughout Scrum, for example, "talking chickens" is a well-known agile phrase.

Just to highlight an important aspect of the responsibilities of the core Scrum roles, the product owner is responsible for the team developing the right things, while the Scrum master facilitates the process to ensure the right things also are developed the right way, which is described in Table B.7. We aim for enduring success, but sometimes we may land in one of the other segments for various reasons.

Table B.7 Product Owner and Scrum Master

Right thing	Quick but unsustainable wins	Enduring success
Wrong thing	Slow failure	Fast failure
	Wrong way	**Right way**

Source: Adapted from Richler (2010).

Scrum ceremonies, artifacts and roles are part of an agile environment where a wide range of terms, tools, and techniques are applied with Scrum in a Scrum environment. Some of the most common terms are defined in Table B.8.

Table B.8   Scrum-Related Terms

Scrum-Related Term	Description
Definition of done	The team agrees on, and displays prominently somewhere in the team room, a list of criteria that must be met before a product increment (often a user story) is considered done. Definition of Done is the same for all work completed during a sprint.
Acceptance criteria	Acceptance criteria are unique for individual user stories. These are the criteria that must be fulfilled before the product owner would approve the user story during the sprint review.
Epic	This is the largest type of task. Epics may exist in the product backlog, if prioritization is low. Otherwise, epics would be decomposed into user stories.
User story	A user story is a statement (or a group of statements) that expresses a desired end user functionality. Usually, it is broken down into a sequential block of tasks. User stories are defined in the product backlog and if prioritized moved to the sprint backlog during the sprint planning.
Task	The smallest part of a task. Tasks are found in the sprint backlog.
Persona	Personas help the team better understand users, and their requirements and goals. They are highly detailed fictional characters that represent most users and other stakeholders. Personas are often used with user stories and epics, so it is clear why the user has the stated requirements and how they would prefer to use the solution.
MVP	The smallest collection of features that can be included in a product for customers to consider it functional.
WIP limit	Work in progress limit is a Lean term where the Scrum team can limit work, i.e., "in progress," to reduce multitasking and bottlenecks. The Scrum team may agree on a WIP limit of 1, so they can work on one task in the column on the Scrum board.
Velocity	Velocity is the capacity of the Scrum team, often measured in story points.

Exercise B.4 Scrum methodology and Scrum roles – Who owns what? Mark an X the blanks in Table B.9. Several roles may share one item.

_____

_____

_____

Table B.9   Scrum Methodology and Scrum Roles

	Product Owner	*Development Team*	*Scrum Master*
Product backlog (artifact)			
Sprint retrospective (ceremony)			
Sprint planning ceremony)			
Sprint backlog (artifact)			
Sprint review (ceremony)			
Daily scrum (ceremony)			
Team size			
Sprint length			
Support for distributed teams			
Definition of done			
System criticality			
Process adherence			
Knowledge sharing			
Agile coaching			
Velocity predictions			
Estimates			

Answers: See Table B.10.

Table B.10   Scrum Methodology and Scrum Roles

	Product Owner	*Development Team*	*Scrum Master*
Product backlog (artifact)	X		
Sprint retrospective (ceremony)		X	X
Sprint planning (ceremony)		X	X
Sprint backlog (ceremony)	X	X	
Sprint review (ceremony)	X		
Daily scrum (ceremony)		X	X
Team size		X	
Sprint length	X	X	X
Support for distributed teams	X	X	X
Definition of done (artifact)	X	X	X
System criticality		X	
Process adherence			X
Knowledge sharing		X	X
Agile coaching			X
Velocity predictions		X	
Estimates		X	

Scrum's roles, artifacts, ceremonies, and best practices are immutable. Implementing only parts of Scrum is possible, but the result is not Scrum. Scrum exists only in its entirety and functions as well as a container for other techniques, methodologies, and practices.

B.3 Risk Management in Scrum

"If there's no risk on your next project, don't do it" (Demarco et al., 2003).

Agile risk management is integrated into everything the Scrum team does, to maximize business value by reducing risk by guiding the Scrum team do the hard things first and such. The basic problem of software development is risk in terms of the team not completing the work during the sprint, business misunderstood by the product owner, Scrum team produces code that involves a high defect rate, etc. These risks act as a multiplier on the team's estimates, doubling or tripling the amount of time and sprints it takes to finish the prioritized work.

The essence of risk management lies in maximizing the areas where the core Scrum roles have some control over the outcome, while minimizing the areas where the core Scrum roles have absolutely no control over the outcome, and the linkage between effect and cause is hidden from us.

In the 2021 "State of Agile" survey, 49% of all responses stated that they reduce risk by using an agile approach. In Scrum we have evidence of minimizing risks due to the following factors:

■ Flexibility reduces business-environment-related risk
■ Regular feedback reduces expectations-related risk
■ Team ownership reduces estimation risk
■ Transparency reduces non-detection risk
■ Iterative delivery reduces investment risk

Today, risk management is more important than ever before and remains an essential discipline when managing the agile team efforts. The reason for this is that epics, user stories, and tasks, to some degree, are built on assumptions, which is why the likelihood of their results becomes questionable by the product owner. The product owner would then be looking at all the factors that may influence the end results and need to be watched for, and all these factors are included under risk management performed by the core Scrum roles.

Warren Buffet said, "Risk comes from not knowing what you're doing." The challenge is that "the risk of team failure increases greatly over time" (Rasmusson, 2010), which leaves teams to overpromise and underdeliver, which is what we seek to avoid. The process of risk management in agile environments such as Scrum includes the following steps, as illustrated in Figure B.7.

Figure B.7   The process of agile risk management.

The first step is Identify, which in Scrum involves identification of risk and may be conducted during any Scrum ceremony. Table B.11 has the overview by combining the Scrum ceremonies and the process of risk management.

Table B.11   Risk Management Activities during Scrum Ceremonies

Agile Process	*Identify*	*Assess*	*Respond*	*Respond*	*Respond*	*Review*
Risk management ceremonies	Identification	Assessment	Create response	Implement response	Risk approval	
Sprint planning	YES	YES	YES	NO	NO	
Daily scrum	(YES)	(YES)	(YES)			
Sprint review	(YES)	(YES)	(YES)			
Sprint retrospective					YES	YES
During the sprint				YES		

Note: *YES* means that it should be done every time. *(YES)* means it is possible, if needed.

An alternative approach to the process discussed Figure B.7 is aligning the risk management activities with the PDCA cycle, as shown in Table B.12.

Table B.12   Risk Management Activities Aligned with the PDCA Cycle

PDCA Cycle	Risk Activity
Plan	Identify
Do	Assess
Check	Review
Act	Respond

During the Identify step, the core Scrum team identifies risks, which mostly are completed during the sprint planning and sometimes during daily Scrum and sprint review, as shown in Table B.11. Keep in mind that in Scrum risk identification happens on multiple levels, these being

- Product vision
- Product roadmap
- Release planning
- Sprint planning
- Daily standup

The tools and techniques for risk identification applied by the core Scrum roles varies, however, the most common tools and techniques are described in Table B.13.

Table B.13 Technique for Risk Identification

Technique	Description	Perspective
Brainstorming	Brainstorming is a group-based or individually performed creative technique, through which efforts are made to find a conclusion to a specific problem by gathering a list of ideas spontaneously contributed by all the member(s) participating in the technique.	Future
Brainwriting	A written form of brainstorming, where each participant writes one risk on a piece of paper before passing it on.	Future
Interviews	One-on-one interviews on risk identification.	Current
Root-cause	See PMBOK 6. edition, page 292 for details	Current
Delphi	The original version of the Delphi method was first applied in the 1960s. The concept was to ask a panel of experts to identify risks. The experts were all placed in different isolated locations so that they were unable to communicate with one another. This helped in reducing the influence of one expert's views on the others' responses.	Current
Delphi, wideband	The wideband Delphi is a process that a team can use to identify risks. The project manager chooses an estimation team and gains consensus from that team on the results. Wideband Delphi is a repeatable process, because it consists of a straightforward set of steps that can be performed the same way each time.	Current
SWOT analysis	See PMBOK 6. edition, page 415 for details	Current
Pre-mortem	The team imagines that a project or organization has failed or succeed, and then works backward to determine what potentially could lead to the success or failure of the project or organization.	Current
Change of perspective; Edward de Bono's six thinking hats	White hat – factual view of the subject of discussion Red hat – emotional, allows one's emotions to run wild Black hat – finds negative aspects and risks (pessimist) Yellow hat – discovers positive aspects (optimist) Green hat – creative, searches for alternatives (usual brainstorming) Blue hat – control and organization of the thinking process Sequence of methods for the identification of risks and opportunities: Clarification of the problem	Current

(Continued)

Table B.13 (Continued)   Technique for Risk Identification

Technique	Description	Perspective
	Putting on the white hat to collect facts and figures relevant to the topic (flipchart, Post-its on pin wall) Similarly, putting on all hats, one at a time, to think accordingly about the risks, for instance, putting on the black hat to identify risks	
Document-centric techniques	Investigate documentation for risks, e.g., software requirements, contracts, legacies, and other such documentations	Past
Survey techniques	Interviews, qualitative and quantitative surveys	Current
Analogy techniques	The basis of the analogy technique is to describe (in terms of several variables), the project for which the risk identification is to be made, and then to use this description to find other similar projects that have already been completed	Past
Observation techniques	Field observation and apprenticing	Current
Storyboarding/ prototypes	Build a prototype or create a storyboard from which risks can be derived	Current
Focus groups or facilitation	Structured interviews of several participants in a facilitated manner	Current
Artifact risk identification	Risk identification based upon solid artifacts, e.g., former car model or item sold	Past
Crawford slip method	Step 1: Explain the process Step 2: Define the terms Step 3: Ground rules Step 4: Pass out the sticky notes before asking the question Step 5: Ask the question Step 6: Evaluate your answers Step 7: Stick the answers on the wall and arrange these responses into categories Step 8: Go through the categories Step 9: Next steps	Current
My worst nightmare	Draw your worst risk and explain it to your team	Current

Once the risks are identified, the next step is for the core Scrum roles to Assess, or make some assessment on how to proceed with the risks. The assessment is a qualitative risk analysis. All risks are assessed in terms of probability and impact. The assessment is then documented by the Scrum team on the Scrum board/information radiator, which rates probability and impacts from high to low or from 1 to 5. It offers a good view of the identified risks for all team members. The process in agile can also be conducted on user stories where each story has an impact and probability of high, medium, or low, as illustrated in Table B.14.

Table B.14   Risk Ratings

High Impact	Medium Impact	Low Impact
User story 1 User story 5 User story 6	User story 2 User story 7	User story 3 User story 4 User story 8 User story 9

Some Scrum teams divide the Assess step into two smaller steps: one qualitative, the other quantitative. The first part was the qualitative assessment just described (Pandian, 2006), which some Scrum teams supplement with a risk screening, top ten list, internal–external risk distribution, or time analysis.

The second part of the Assess step is the quantitative risk assessment, which can be supported by calculations and simulations to perform a sensitivity analysis, Monte Carlo simulations, failure mode effect analyses, case-effect diagrams, affinity diagrams, or decision tree analysis. This assessment may be combined with risk spikes, which are covered later in this chapter.

The next step is the Respond step, which can be created at any time (see Table B.11) and is often implemented anytime during the sprint. The risk responses may differ depending on whether the risk is positive or negative. The common risk responses are listed in Table B.15.

Table B.15   Risk Responses

Negative Risk Response	Description	Positive Risk Response
Escalate	Escalate the risk to outside the team	Escalate
Avoid	Eliminate the threat of a risk by eliminating the cause or ensure it will occur	Exploit
Accept	Do nothing or create a contingency plan	Accept
Transfer	Assign the risk to someone else by subcontracting or buying insurance, or sharing it with another team	Share
Mitigate	Reduce or increase probability or impact of occurrence	Enhance

Michele Sliger and Stacy Broderick (2008) have in their book *The Software Project Managers Bridge to Agility* a slightly different view on the risk response planning (described in Table B.16). The terms are similar, but we may see major changes in the process.

Table B.16   Risk Response Planning

Traditional	Agile
One or more people are assigned to develop strategies to …	The team brainstorms strategies to …
Avoid	Avoid
Mitigate	Mitigate
Plan contingency	Contain
Accept	Evade

The use of negative risk responses depends on the impact and probability, where a high probability and high impact should be handled with the avoid responses, while the low impact and low probability risks can be evaded/ accepted, as shown in Table B.17 (based on work by Geiger, 2007).

Table B.17   Negative Risk Response Strategies

High Impact	Transfer	Avoid
Low Impact	Accept	Mitigate
	Low Probability	High Probability

An alternative approach to the negative risk response strategies is illustrated in Table B.18 (from Griffiths, 2014). It highlights the importance of selecting the right risk response strategy to retain business value.

Table B.18   Negative Risk Response Strategies

Business Value Retained	Avoid	Mitigate	Transfer	Accept
	Best			Worst

A similar alternative to handling the relationship between risk and value is presented in Table B.19 where it is clear to start with high risk and high value, with low risk and low value coming last.

Table B.19   Risk and Value: What to Do

High Risk	Avoid	Do first
Low Risk	Do last	Do second
	Low Value	**High Value**

The following sections cover the two artefacts, the risk adjusted backlog and the risk burndown chart and the essential risk activity of using risk spikes.

Risk-Adjusted Product Backlog

The main principle behind a risk-adjusted product backlog is to have a smart blend of value-generating business features and risk-reduction actions. This means the risk-adjusted backlog equals features and risks. The first step is to develop a prioritized list of user stories or features using, for example, MoSCoW, as shown in Table B.20. This is part of the backlog refinement activity conducted by the product owner.

Table B.20   Risk-Adjusted Backlog

Must Have	*Must Have*	*Must Have*	*Should Have*	*Should Have*	*Could Have*	*Could Have*
User story	User story 1	User story 3	User story 2	User story 6	User story 4	User story 5
ROI	$500	$800	$500	$400	$100	$700
Probability	20%	20%	20%	20%	10%	10%
Impact	$200	$200	$300	$300	$50	$400
Story value	$460	$760	$440	$340	$95	$660

During the next step, return on investment (ROI) or similar financial calculation is calculated for each of the user stories. Next, the risk probability and risk impact to each user story is included in the risk-adjusted product backlog. Last, the product owner calculates the story value. The result is that user story 3 now takes the first spot from user story 1 as the story value is higher than user story 1. User story 5 and user story 4 also change places. Keep in mind that must have, should have, and could have cannot change places, as it is the prioritization of the business value, which now has been adjusted in terms of risk measured toward return on investment (ROI) in this example.

The product backlog is used for managing changes, while the adjusted backlog helps the team to tie risk to value.

Risk Burndown Chart

A risk burndown or burnup chart is where the risk to project success associated with each story point or feature is displayed, as shown in Figure B.8. The project risk will burn down and decrease as the project progresses and the functionality is completed. The chart demonstrates how the risk reduces as the project proceeds. The risk exposed is on the Y-axis and the number of iterations is on the X-axis. Risk burndown charts are easy to create and make communication within the Scrum team a lot easier and can be found on the information radiator.

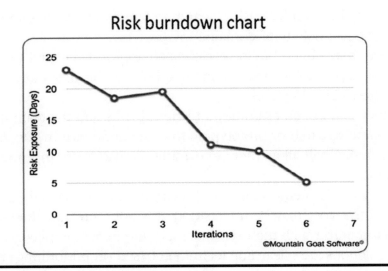

Figure B.8 Risk burndown chart (Cohn, 2012).

Risk-Based Spikes

In agile, a spike is like a fork in the road. The team or customer, or both, may be uncertain of the way ahead, often a user story that cannot be estimated. Spikes often become a technical, architectural, and development investigation between sprints to research an answer to a problem. Risk-based spikes underlay the concept of failing fast, as spikes are quickly tested, and resolution is drawn. This means that risk-based spikes are quick time-boxed experiences used to help the team answer a question and determine a path forward.

"Architectural spike" is a term that comes from the Extreme Programming (XP) practice. The goal is to reduce the risk of a technical problem or increase the reliability of a user story's estimate. The duration and objective(s) of a spike should be agreed between the product owner and team before the start. A spike is an experiment that allows developers to learn just enough about the unknown elements in a user story. The concept of the spike is often used in conjunction with an architectural issue. An architectural spike is a thin slice of the entire application built for the purpose of determining and evaluating a potential architecture. Often, a spike is a quick and dirty implementation, a prototype that will be thrown away. Sometimes architectural spikes are the first iterations, sprint zero to prove a technological approach.

Why Use Risk-Based Spikes?

Spikes, another invention of XP, is a special type of story used to drive out risk and uncertainty in a user story or other project facet. Spikes may be used for several reasons:

■ Spikes may be used for basic research to familiarize the team with an innovative technology of domain.

■ The story may be too big to be estimated appropriately and the team may use a spike to analyze the implied behavior so they can split the story into estimable pieces.

■ The story may contain significant technical risks and the team may have to do some research or prototyping to gain confidence in a technological approach that will allow them to commit the user story to some future time box.

■ The story may contain significant functional risk, in that although the intent of the story may be understood, it is not clear how the system needs to interact with the user to achieve the benefit implied.

■ Spike solutions are a learning technique based on performing small, concrete experiments.

■ If something does not work as expected, is it because your understanding of the technology is wrong? Is it due to an unseen interaction with the production code or test framework? Standalone spikes eliminate this uncertainty.

■ For stories that you cannot estimate accurately, an alternative to scheduling a spike story is to provide a high estimate. This is risky, because some stories will take longer than your highest estimate, and some may not be possible at all.

■ Another option is to research problems by reading about the underlying theory and finding code snippets in books or online. This is often an effective way to get started on a spike, but the best way to really understand what's going on is to create your own spike.

The former United States secretary of defense, Donald Rumsfeld, gave a talk in 2002 to the Department of Defense, which later was called the "known knowns," which are shown in Table B.21 as the Rumsfeld matrix. Some risks are identified as risks that the Scrum team knows (known knowns). Other risks are the ones the Scrum team knows that the Scrum team does not know (known unknowns), but the Scrum team gets lucky enough to cover during various activities. However, the Scrum team can be unaware of the fact that the other Scrum team members know the risks (unknown knowns). The challenge is how to manage the risks the Scrum team does not know. Unknown unknowns have some similarities with the black swan theory, which is a metaphor for events that come as a surprise and have a major effect. Risk-based spikes is an investigation of the known unknowns.

Table B.21   The Rumsfeld Matrix

	Level of Observability	
Level of Risk	**Known knowns** (Things we know we know)	**Unknown knowns** (Things we don't know we know)
	Known unknowns (Things we know we don't know)	**Unknown unknowns** (Things we don't know we don't know)

Exercise B.5 Know your keywords – Match the keywords, 1 to 3, to their definitions, A to C.

1. Risk-adjusted backlog
2. Risk burndown chart
3. Risk-based spike
A. Chart where the risk to project's success associated with each feature is displayed
B. Value-generating business features and risk-reduction actions
C. Quick experience used to help the team answer a question and determine a path forward

_____
_____
_____
_____

Answers: 1B, 2A, and 3C

Risk management is an organic component of Scrum and owned by the core Scrum team. The process of risk management in Scrum follows the steps of planning, identifying, qualifying, and quantifying, and ensuring proper actions to deal with the risks. Many of the tools and techniques of tradition project management, such as Monte Carlo simulations and expected monetary value, are like those used in Scrum. They vary in when and how we apply the tools and techniques. In addition, Scrum brings the risk-adjusted backlog, risk burndown chart, and risk-based spikes to the table to create collaboration, coordination, and communication on risk management.

B.4 Sample PMI-RMP Exam Questions on Scrum and Risk Management in Scrum

This section contains five short exam questions in the PMI-RMP format for you to check your knowledge of the content presented in this chapter and to check your readiness for the PMI-RMP exam. The answers will be provided in boldface following in questions section. If you make mistakes, you should go back and learn why mistakes were made. Do not learn the questions and answers, learn the content.

B.4.1 Questions

1 Why does the team put risks in the backlog?
   A. Avoid having to keep separate risk lists
   B. Keep the team focused on risks
   C. Ensure that the risks get worked on in the early iterations
   D. Prevent the team from forgetting about the risks

2 Which of the following is an agile risk strategy?
   A. Accept
   B. Plan contingency
   C. Avoid
   D. Transfer

3 During risk management, the team uses the review process to examine which of the following?
   A. Sprint planning
   B. Sprint review
   C. Sprint retrospective
   D. Daily scrum

4 Which risk-based spikes can be used across all agile projects?
   A. Sensitivity analysis and decision tree analysis
   B. Expected monetary value analysis and simulations
   C. A and B
   D. Qualitative and quantitative measurements

5 What does the risk burndown chart display?
   A. Risk exposed
   B. Number of iterations
   C. Risk assessment
   D. A and B

B.4.2 Answers

1 Why does the team put risks in the backlog?
   A. Avoid having to keep separate risk lists
   B. Keep the team focused on risks
   C. **Ensure that the risks get worked on in the early iterations**
   D. Prevent the team from forgetting about the risks
   Explanation: The team puts risks in the backlog to ensure that they get
   to work on the early iterations (C), and not to avoid having to keep sepa-
   rate risk lists (A), as the product backlog includes the risks. This keeps
   the team focused on risks (B), however, it is not the best of the alternatives nor does it prevent the team from forgetting about the risks (D).

2 Which of the following is an agile risk strategy?
   A. Accept
   B. Plan contingency
   C. **Avoid**
   D. Transfer
   Explanation: Avoid is the only agile strategy (C), while the other options are traditional risk responses.

3 During risk management, the team uses the review process to examine which of the following?
   A. Sprint planning
   B. Sprint review
   C. **Sprint retrospective**
   D. Daily scrum
   Explanation: During risk management, the review process is used by the team to examine the sprint retrospective (C).

4 Which risk-based spikes can be used across all agile projects?
   A. Sensitivity analysis and decision tree analysis
   B. Expected monetary value analysis and simulations
   C. **A and B**
   D. Qualitative and quantitative measurements
   Explanation: Risk-based spikes that can be used across all agile projects are sensitivity analysis and decision tree analysis (A), and expected monetary value analysis and simulations (B), which makes A and B (C) the best choice. Qualitative and quantitative measurements (D) is wrong.

5 What does the risk burndown chart display?

A. Risk exposed

B. Number of iterations

C. Risk assessment

D. **A and B**

Explanation: The risk burndown chart may display risk exposed (A) and number of iterations (B), which makes A and B (D) the best choice. While risk assessment (C) is relevant, it is not the best option for this question.

Appendix C: Hybrid Project and Risk Management

Everything is hybrid these days. In early 2022 one hot topic was hybrid workplaces. Should we work onsite or from home or a hybrid workplace with a couple of days each place. Does this sound familiar to you? If you work in information technology you might also be familiar with this talk. Should the solution be on-premises or in the cloud or a hybrid cloud on-premises solution. It is often not clear which is the better of the solutions.

C.1 Hybrid Project Management

In project and risk management, we have been having the same kind of talks for the last 10 to 20 years. It all started in the 1970s with the development of the waterfall approach by Winston Royce. This approach is the so-called predictive or traditional approach. Years later the predictive approach ran into debate as projects took too long and documentation was perhaps a bit too extensive. At the end of the 1990s, the search for solutions to these predictive impediments led to the emergence of practices that became known as agile. Agile was based upon the spiral development approach developed by Barry Boehm. Agile worked well for some projects for years but not for others. Now it was agile's turn to face various issues, as not two projects are the same. This led to an increased popularity about hybrid project management due to its ability to effectively bridge the predictive and agile approaches.

The *PMBOK Guide* – Sixth Edition came out with the *Agile Practice Guide*, and it was labelled "Open Minds. Multiple Approaches. One Goal," highlighting no single best development approach is available. Project hybrid management combines the techniques and processes of both the predictive and agile approaches to increase the probability of project and organizational success.

Project hybrid management is the concurrent use of traditional and agile methods. When choosing two methodologies, it is important to identify what you like and don't like about them, regularly reevaluate, and adjust. If performed right, hybrid approaches can help realize the benefits and set off the disadvantages of both agile and traditional approaches.

On the other hand, hybridity is a natural phenomenon when adopting some style of project management, because there is an intrinsic need to adapt to the needs of the environment, in which the combination of practices and processes of the agile and traditional approaches is a way of dealing with the trade-off between the need for agility and project control.

There is confusion in industry about what risk management is in a hybrid project environment. Some argue this is driven by the lack of practical understanding of risk management basics and further compounded by confusion on how traditional and agile approaches may be successfully integrated to increase the probability of project and organizational success.

Hybrid is more or less of one of the other. The various opportunities to combine predictive and agile are covered later in this section. The purpose is to create something that really works. This might be easier if deliverables are modularized. The result will be a more robust, flexible process that evolves in response to the situation rather than a well-documented, inflexible process that assumes that all problems are the same. We want to be more agile than the standard predictive approach but less agile than the purely agile approach, so something in between. So, is hybrid just agile not being fully agile, or waterfall not being fully waterfall? I think hybrid agile methods are a reality in most agile implementations. One explanation is that this happens in part because agile adoption has been practitioner-led, leading teams to focus on domains they can influence, mainly the team itself. Areas outside of their control continue to follow more traditional approaches.

We know from PMI research that Hybrid approaches also help reduce complexity, creating clear scope requirements, and maintaining a high level of stakeholder engagement had positive effects on all measures of project success.

Some might argue that we already have this approach with the rise of disciplined agile. Just think about the inception, construction, and transition phases. Is inception and transition predictive with an agile construction phase?

I read a PMI research paper titled "Agile, Traditional, and Hybrid Approaches to Project Success: Is Hybrid a Poor Second Choice? Is Hybrid a Poor Second Choice?" (Gemino, Reich, and Serrador, 2020), and I was in doubt about what to expect. However, results from this international study, including 477 cross-industry projects, indicated that 52% of projects could be categorized as hybrid approaches. A regression analysis using multiple outcome measures indicated substantial explanatory power ($0.21 < R^2 < 0.41$). Analysis suggested that hybrid and agile approaches significantly increase stakeholder success over traditional approaches, while achieving the same budget, time, scope, and quality outcomes. Hybrid approaches were found to be similar in effectiveness to fully agile approaches. That is interesting!

The same PMI research examined "why organizations might move from traditional approaches toward more agile practices, but do not commit wholly to an agile approach", and it was due to these reasons:

- Governance and compliance requirements
- Safety and robustness requirements
- Documentation requirements
- Pre-set budgetary and time requirements
- Managing large, complex projects

So, what do you really do? Mike Griffith (2022), on his PM illustrated website, talks about layering, which includes a horizontal and vertical approach and most variants of hybrid approaches. The horizontal layer implies we do predictive and agile at the same time. That could be high-level predictive planning and governance with agile as a delivery mechanism on the team level. The vertical approach (an agile or predictive approach followed by an agile or predictive approach) is like using predictive and agile in various parts, stages, or phases of a project. It could include upfront predictive planning, agile development, and predictive rollout. Predictive, agile, and predictive again. A friend of mine called the rest of the approaches (largely agile or predictive with agile or predictive components) superficial, meaning applying one approach, let's say predictive, and then using bits and pieces from agile. Again, hybrid project management has many names and approaches, but the bottom line remains the same. We pick and choose what fits the needs of the projects.

To analyze these hybrid approaches in more detail, it comes down to the people, processes, and business environment. People involve conflict management, leadership, team performance, stakeholders, and such, while processes manage all the constraints, that's time, cost, scope, quality, and such, also risk. More on hybrid risk management later in this chapter. Lastly, for the business environment, a common topic here is compliance.

C.2 Hybrid Risk Management

Before attempting hybrid risk management, you need to be comfortable with predictive and agile risk management. Revisit Chapters 5–9 for predictive and Appendices A and B on agile, if in doubt.

First, one approach is the superficial approach (largely agile or predictive with agile or predictive components), meaning selecting one approach and then adding bits and pieces from the other approach. So, let's do predictive risk management with emphasis on the risk management plan, identification of risk, qualitative risk assessment, quantitative assessment, and risk responses in sequence. The findings are documented in the risk register. This is predictive risk management. Let's add a few agile components. Place the risk register on the board (information radiator). After each step or phase, plan a meeting where we look for continuous improvements including risk management practices, like a sprint retrospective in Scrum. Include an agile delivery team and so on. The possible combinations are endless.

Another layering approach is the horizontal approach (combined agile and predictive approaches used simultaneously). One application is an overall predictive risk management approach with upfront identification and analysis combined with the iterative agile approach we know from Scrum. This would combine most of the tools and technique discussed in this book one way or the other. We might have a risk register and a product backlog. The risks managed from the team are documented in the risk register and prioritized in the product backlog. The project may have a major risk workshop followed by daily risk management activities during the sprint. The possible combinations are endless.

The vertical approach (an agile or predictive approach followed by an agile or predictive approach) is where predictive and agile are fully applied but in various steps or phases of the project. The predictive would work for detailed planning and early risk identification, while agile is strong for execution followed by a planned-based rollout. In this situation we might start with a risk management strategy and risk management plan followed by populating a risk register based upon a workshop. During execution the risks from the risk register might be included in the product backlog and prioritized. Risk management activities would then follow a strictly agile format using ceremonies, team ownership, and boards. After execution, the project can return to the risk register, do ongoing risk identification workshops, risk audits, assign new risk owners, and so on. The possible combinations are endless.

A more appropriate approach is perhaps to view risk management as core to the overall project management approach. The possible combinations are endless.

The ways the different approaches deal with these risks are fundamentally different. Therefore, the project manager or PMO should consistently assess, monitor, and manage these risks and assumptions across the different parts and approaches of a project.

Appendix D: PMI Code of Ethics and Professional Conduct

The concept of a professional code of ethics and professional conduct has been common throughout history, as evidenced by the early use of the Hippocratic oath within healthcare. Ethics has been defined as involving the systematic application of morals, rules, standards, or principles to concrete problems. Ethics involves learning what is right or wrong and then doing the right thing.

Aside from the obvious, the reasons for ethical behaviors are many. One is the retention of high-quality employees. Another, according to respected leaders, is that it is a requirement for long-term success and media exposure. Ethics and project management are closely related and are part of the day-to-day project management activities, whether that be dealing with the objectives of the project, stakeholders, risks, or the project team.

We live with the assumption that "the modern day, well-educated and responsible project manager must possess the knowledge and skills to be able to discern and debate ethical issues" (Helgadóttir, 2007). This is where the PMI Code of Ethics and Professional Conduct springs into action.

> Codes of ethics are valuable as they both raise awareness of ethical issues and dilemmas that professionals may potentially face and serve to enhance the public profile of the profession. Furthermore, codes of ethics may provide clarifications about the conduct deemed acceptable in client-professional relationships.

(Davison, 2000)

In general, ethics can be outcome or process oriented. The PMI Code of Ethics and Professional Conduct seems to be inspired by the outcome-oriented virtues in terms of virtue ethics, the mark of the profession and utilitarianism, where we conduct our tasks as project managers or agile

293

team members for the benefit of as many people as possible. The process-oriented ethics of deontology and egoism are at bay while preserving the natural rights of others and being respectful of their duties comes to the fore. Table D.1 illustrates the nature of ethics (Wood-Harper et al., 2010).

Table D.1   Nature of Ethics

Label	Beneficiary	Objective	Good
Deontological	Not considered	Follow the rules	Follow the rules
Individual consequentiality (ethical egoism)	Individual	Maximize good for individual	Happiness well-being, fame, riches
Group consequentiality	Group (social group, organization nation)	Maximize good for group	Survival, autonomy, ascendancy
Utilitarian	Society as a whole	Maximize good for human race or all sentient beings	Life, liberty, standard of living

PMI developed the PMI Code of Ethics and Professional Conduct to provide some guidance to all PMI members and credential holders to adhere to a high standard of ethical behavior. Ethical behavior is important in satisfying basic human needs, as many professionals have a need to work in an ethically sound way. Some academics argue that ethical behavior creates credibility, which can help during the project to make things work. Unethical behavior is a strong force for conflict in projects, while ethical behavior can unite people and help create a strong basis for good project execution.

Ethical behavior is also a robust basis for decision-making. IBM's global CEO study "Leading through Connections 2012" based upon interviews with 1709 CEOs in 64 countries and 18 industries revealed that when it comes to the organizational attributes that engage employees to draw out the best in their workforces, CEOs are most focused on ethics and value. Ethical behavior has a wide range of long-term gains, while the lack of ethical behavior can cause its own wide range of distress for most projects and participants. Table D.2 illustrates how the ethical approaches of different stakeholders affect their decision-making and behavior.

Table D.2   Ethical Approaches of Different Stakeholders

Stakeholder	Ethics	Example
Government	Group consequentiality	Triage rules and other service trade-offs
Clinical Healthcare Service (CHS), eg., hospital	Deontological egoist	Legal compliance and continued funding
Business manager	Egoist group consequentiality	Salary increase and group harmony
Nurse	Deontological	Follow management directives
Client/patient	Egoist	Increase good health

An article by Aiken et al. (2004) titled "Using Codes of Conduct to Resolve Legal Disputes" highlighted another key aspect of the application of code of conducts: court evidence. The customer would expect and state in most types of contracts that the vendor follow best practices and codes of conduct within the industry. If things go bad in the project and in the negotiations following, the project may end up in court, where the code of conduct may be applied against the vendor.

Vision

PMI created a vision for ethical behavior:

> As practitioners of project management, we are committed to doing what is right and honorable. We set high standards for ourselves, and we aspire to meet these standards in all aspects of our lives – at work, at home, and in service to our profession.

This code of ethics and professional conduct describes the expectations that we have of ourselves and our fellow practitioners in the global project management community. It articulates the ideals to which we aspire as well as the behaviors that are mandatory in our professional and volunteer roles.

Purpose

The code of PMI enhances the profession and helps us become better professionals:

> The purpose of this Code is to instill confidence in the project management profession and to help an individual become a better practitioner. We do this by establishing a profession-wide

understanding of appropriate behavior. We believe that the credibility and reputation of the project management profession is shaped by the collective conduct of individual practitioners. We believe that we can advance our profession, both individually and collectively, by embracing this Code of Ethics and Professional Conduct. We also believe that this Code will assist us in making wise decisions, particularly when faced with difficult situations where we may be asked to compromise our integrity or our values. Our hope that this Code of Ethics and Professional Conduct will serve as a catalyst for others to study, deliberate, and write about ethics and values. Further, we hope that this Code will ultimately be used to build upon and evolve our profession.

It would be great if this code could apply to all agile practitioners and professionals in project management, but that is hardly the case, as most outside the PMI world are unfamiliar with this code. This means that the PMI Code of Ethics and Professional Conduct only applies to PMI members and individuals who are not members of PMI but meet one or more of the following criteria (PMI.org):

- Non-members who hold a PMI certification
- Non-members who apply to commence a PMI certification process
- Non-members who serve PMI in a volunteer capacity

Those who do not follow the code miss the opportunity to give something back to the project management profession and improve themselves as practitioners. At a formal level, failure to follow the code may also mean that PMI members can be expelled, but that is another story.

Structure

The PMI Code of Ethics and Professional Conduct is divided into sections that contain standards of conduct that are aligned with the four values. These values were identified as most important to the project management community:

- Responsibility
- Respect
- Fairness
- Honesty

Each section of the Code of Ethics and Professional Conduct includes both aspirational standards and mandatory standards. The aspirational standards describe the conduct that we strive to uphold as practitioners.

Although adherence to the aspirational standards is not easily measured, conducting ourselves in accordance with these is an expectation that we have of ourselves as professionals – it is not optional.

The mandatory standards establish firm requirements and in some cases limit or prohibit practitioner behavior. Practitioners who do not conduct themselves in accordance with these standards will be subject to disciplinary procedures before PMI's Ethics Review Committee (PMI, 2012).

Responsibility

The first of the four general values are responsibility. It is a basic standard for ethical behavior and is spelled out by several mandatory and aspirational standards. Hopefully, most agile practitioners should be able to recognize and commit to the mandatory values without having to make too many changes in their life. The aspirational standards falling under the category of responsibility may be slightly more abstract, but they too contain many good concepts to bear in mind. Included in the standard of responsibility are several mandatory standards of responsibility.

Mandatory Standards of Responsibility

- We inform ourselves and uphold the policies, rules, regulations, and laws that govern our work, professional, and volunteer activities.
- We report unethical or illegal conduct to appropriate management and, if necessary, to those affected by the conduct.
- We bring violations of this Code to the attention of the appropriate body for resolution.
- We only file ethics complaints when they are substantiated by facts.
- We pursue disciplinary action against an individual who retaliates against a person raising ethics concerns.

Aspirational Standards of Responsibility

- We make decisions and take actions based on the best interests of society, public safety, and the environment.
- We accept only those assignments that are consistent with our background, experience, skills, and qualifications.
- We fulfill the commitments that we undertake – we do what we say we will do.
- When we make errors or omissions, we take ownership and make corrections promptly. When we discover errors or omissions caused by others, we communicate them to the appropriate body as soon they are discovered. We accept accountability for any issues resulting from our errors or omissions and any resulting consequences.

- We protect proprietary or confidential information that has been entrusted to us.
- We uphold this Code and hold each other accountable to it.

In an agile context, the value of responsibility lies in making ethical decisions and reporting unethical behaviors. In agile, ethical decisions are made by the empowered teams made up of five to nine people. A group this size gives a good base for ethical decisions, as most of the members can guide one or two confused agile practitioners. Several of the agile methodologies are based upon values like the PMI Code of Conduct. Extreme programming has the core values of respect and courage, which are closely related to the PMI view on responsibility.

Exercise D.1 Missing words

1. In the case of a contracting arrangement, we <<Missing Word1>> bid on work that our organization is <<Missing Word2>> to perform and we assign <<Missing Word1>> <<Missing Word2>> individuals to perform the work. What are the two missing words?
2. In the following, insert "do" or "do not" in <<HERE1>> or <<HERE2>>.

As practitioners and representatives of our profession, we <<HERE1>> condone or assist others in engaging in illegal behavior. We <<HERE2>> report any illegal or unethical conduct.

_____

_____

_____

_____

_____

Answers: 2. HERE1 is "Do not," while HERE2 is "Do."

Respect

The second value is respect. The fact that it is second on the list does not imply that respect is second to responsibility. All four core values are equally important. Respect is perhaps the one of the four that is the most integral to agile DNA.

Respect includes negotiating in good faith. Part of the Agile Manifesto is the commitment to seek customer collaboration over contract negotiation. This certainly implies that we negotiate in good faith and will go a long way to find a proper solution rather than resort to a legal solution.

Negotiations are also an integrated part of working in agile. We talk or negotiate all the time, whether it is with the product owner or in the team when we make estimates. Respect also means that we do not use our position to gain favor. This is a misuse of leadership. In agile, we favor servant leadership. Leaders who serve the team will not use an opportunity to use their position over those lower in the hierarchy. The team is empowered and consists of individuals who can make it difficult for one or two team members to use their positions in self-serving ways.

Respect also applies to how we relate to other cultures or people who are different. In agile, we work in a global environment, whether the teams are collocated or distributed. We put great effort into creating high-performing teams where cultural differences and diversity are strengths rather than weaknesses. Agile is global-born. Ideas and concepts flow globally and are established in respect for the work being done. If a team struggles with the proper level of respect, we have in place methods for conflict resolution, coaches, and monthly retrospectives that give the team a range of opportunities to tackle the issue.

Mandatory Standards of Respect

- We negotiate in good faith.
- We do not exercise the power of our expertise or position to influence the decisions or actions of others to benefit personally at their expense.
- We do not act in an abusive manner towards others.
- We respect the property rights of others.

Aspirational Standards of Respect

- We inform ourselves about the norms and customs of others and avoid engaging in behaviors they might consider disrespectful.
- We listen to others' points of view, seeking to understand them.
- We directly approach those persons with whom we have a conflict or disagreement.
- We conduct ourselves in a professional manner, even when it is not reciprocated.

Exercise D.2 Turn to your neighbor – When a portion of the lecture has ended, have participants turn to each other and discuss the two or three main points learned.

_____

_____

_____

_____

_____

Answer: Review the main points if necessary.

Fairness

The value of fairness includes an aspirational standard of transparency. This is very much in line with agile thinking as we go to great lengths to demonstrate transparency. In agile, we communicate frequently and maintain a high level of information within the team. Information is posted on information radiators and boards for various purposes, not the least of which is the need for transparency.

Fairness also deals with resolving conflicts. Agile has the tools and procedures in place to deal with them quickly and in a fair manner. Conflicts are part of working in agile, so it is not a big deal. People in teams are experienced in handling them effectively. Fairness also contains an element of non-discrimination, which can be an issue with distributed teams who might work under different conditions. Agile cannot prevent unfair events because agile is like a human being, who can be by nature unfair. But agile techniques and concepts offer tools and techniques that address unfairness.

Mandatory Standards of Fairness

- We proactively and fully disclose any real or potential conflicts of interest to the appropriate stakeholders.
- When we realize that we have a real or potential conflict of interest, we refrain from engaging in the decision-making process or otherwise attempting to influence outcomes, unless or until: we have made full disclosure to the affected stakeholders, we have an approved mitigation plan, and we have obtained the consent of the stakeholders to proceed.
- We do not hire or fire, reward or punish, or award or deny contracts based on personal considerations, including, but not limited to, favoritism, nepotism, or bribery.
- We do not discriminate against others based on, but not limited to, gender, race, age, religion, disability, nationality, or sexual orientation.
- We apply the rules of the organization (employer, Project Management Institute, or other group) without favoritism or prejudice.

Aspirational Standards of Fairness

- We demonstrate transparency in our decision-making process.
- We constantly re-examine our impartiality and objectivity, taking corrective action as appropriate.
- We provide equal access to information to those who are authorized to have that information.
- We make opportunities equally available to qualified candidates.

Honesty

The fourth value is honesty, and one might wonder why such a basic ethical behavior is highlighted. Still, consider that the concept of honesty might vary quite a lot between people, nationalities, or cultures. Transparency is part of being honest about what we are doing. This works well with agile practices with public truthful communications and accurate information. In addition, we use techniques like value-driven development to understand the truth to deliver value to our customers.

Mandatory Standards of Honesty

- We do not engage in or condone behavior that is designed to deceive others, including, but not limited to, making misleading or false statements, stating half-truths, providing information out of context, or withholding information that, if known, would render our statements as misleading or incomplete.
- We do not engage in dishonest behavior with the intention of personal gain or at the expense of another.

Aspirational Standards of Honesty

- We earnestly seek to understand the truth.
- We are truthful in our communications and in our conduct.
- We provide accurate information in a timely manner.
- We make commitments and promises, implied or explicit, in good faith.
- We strive to create an environment in which others feel safe to tell the truth.

D.1 Sample PMI-RMP Exam Questions on Code of Ethics and Professional Conduct

This section contains five short exam questions in the PMI-RMP format for you to check your knowledge of the content presented in this chapter and to check your readiness for the PMI-RMP exam. The answers will be provided in boldface following the questions section. If you make mistakes, you should go back and learn why mistakes were made. Do not learn the questions and answers; learn the content.

D.1.1 Questions

1 What is the difference between aspirational and mandatory standards, as referred to in the PMI code?

A. Aspirational standards are not mandatory but good practice and encouraged.

B. Aspirational standards are backed by federal law and mandatory standards backed by state and local law.

C. Aspirational standards are enforced by state law and mandatory standards are backed by federal law.

D. Both are compulsory standards and backed by law.

2 While leading a risk workshop, a subject matter expert disagrees with a decision you have made and makes it a point to be very vocal about it. He uses the meeting to express his doubts about your skills and even goes so far as to suggest that your race plays a part in the way you make decisions. How should you react?

A. Do nothing. File a complaint with the manager's boss after the meeting.

B. Use your authority as the meeting leader to take control of the discussion and present your rebuttal.

C. Suggest an immediate meeting between the two of you to discuss your differences.

D. Bring the manager's boss into the meeting and ask for assistance in addressing his comments.

3 A team member is stealing from the company. Which value is violated?

A. Responsibility

B. Respect

C. Fairness

D. Honesty

4 You work for a European-based company hired to perform risk management services in a foreign country. Other companies who have done business in this country inform you that gifts must be made to the government to obtain the necessary approvals. What do you do?

A. Offer the recommended gifts to obtain project approvals

B. Do not offer gifts to obtain project approvals

C. Ignore the need for project approvals

D. Both B and C

5 You are responsible for developing a cost estimate to bid on a government contract. The scope was set by the government. Your supervisor says the cost estimate is too expensive and should be reduced by one-third to ensure your company wins the contract. Your analysis shows that any reduction to the proposed cost estimate makes the project unable to meet the specified scope. What do you do?

A. Reduce the cost estimate and submit the proposal

B. Submit your initial cost estimate without reducing the cost

C. Explain to your supervisor in writing that your analysis shows a reduction in the cost estimate makes the project unable to meet the specified scope

D. Both A and C

D.1.2 Answers

1 What is the difference between aspirational and mandatory standards, as referred to in the PMI code?

   A. **Aspirational standards are not mandatory but good practice and encouraged.**

   B. Aspirational standards are backed by federal law and mandatory standards are backed by state and local law.

   C. Aspirational standards are enforced by state law and mandatory standards are backed by federal law.

   D. Both are compulsory standards and backed by law.

   Explanation: Aspirational standards are standards that every professional should strive to uphold but are not compulsory. Mandatory standards are required and often backed by law.

2 While leading a risk workshop, a subject matter expert disagrees with a decision you have made and makes it a point to be very vocal about it. He uses the meeting to express his doubts about your skills and even goes so far as to suggest that your race plays a part in the way you make decisions. How should you react?

   A. Do nothing. File a complaint with the manager's boss after the meeting.

   B. Use your authority as the meeting leader to take control of the discussion and present your rebuttal.

   C. **Suggest an immediate meeting between the two of you to discuss your differences.**

   D. Bring the manager's boss into the meeting and ask for assistance in addressing his comments.

   Explanation: The PMI Code of Ethics and Professional Conduct requires that you act in a professional manner even when others do not. Answer A is incorrect because doing nothing solves nothing. Going to the manager's boss is likely to make the situation worse, not better. Answer B is incorrect because it is an emotional response, not a professional one. Answer D is incorrect because you should always first attempt to solve differences one-on-one.

3 A team member is stealing from the company. Which value is violated?

   A. **Responsibility**

   B. Respect

   C. Fairness

   D. Honesty

   Explanation: Stealing is a case of many broken values; however, it is considered part of responsibility (A), which is probably the best answer. However, options B, C, and D, to some degree, are also violated.

4 You work for a European-based company hired to perform risk management services in a foreign country. Other companies who have done business in this country inform you that gifts must be made to the government to obtain the necessary approvals. What do you do?
A. Offer the recommended gifts to obtain project approvals
B. **Do not offer gifts to obtain project approvals**
C. Ignore the need for project approvals
D. Both B and C
Explanation: Answer A is not correct because you have a responsibility to refrain from offering inappropriate gifts for personal gain. Thus option B is correct. The exemption regarding conformity with applicable laws or customs of the country where project management services are being performed does not apply because you are working for a European-based company and are subject to EU law. Answers C and D are incorrect because you have a responsibility to comply with laws and regulations in the country where providing project management services requires project approvals.

5 You are responsible for developing a cost estimate to bid on a government contract. The scope was set by the government. Your supervisor says the cost estimate is too expensive and should be reduced by one-third to ensure your company wins the contract. Your analysis shows that any reduction to the proposed cost estimate makes the project unable to meet the specified scope. What do you do?
A. Reduce the cost estimate and submit the proposal
B. Submit your initial cost estimate without reducing the cost
C. **Explain to your supervisor in writing that your analysis shows a reduction in the cost estimate makes the project unable to meet the specified scope**
D. Both A and C
Explanation: You have a responsibility to provide accurate and truthful representations in the preparation of estimates concerning costs, services, and expected results, so option C is correct. This responsibility makes options A and D inappropriate. You have accountability to your management, and option B is not appropriate because you are usurping your manager's authority and undermining your own professional conduct by doing so.

Appendix E: Cross-Reference Guide

The Cross-Reference Guide aligns the terminology of the three approaches (predictive, hybrid, and agile) with the five domains of the *PMI Risk Management Professional (PMI-RMP) Exam Content Outline and Specifications* (updated March 2022). A blank space means the terminology is not commonly applied during the domain, whereas an "X" indicates that the terminology is commonly applied.

Terminology (Predictive)	Risk Strategy and Planning	Risk Identification	Risk Analysis	Risk Response	Monitor and Close Risks
Assumption		X			
Assumption and constraint analysis		X	X		
Assumption log	X			X	
Alternative analysis				X	
Benchmarking	X				
Brainstorming			X		
Conflict resolutions	X				
Constraints	X	X			
Checklists			X		
Critical path			X		
Contingency plan				X	

(*Continued*)

Terminology (Predictive)	Risk Strategy and Planning	Risk Identification	Risk Analysis	Risk Response	Monitor and Close Risks
Cost–benefit analysis				X	
Change logs					X
Cost baseline					X
Development approach	X				
Document review	X		X		
Enterprise environmental factors	X				
Expected monetary value			X		
Fallback plans				X	
Historical information	X				
Hierarchical charts			X		
Impact		X	X		
Influence diagrams			X		
Interviews		X	X		
Issue log	X				
Lessons learned	X			X	X
Lessons learned register	X			X	
Monte Carlo analysis			X		
Multicriteria decision analysis				X	
Opportunity	X	X	X		
Organizational process assets	X				
Performance measurement baseline					X
PESTLE	X				
Plan risk response				X	
Probability		X	X		

(Continued)

Terminology (Predictive)	Risk Strategy and Planning	Risk Identification	Risk Analysis	Risk Response	Monitor and Close Risks
Probability and impact matrix			X		
Project charter	X				
Project communication management	X				
Project management information system	X				
Project management plan	X				X
Project team assignments				X	
Prompt lists			X		
Project documents					X
Project management plan	X				
RACI chart	X				
Residual risks				X	X
Responsibility assignment matrix (RAM)	X			X	
Risk acceptance				X	
Risk action				X	
Risk action owner				X	
Risk audit					X
Risk avoidance				X	
Risk appetite	X				
Risk attributes		X			
Risk breakdown structure	X		X		
Risk categories	X		X		
Risk escalation				X	
Risk exploiting				X	
Risk management plan	X		X		

(Continued)

Terminology (Predictive)	Risk Strategy and Planning	Risk Identification	Risk Analysis	Risk Response	Monitor and Close Risks
Risk management strategy	X				
Risk mitigation				X	
Risk owner				X	
Risk principles	X				
Risk rating			X		
Risk reassessment					X
Risk register	X	X	X	X	X
Risk report	X		X	X	X
Risk sharing				X	
Risk transference				X	
Risk thresholds	X	X			
Root-cause analysis			X		
Scope baseline					X
Servant leadership	X				
Secondary risk				X	X
Sensitivity analysis			X		
Simulations			X		
Stakeholder analysis	X				
Stakeholder engagement plan	X				
SWOT analysis	X		X		
Threat	X	X	X		
Trigger condition		X			
Variance analysis					X
Work package					X
Work performance data					X
Work performance information					X
Work performance reports					X

(Continued)

Terminology (Agile)	Risk Strategy and Planning	Risk Identification	Risk Analysis	Risk Response	Monitor and Close Risks
Agile principles	X	X	X	X	X
Agile Manifesto	X	X	X	X	X
Burndown chart		X	X	X	X
Backlog refinement	X				X
Definition of done		X	X	X	X
Definition of ready	X				
Ground rules	X	X	X	X	X
Information radiator		X	X	X	X
Lean	X	X	X	X	X
Product backlog	X				
Product owner	X	X	X	X	X
Product roadmap	X				
Scrum master	X	X	X	X	X
Scrum team	X	X	X	X	X
Sprint					
Sprint backlog		X	X	X	X
Sprint planning		X	X	X	
Sprint review		X	X	X	
Sprint retrospective		X	X	X	
Story point	X				
Velocity	X				

Appendix F: Tasks Placemat

The Tasks Placemat provides a high-level overview of the five domains of the *PMI Risk Management Professional (PMI-RMP) Exam Content Outline and Specifications* (updated March 2022). Tasks marked in boldface are extremely close to the content of the similar process in the *PMBOK Guide* – Sixth Edition, "Knowledge Area Risk Management."

Risk Strategy and Planning	*Risk Identification*	*Risk Analysis*	*Risk Response*	*Monitor and Close Risks*
Perform a preliminary document analysis	**Conduct risk identification exercises**	**Perform qualitative analysis**	**Plan risk response**	Gather and analyze performance data
Assess project environment for threats and opportunities	Examine assumption and constraint analyses	**Perform quantitative analysis**	**Implement risk response**	Monitor residual and secondary risks
Confirm risk thresholds based on risk appetites	Document risk triggers and thresholds based on context/ environment	Identify threats and opportunities		Provide the information required to update relevant project documents
Establish a risk management strategy	Develop risk register			**Monitor project risk levels**
Document the risk management plan				
Plan and lead risk management activities with stakeholders				

Source list of Terms and Acronyms

Note: PMI Standard (2019) refers to *The Standard for Risk Management in Portfolios, Programs, and Projects* (2019), Project Management Institute; PMI Standard (2009) refers to the *Practice Standard for Project Risk Management* (2009), Project Management Institute; and PMBOK Guide – Sixth Edition refers to *A Guide to the Project Management Body of Knowledge (PMBOK Guide)* – Sixth Edition, Project Management Institute.

A

Assumption	PMBOK Guide – Sixth Edition	699
Assumption and constraint analysis	PMI Standard (2019)	131
Assumption log	PMBOK Guide – Sixth Edition	699
Alternative analysis	PMBOK Guide – Sixth Edition	699

B

Benchmarking	Missing reference information	Generic
Brainstorming	PMI Standard (2019)	131

C

Conflict resolutions	Missing reference information	Generic
Constraints	PMBOK Guide – Sixth Edition	701
Checklists	PMI Standard (2019)	131
Critical path	PMBOK Guide – Sixth Edition	704
Contingency plan	PMI Standard (2009)	109
Cost-benefit analysis	PMBOK Guide – Sixth Edition	703
Change logs	PMBOK Guide – Sixth Edition	700
Cost baseline	PMBOK Guide – Sixth Edition	703

D

Development approach	PMBOK Guide – Sixth Edition	704
Document review	PMBOK Guide – Sixth Edition	705

E

Enterprise environmental factors	PMBOK Guide – Sixth Edition	706
Expected monetary value	Missing reference information	Generic

References and Additional Readings

Aiken, P., Stanley, R. M., Billings, J., & Anderson, L. (2004) Using Codes of Conduct to Resolve Legal Disputes. *Computer*, 43(4), 29–34.

Beck, K. (2000) *Extreme Programming Explained: Embrace Change*. Longman Higher Education.

Beck, K. (2007) A Theory of Programming. *Dr. Dobb's Journal*, November 2007.

Bissonette, M. M. (2016) *Project Risk Management: A Practical Implementation Approach*. PMI.

Davison, R. M. (2000) *Professional Ethics in Information Systems: A Personal Perspective by R.M.* Association for Computing Machinery.

Dweck, C. S. (2006) *Mindset*. Ballentine Books.

Dweck, C. S. (2016) What Having a "Growth Mindset" Actually Means. *Harvard Business Review*.

Fraser, J., Quail, R., & Simkins, B. (2021) *Enterprise Risk Management: Today's Leading Research and Best Practices for Tomorrow's Executives*, 2nd edition. Wiley.

Gemino, A., Reich, B. H., & Serrador, P. M. (2021) Agile, Traditional, and Hybrid Approaches to Project Success: Is Hybrid a Poor Second Choice? *Project Management Journal*, 52, 161–175.

Helgadóttir, H. (2007) *The Ethical Dimension of Project Management*. Nordnet. Projects under Risk.

Highsmith, J. (2002) *Agile Software Development Ecosystems*. Addison–Wesley.

Hillson, D., & Simon, P. (2020) *Practical Project Risk Management: The ATOM Methodology*, 3rd edition. Berrett-Koehler Publishers.

Hoda, R., Kruchten, P., & Noble, J. (2010) Agility in Context. *OOPSLA/SPLASH'10*, October 17–21, 2010, Reno/Tahoe, NV, USA.

Kendrick, T. (2015) *Identifying and Managing Project Risk*, 3rd edition. AMACOM.

Larman, C., & Vodde, B. (2008) *Scaling Lean and Agile Development: Thinking and Organizational Tools for Large-Scale Scrum*. Addison-Wesley.

Poppendieck, M., & Poppendieck, T. (2003) *Lean Software Development: An Agile Toolkit*. Addison-Wesley Professional.

Project Management Institute (2009) *The PMI Practice Standard for Project Risk Management*.

Project Management Institute (2017) *A Guide to the Project Management Body of Knowledge* (PMBOK Guide), Sixth edition.

Project Management Institute (2019) *The Standard for Risk Management in Portfolios, Programs, and Projects*.

Reinertsen, D. G. (2009) *The Principles of Product Development Flow.* Celeritas Publishing.

Ries, E. (2011) *The Lean Startup.* Crown Publishing Group.

Sidky, A. S. (2007) *A Structured Approach to Adopting Agile Practices: The Agile Adoption Framework.* PhD thesis. Virginia Tech, 2007.

Sliger, M., & Broderick, S. (2008) *The Software Project Manager's Bridge to Agility.* Addison-Wesley.

Williams, L. (2012) What Agile Teams Think of Agile Principles. *Communications of the ACM,* 55(4), 71–76.

Womack, J. P., Jones, D. T., & Roos, D. (2007) *The Machine that Changed the World: The Story of Lean Production.* 2007 updated edition. Free Press.

Wood-Harper, A. T., Corder, S., Wood, J. R. G., & Watson, H. (1996) How We Profess: The Ethical Systems Analyst. *Communications of the ACM,* 39(3), 69–77.

Index

For Product Safety Concerns and Information please contact our
EU representative GPSR@taylorandfrancis.com Taylor & Francis
Verlag GmbH, Kaufingerstraße 24, 80331 München, Germany